# AN INTIMATE COLLISION

# AN INTIMATE COLLISION

## ENCOUNTERS WITH LIFE AND JESUS

### CRAIG D. LOUNSBROUGH

WIPF & STOCK · Eugene, Oregon

Wipf and Stock Publishers
199 W 8th Ave, Suite 3
Eugene, OR 97401

An Intimate Collision
Encounters with Life and Jesus
By Lounsbrough, Craig D.
Copyright©2013 by Lounsbrough, Craig D.
ISBN 13: 978-1-5326-4158-9
Publication date 10/2/2017
Previously published by Ambassador International, 2013

## Dedication

Humanity is wonderfully diverse. The privilege to walk among so many lives and to experience that diversity is both staggering and magical. I am profoundly humbled that so many have invited me into their journeys and have permitted me to walk alongside them for periods of time both long and short, in times of both great joy and horrific pain.

Writing a book of this sort could only be accomplished because of these incredible people and the journeys that they selflessly invited me to participate in. The invitation to walk with them was an honor, and the rich memories of those journeys remain an honor. The opportunity to be transformed by their journeys was a privilege. The memories left in the wake of them are priceless. The way they caused me to grow remains unfathomable. I simply cannot write a book like this without acknowledging these wonderful people and the stories of their lives that fill the pages that follow. As you meet them, may you be as captivated by them as I was ... as I am.

Yet, it was my own parents and the journey they invited me to walk that gave me eyes to see, ears to hear, and a heart that yearned. Without Mom and Dad, I would never have been in a place to know that such a journey was even possible, much less that it existed. Neither would I have known of my ability to write of it. Both Mom and Dad have passed on, but their legacy lives on. And so I appropriately dedicate this book to David and Donna Lounsbrough. While you have both gone on to be with the Lord, you are an inspiration in ways that you cannot imagine.

The arduous journey of writing such a book left me exhausted more times than I care to remember. Writer's block and literary doubt were frequent companions along this journey. Yet, my children proved a constant source of inspiration. Indeed, they remind me of how great young people can be and how much hope there is for the future. It is my hope that this book will make the world that they live in a better place for them, as they themselves make it better through the living out of their own remarkable lives. Therefore, I likewise dedicate this book to Cheyenne and Corey. You two bless me so very much. Dad loves you!

Finally, my profound thanks to all those at Ambassador International who faithfully partnered in the creation of this book. I cherish your commitment to God, your passion for the craft of publishing, and your always fresh vision. It has been a privileged journey.

# TABLE OF CONTENTS

**FOREWORD –**
An Intimate Collision ............................. 11

**CHAPTER 1**
**"I LOVE YOU"**
Love Strong Enough to Reside in Our Pain .................. 15

**CHAPTER 2**
**THE POOL**
Embracing Our Handicaps ................................ 31

**CHAPTER 3**
**DARREN AND A PLASTIC FISH**
How Far Have I Drifted? ................................. 45

**CHAPTER 4**
**A LEATHER BELT AND A THREE-DOLLAR BUCKLE**
What Defines My Life? ................................ 61

**CHAPTER 5**
**CONVERGING WITH MY LOSS**
Do I Want the Dead Raised? ........................... 75

**CHAPTER 6**
**JUDGING IN THE COURTYARD**
Stripping Away Appearances .......................... 93

**CHAPTER 7**
**ASIDE WITH GOD**
What Am I Hearing? ................................ 109

**CHAPTER 8**
# ON THE ROADSIDE
Do I Really Want to See?.................................129

**CHAPTER 9**
# I AM THAT "ONE"– SHEEP IN THE CESSPOOL
Am I More?...........................................143

**CHAPTER 10**
# SEVENTY CENTS OF SIMPLICITY
Richness Through Developing Childlike Eyes...............155

**CHAPTER 11**
# HOW VERY MANY YEARS
Rejecting the Pain of the Past...........................165

**CHAPTER 12**
# PINE TREES AND SLIPS OF PAPER
Seeing Birth in Death...................................179

**CHAPTER 13**
# TWO THIN ONES
Purposefully Gain to Purposefully Give...................191

**CHAPTER 14**
# A RED RYDER BB GUN
The Plain Power of Legacy..............................205

**CHAPTER 15**
# A BLIZZARD OF BLOSSOMS
Seeing Endings as Beginnings...........................217

**CHAPTER 16**
# "WHY ARE YOU DOING THIS?"
Worth Unimagined......................................229

**CHAPTER 17**
# AND IT IS SATURDAY
Living in the In-Between of Life.........................239

**CHAPTER 18**
## SNOWSCAPES OF THE HEART
Looking Ahead by Not Looking Behind . . . . . . . . . . . . . . . . . . . . . . 253

**CHAPTER 19**
## THE NEW ERA
Impossible New Beginnings . . . . . . . . . . . . . . . . . . . . . . . . . . . . . 265

**CHAPTER 20**
## THE MINER'S HUT
Hints of Eternity Here and Now . . . . . . . . . . . . . . . . . . . . . . . . . . 275

**CONCLUSION**
## A COLORLESS CANVAS
A Collision of Color . . . . . . . . . . . . . . . . . . . . . . . . . . . . . . . . . . . 287

# FOREWORD
## An Intimate Collision

**OFTEN I WANDER THROUGH THE** meandering back roads of my mind. The paths are peaceful, softly winding to gentle places. There are memories both abundant and abounding, each one iced with a bit of the frosting of idealism, but real nonetheless. The memories paint a magical canvas that inspires me each time I gaze at it.

They are laced sweet by spring's blossoms and speckled gold by the sea of dandelions that seem as spots of brilliant yellow pigment liberally splattered from an artist's palette. Frosty root beer floats on heavy, tepid nights. There were raucous hours splashing in the pool under lazy, drifting summer skies. The lingering call of geese hauntingly plied fall's brisk horizon, lulling the final reds and golds of fall to a deep, seasonal slumber. There were crackling fires on bitter winter nights, confidently holding the cold at bay. Dad's never-ending knack at fixing everything, our hearts and our hurts included. Mom's timely arrival with thick, steamy hot chocolate on cold winter days, or brisk iced tea to cut summer's humidity; her knowing presence discerning our need before we knew it, and filling it before we felt it. The memories are peppered with fishing and frolicking, trees and toads, bikes and BB guns, paper routes and pliable hearts.

These places are a deep sanctuary, a point of restorative refuge in a world deluged with destruction and pervaded with pain. But, to ascribe them as memories only is to rob and pillage them. It is in essence to strip them of their treasures, for they are rich beyond wealth. They are the raw fabric and essence of life fully playing out in the freedom of innocence that was yet to be lost. They were seen through young eyes that captured life and froze it into the storehouses of our memories before those eyes clouded with the pessimism of adulthood. Hearts yet unacquainted with the savage recoil of life remained widely open to every experience.

We were granted the inestimable privilege of drinking in each moment and committing those moments to memory for ready retrieval in darker days. Strands of memory that when gingerly but carefully woven through the tapestry of our lives provided us illuminating meaning, profound understanding, soothing comfort, and unimaginable fortitude. The deep well of the past was there to draw into the present in order that it might spill upon the often-parched landscape of now.

This rich foundation gave my brothers and me a sustaining strength to navigate the bleaker realities of adulthood. The torrential winds of adversity are more easily tolerated when you've had ample time on the sea of tranquility. And so, I was able to intersect hurting and scarred lives with the unshakable knowledge that all seas eventually turn calm. Therefore, this book is written with eyes of wonderment shaped in childhood, with those eyes brought to bear on the blackness of adulthood in a manner that lends the fullest credence to pain, while concurrently possessing the fullest of faith in something greater than pain.

I realize that the memories of many individuals are none of the sort described in this book. That is part of the purpose in writing it. The pages to come were penned not only to provide readers the ability to access the riches of their past but also to allow those without a rich past to borrow mine and that of others in a manner that might undergird and possibly enrich them in their own journey. Hopefully I will have succeeded on both fronts.

The title of the book arises from the times when God encountered me in these places, both past and present. Those "intimate collisions" that left me astounded, mesmerized, often entranced, and always spiritually enriched by their intimacy, their power, and their raw authenticity. Those kinds of collisions that don't come every day but come frequently enough to leave us gasping and gaping at the magnitude of God moving in the deepest currents of our existence. Those collisions that, unlike the kind we have in our finite existence, allow us to walk away incalculably better than we were before the collision. These divinely superb collisions that yield transformations so substantial they defy words and effortlessly thrust us past our loftiest expectations.

Isaac Bashevis Singer wrote, "Life is God's novel. Let him write it." It seems that His chosen instrument in penning our novels is the collisions that we have with Him, or He has with us. Here, in those glorious and sometimes painful encounters, the writing of our novels is penned with great flourish and stamina. In these collisions, the finest chapters of our lives are composed.

This book outlines those "intimate collisions" that stand as marvelous moments in my own life and in the multitudes of lives that I have been privileged to participate in. Some of them are but a sentence jotted in someone's novel, while others are full chapters. Whatever the case might be, may these "collisions" cause your own collision with God in a manner that is entirely life changing and passionately transforming for you. If you have but one "intimate collision" with God by reading this book, then the efforts expended here were entirely worth every ounce of energy and every hour given over to this text. May God run right into you!

**CHAPTER 1**

# "I LOVE YOU"

## Love Strong Enough to Reside in Our Pain

*"No, the Father himself loves you because you have loved me and have believed that I came from God."*

John 16:27

*"One word frees us of all the weight and pain of life: That word is love."*

~ Sophocles

**AT THREE YEARS OF AGE,** the mesmerizing excitement of Christmas drains little bodies that happily expend themselves in the wide-eyed savoring of tinsel, glass bulbs, twinkling lights, and brightly wrapped packages. For children, Christmas is magic that falls as pixie-dust on a normally normal world, transforming even the most mundane things into something brilliantly enchanting. As Norman Vincent Peale aptly put it, "Christmas waves a magic wand over this world, and behold, everything is softer and more beautiful." So it was for a three-year-old heart seized by wonder.

Completely spent from her daylong embrace of all the enchantment, I carried my three-year-old daughter to bed in the waning, sleepy hours of Christmas Eve. Her arms and legs hung limp, having felt and touched and run through the wonder of the season until they simply had no energy to feel and touch and run any more. She had expended herself in wonder, which is an utterly wonderful way to expend oneself.

Slowly and methodically, I ascended the stairs as if there needed to be something respectful and therefore formal about closing out such a magnificent day. With her body draped in my arms, I gently nudged open the door of her darkened bedroom. In those mystical kinds of circles that life moves in, I found myself stepping into her room and into the end of a long day. Tenderly placing her within the thick folds of the awaiting blankets, her heavy eyes opened ever so slightly. Laced with the haze and mist of exhaustion, yet sprinkled at the edges with some slight bit of remaining magic, she looked into my eyes and said the four words that no gift awaiting me under any tree could possibly say as well. Softly, she mumbled the words "I love you, Daddy." A tiny smile curled across her sleepy lips. Then she rolled over and drifted off to sleep.

Pausing in the darkness, I placed my hand on her tiny shoulder and pondered how priceless she was and how indescribably precious her words were. I tucked all of them into the folds of my mind, tucked in the loose corners of her comforter, and turned and walked out of her room.

As I descended the stairs, they somehow looked different. Sometimes we experience events that alter us at some profoundly core place. When that happens, our perspective is canted just enough that things look oddly and unexplainably different. Yet, it may be that what appears oddly different is really what the reality of the thing has been all along. The oddity rests only in the fact that we've just not been able to perceive it sufficiently.

Settling into my chair, I stared intensely into the seemingly regal boughs of the Christmas tree. The lights sparkled as they always had, dancing amongst the evergreen branches. The ornaments effortlessly reflected an array of dancing lights off their mirrored surfaces. Yet now, they had some meaning other than being simply ornamental ... a meaning previously missed and oddly different to which I had been indifferent. Somehow, the holiday was no longer commercial. The cheap plastic veneers of the holiday melted away, revealing shades of something much more profound, much more alive, much more intentional and real. Something coalesced out of all the trappings that was almost tangible, something that had a voice that was properly silent but blaringly loud.

The intent of the holiday became distinctly sharper, like a figure emerging from the recesses of a deep fog. All the trappings strained to embrace one single message. The superficial stuff of Christmas that we have liberally manufactured are really our feeble attempts to somehow articulate and voice the message we are all desperate to hear. It's a message that we all frantically hope is what the season's really all about—that life is all about. Yet, we're too dreadfully fearful to find out that it might not actually be that message, or that the message might not exist at all. The message that we yearn and hope for is the message, "I love you." My daughter said it. It was authentically compelling, but it somehow felt vulnerable and far too delicate to be anything of substance when held against the toxicity of a fallen world. Was it that innocent and that simple? Is that what God said on that Bethlehem night?

As I eased into the embrace of my chair, the message dissipated all too quickly, as the authentic messages in life tend to do. It swiftly became lost in the spinning vortex of reality that Christmas intersects once a year. I am inundated by pain both in my own life and in the lives of those around me. Christmas and the assorted trappings seem an effort to grasp at some scattered fragments of what should be in life, but what it is not.

The story of love seems to rise out of a longing for something innately deep with its themes incessantly repeated because of love's absence, not its presence in the grind of real life. If somehow we recite the story of love and the themes of love with enough frequency, we can at least believe we are capable of articulating love. If we can at least articulate it, it's not entirely lost to us, even though we have failed miserably in achieving it. And if we can hold onto even some precariously thin thread of this thing we call love, maybe there is hope ... just maybe.

While I desperately want to believe that the words of my daughter have within them the original shards of something astoundingly divine that will stand superior to the horrendous realities of life, my mind tells me otherwise. That love, even from the lips of an innocent three-year-old is, in the end, meaningful but largely powerless. My mind says life is too awful and love seems too idealistic, rendering it the stuff of fairytales, teary-eyed idealists, and naive religious fanatics too fearful of theological deficiencies to set Scripture squarely against life. Like so much in life, there are so many things that we desperately wish were true, and yet we find ourselves desperately disappointed when we discover that they are not. Tangible, authentic, and completely undiluted love seemed to be one of those things.

As I sat there, my jaded nature overcame me as a descending fog that slowly enveloped and suffocated my daughter's words. The power of those simple words quickly evaporated in the mist despite my frantic attempts to grasp them before they vanished. Was my realism justified? Is love nothing more than what we would like, being the stuff of idealistic projection that we can never achieve? Is love a hopeless hoax perpetrated upon mankind? Is it a genuinely nice idea, but an entirely substance-less one? And because it's substance-less, will we always possess the idea but never the substance? And does that mean that mankind is doomed to chase empty mirages out of the hope that life is more than we think it is? How does love as exhibited by God on that night so many years ago stand up against everything that would appear capable of crushing it with the simplest of ease?

As a pastor and a therapist, I have seen pain in others, whether that be the horrific violation of sexual abuse or the trauma of the sudden abandonment by a spouse. I have watched helplessly as terminal illnesses instantly redrew the line of death from somewhere out on the horizon of people's lives, suddenly scrawling its blackness directly at their feet. I have witnessed the inexplicable death of a child that begs for some thin thread of explanation that never comes, that never fills the gaping hole left in a parent's heart in order to give reason to tragedy. I have seen jobs vanish, bodies deteriorate, plans detonate, and hope dissipate. Pain takes many forms—so many that we will never be rid of it.

Then, there is my own pain on innumerable fronts that has frequently left me a crippled mass of emotional flesh, engulfed in agonies that cruelly defy words that might somehow capture my pain and give it an identity. If words were given to frame my pain, they might provide me recourse against the pain. But far too often, words are absent because sometimes they're just too shallow and effortlessly crushed like a piece of tissue paper. I find myself slogging about in the swill of it all, having to carry the crippling weight of my own agony while simultaneously helping others survival theirs. Too many times, I have gone to bed at night with no idea of how I survived the day. Too many times, I have awakened entirely uncertain of how I'm going to be able to face the next one. How does love stand in the face of these horrors and a million others like them?

"I am jaded," I thought as I stared into the twinkling lights, "and for good reason." My mind drifted …

## Love Comes

It stretched sixty miles, every inch paved with unrelenting contractions. Birth was being held at bay in the choking dust of pain and the sticky lathering of thick sweat. There was a deep confusion listing Mary's mind, much like dropping a plumb line of disorienting doubt into a young soul, a line that can find no bottom. Nothing fit in everything that was happening. How could the Son of God be born like this, under these circumstances and in this situation? Who would reasonably construct a plan that even remotely looked like this? The chaos of events, of timing, and of untimely circumstance hardly set the stage that one would visualize for a coming King. How was all of this the stuff of royalty? None of the events remotely reflected the birth as Mary had conceptualized it for the past nine months. Everything seemed to be at terrible odds with the message of the angel and how she had imagined it all happening. Why the census now? Why the census at all? Imperial Caesar had set the stage for an intimate collision without even knowing it.

There's the plan of God, and then there is how we perceive that plan. The two are most often strikingly different, at times incongruent beyond the scope of human logic. An unknown author said, "Faith is trusting in God's plan, not trusting God will give us our plans ..." The difference between the two can stymie us.

We can bring the full press of our minds to bear on the contradiction and still not obtain a common ground. The difference between God's plan and how we conceptualize that plan leaves all the might of our mental processes incapable of achieving even the remotest shred of reconciliation. The unresolved residue that bubbles up from the contradiction turns into doubt that then wreaks spiritual debilitation. And for Mary, God's plan and how she had perceived it were terribly at odds, creating an emotional angst that matched the unrelenting contractions that pressed ever harder.

The donkey misstepped. Mary was jostled, and the contractions, as well as the contradictions, surged yet again. As had happened throughout the long arduous day, the barren landscape vanished once more in the tidal surge of blurring pain. The thoughts of a teenage Jewish girl were obscured by pain and equally smeared by uncertainty.

Bethlehem sat on a limestone ridge framed by two summits that seemed to have drawn themselves up from the plains. A saddle-like hollow between them gently cradled the city, giving it an abeyance of antiquity seasoned as a stalwart nursemaid awaiting a new birth. The city was set in an amphitheater of hills as if anticipating a grand drama, a most masterful drama set to unfold on a stage of obscurity. The climb was a demanding one, rising two thousand five hundred feet in height. The ascent was achingly laborious, layering exhaustion upon exhaustion for this teenage girl.

The arrival was marked by yet another ascent, that of navigating the jostling crowds. Vendors called out in boisterous tones, hawking their wares amid droves of sweaty pack animals. Shuffling, startled, lowing, fighting attending reins, they coursed resistantly through tight streets into the deepening throng, finding themselves caught in the suction of the masses.

Pigeons burst from lofty precipices in a flush of frantic feathers … circling, regrouping, and then landing high above the bustle on precarious stone ledges. Their bobbing heads frantically attempted to discern any potential threats that might arise from the predatory landscape that milled about below them. Squads of armored centurions walked in lockstep formation, the thick metallic rattle of swords and sabers accentuating each step. Cavernous alleys stood rock tight, refusing to submit to the crowds that pressed against their cold limestone walls as they navigated into the bowels of the city. Bethlehem was mayhem.

Somewhere in the sea of pressing humanity, a busy innkeeper paused long enough to offer this winsome teenage couple some shelter. It was nothing more than a cave, but it was nothing less; crudely carved out of the lifeless limestone ridge that generally sat below the place of residence. Mary and Joseph stared at each other, trying to mine out a decision buried underneath the bedrock of exhaustion. Exhaustion had washed their faces with furrowed lines and set eyes deep in darkened sockets. At least the stable has been cleaned, feed and hay had been put up in preparation for the census. The animals were bedded for the night, providing some slight measure of privacy. It was theirs if they wanted it. In the midst of their exhaustion, they agreed simply because exhaustion seeks reprieve regardless of the manner in which it's obtained.

Once again, they set out, except this journey was but a few hundred feet to a limestone stable. The door relented and creaked open, sounding something like poverty drawing itself up and heralding royalty as best it can. The couple was met by the sharp smell of fresh urine. Musty odors lent a heavy feeling to the air, almost dragging it to the floor. The stable was permeated by a dense mixture of manure, straw, feed, and the thick coats of stable animals that caught a slight breeze and wafted thick through the damp air. The innocent bleating of sheep was absorbed in soft piles of fodder. The unsettled jostling of cattle in their stalls gave depth to the darkness. Donkeys shifted in some sort of tentativeness, the soft thud of their hooves suggesting a silent anticipation.

Mice scurried anxiously along walls into dark corners, vanishing in deep mounds of fresh hay. An owl greeted the night, the call distant, haunting, and masked in the darkness. The barking of a dog floated in from the advancing twilight as nightfall rendered the world weary and heavy with sleep. The muffled voices of a world settling in for the night drifted down vacant streets in scant and ever blurry tones, hushing itself to bed. A dim light from a flickering lamp cast a vague and tentative glow across a yawning stable; it's soft, dancing light exposed the scene, but silently so.

Joseph's gaze darted around the stable; thoughts racing quickly, he created a place in the fresh hay for the delivery of a fresh life. Soon, the piercing cries of a young woman cut deep into the thick limestone and were then absorbed into the attending mounds of hay.

Animals were startled and then settled. The light remained steady and unabated, as would the light of this Savior. Sweat traced glistening lines down Mary's strained face, collecting and then dripping off her chin. Sweeping strands of hair were thoroughly drenched in heavily soaked tresses flattened against a face caught in the throes of childbirth. Her features were mottled in deep reds, etched with the anguish of birthing a Savior.

Joseph, hesitant, concerned, and beside himself, scurried about in confusion, wanting to take upon himself some of the immense pain of the birth. Yet, he was forced into solitude, as was Mary. He found himself embroiled in the angst of helplessness, stranded dead center in the middle of glory only to watch, to be in company with the rest of creation itself as for a moment all that existed held its breath.

It seems that majesty is majestic because we have no part in it other than the privilege to watch it. While our humanity chafes against our ability to do nothing but watch, it is a privilege despite how unsettling that privilege might feel. So it was with Joseph.

The contractions tightened and came closer, accelerating the pain. History and eternity were about to shift, to pivot on this single moment in this most solitary place. The light flickered, bathing the scene in soft golds that waltzed with flickering shadows that could only admire the light from a distance unless they were to be consumed by it. The animals had settled into a near reverence. Darkness had made way for a myriad of scattered stars to join, ushering in a waiting cosmos that jostled for room above the expectant stable. Something of majesty had been lavished across the stable, rendering the mundane and impoverished as holy. These are the kinds of places that God seems to inhabit, and these are the kinds of times that God seems to embellish with holiness.

The night was not disappointed. Finally, the cry of a newborn replaced the cries of His mother. It was new but strong, breathing into His lungs the heavy musty air around Him. God now felt a body He created, from the inside out. It was strange and entirely unfamiliar.

Instinctively, Mary removed the mucus from His mouth and nose. His soft pink body, trembling at the violent transition from heaven's perfection to earth's alien imperfection was wiped clean of blood and amniotic fluid. In an incomprehensible turn of events, the all-powerful was now completely helpless. Eternal independence was now completely dependent upon a trembling teenage girl soaked in sweat and bathed in the exhaustion of birth.

Mary bared a breast and raised the infant to her. He settled and became calm, easing into the turbulent transition from one world to an immeasurably different one. Tiny fingers that shaped mountains and hurled galaxies into deep space now wrapped themselves around Mary's finger. Trembling legs whose stride could cover infinite expanses in but one step grew calm in the radiant warmth of the swaddling clothes that gently engulfed Him. The God who drew man up from the sparse dust of the earth placed Himself in the very hands of that very creation. God was here … finally.

Thousands of years of prophecies were now completed. The summation of millions of voices whose lips passionately uttered the coming of this moment drew silent. The hope and desire of so many who expectantly scanned the horizons of the future for this very event were now fulfilled. A single expectation that gave untold millions the ability to face their times and their eras with hope was now coddled in the arms of a young girl in a strange town.

Amazingly, all of the future expectations that were woven through innumerable prophecies and endless lives were now a present reality. That very reality that lay only moments old in Mary's arms ushered into that stable an unshakable hope for all men and all women for all of eternity. It was a hope that pressed out of the limestone walls, out beyond the edges of Bethlehem, and out to the fringes of existence itself.

Creation exhaled. Angels shouted. A rousing cheer shook the halls of heaven in wild applause. The invasion had commenced in a way that looked nothing like an invasion at all. Of course, that's the wonder of a magnificently creative God. God smiled, knowing that the event promised from eternity past was completed. It was finished.

### Viable, Believable Love

A manger today would be followed by a cross tomorrow. An entrance set at the lowest recesses of humanity had occurred, with an exit eventually looming at an even lower place. The words "it is finished" would be heard again, only differently. The bookends that would mark the journey of "God among us" were erected in the lowest places imaginable in order that the love they demonstrated would be proven as irrefutably sufficient.

### The Message of Love and Our Disbelief

Both events were emblazoned in love. Perfect love in the form of this infant would come face to face in a raw, primordial clash with every manifest horror of sin. Love would be spared no reprieve. It would be tested in the searing flames and fiery white hot coals of every fire that evil could set. It would have to walk through it all and stand through it all, and it did. Love's power was not the issue, although it appeared to be. The issue was the shallowness of man to grasp the depth of love—my shallowness.

It's our unspoken assumption, set squarely on the thin veneer of human logic that love will eliminate pain, wiping it from the landscape of our lives by its sheer power. It's a rationale quite appropriate for the limitations of human love, but it is sorely inadequate when understanding God's love, that the presumed nature of love is to desire the freedom, or more appropriately, the liberation of that which is loved. Love is about rescue, for anything less would be cruel and hardly loving—or so we believe and so we think.

But love is infinitely more powerful and more profound than simply its ability to eradicate pain ... far more powerful. God designed love to be massive enough to live in pain and subdue pain's attributes for phenomenal growth. In a desperate but profound moment, Jesus

said, "My prayer is not that you would take them out of the world
..." (John 17:15). God's love was designed to be inserted directly
into the world's pain to work pain against itself for our good. James
seized the idea when he wrote, "Consider it pure joy, my brothers,
whenever you face trials of many kinds, because you know that the
testing of your faith develops perseverance. Perseverance must finish its work so that you may be mature and complete, not lacking
anything" (James 1:2–4).

Loves does not live with the insecurities that demand it eliminate
pain in order to insure its own survival. It is able to overpower pain
handily and use pain's energy against pain's intent, seizing the power
of pain and bending it to our growth so that we lack nothing. Love
has the power to change the force, direction, and the nature of pain
so that we gain so very much more than simply the elimination of
pain.

If love is left untainted by our promiscuous meddling, and if it
is left to be everything that God designed it to be, God will use it
to turn pain to our profit in His pursuit of our perfection. Love
turns pain's power in our favor, reaping unimagined growth for us.
Otherwise, that precious growth would be squandered wantonly by
the primitive and rudimentary removal of pain. Paul said that "we
rejoice in our sufferings, because we know that suffering produces
perseverance; perseverance, character; and character, hope" (Romans
5: 3 and 4). Rich is pain in the hands of love.

God's plan did not involve the eradication of pain for the waste
that such an action would incur. Instead, love involved inserting
Himself as perfect love into the middle of all mankind's sordid pain.
The newborn cry that proclaimed the implementation of that plan
rose that night from an isolated manger set deep in the wilderness
of mankind's pain. And from this place, Jesus would walk the back
roads of mankind's pain right up a barren hill set with three crosses.
He did not eradicate pain. He deliberately walked right into it. He
subdued it and forged it into a tool that would forge us into His

image. Love is not lenient. Rather, it is lethal as it kills the "old man" in us and shapes us into His likeness.

The manger settled now. Animals calmed and drifted off to a delicate sleep. Mary and Joseph felt the effects of the events and they settled, drifting into the consuming fatigue. Calm gently enshrouded the barn as God pulled up a blanket of stars and tucked in the horizon. Unbeknownst to those in the manger, the applause of heaven had burst the seams of heaven itself, spilling a cavalcade of angels down to shepherds in fields nearby. They soon would visit and welcome the King: the honored first of billions to be touched by this birth.

The city drifted off to sleep. Business would resume tomorrow. The census would continue. Bartering, bantering, and trading would be transacted in the open-air markets that lined streets now steeped in the subduing darkness. Meals would be cooked. Marriages performed. Clothing mended. Children would romp in dusty streets. Rome would rule. Birth and death would roll on in the unfolding human drama. Eternity had been shaken, but earth felt not a ripple. God had come, disguised, quietly and unobtrusively, slipping into human history and human pain. The Creator entered His creation on tiptoe, saying in the most profound way, "I love you."

### BACK HOME

A hand on my shoulder drew me back to the tree. My wife's gentle smile carried its own illumination. The lights twinkled in pinpoints of excitement. My daughter's words settled in my head, warm and inviting recollection over and over. Finally, I got it. I realized that my daughter's words were not designed to eliminate my pain or the horrors of life around me. Pain and love are not the "either or" of life, being somehow mutually exclusive. Opposite though they may be, it is the energy of the friction between them that, when harnessed, molds us into Christ-likeness. Life's assorted horrors bespeak of opportunities that love desires and dares to seize in building Christ-likeness into our lives.

Her love took my pain and turned it against itself, harnessing its power to be unleashed in my life in order to bring remarkable growth. Suddenly, it made sense. Love does not eradicate pain; it turns it back on itself for my good. Pain then is growth waiting to happen. It is the ingredient that God uses to bring Christ-likeness to my life.

How immense to be loved by God with the same love that drove Him to slice open the expanse of the eternal in order to step into the carnage and filth of this place. How much more unimaginable to realize not simply that He came but what He came to do. Only love, that marvelously powerful, mystically veiled, yet wholly unstoppable force could compel actions like that.

The lights seem brighter now, the season immeasurably fuller. The words "I love you" emanate from the heart of a daughter and the heart of God Himself. My heart was now full with the applause of heaven resonating in my soul, bursting yet contained so that I might not lose so much as a drop of its nectared tonic. Life was now given fresh meaning in light of the pain around me. I find myself savoring the words "I love you" as this night demands they be savored. It is truly a wonderful time of the year.

**PONDERING POINT**

Our society's view of love is poorly conceived and terribly marginal. The voice of our culture espouses love based on pay-offs, conditional returns, feel-good experiences, and the promised eradication of pain. Such a love as that is not love at all but a modality of trading affection for the acquisition of some desired asset or refuge with no intent for growth. But we have embraced such transactions and definitions as love, thereby forfeiting by our own ignorance the power and irrepressible magnitude of love to cause "all things [to] work together for good" (Romans 8:28, KJV).

Love was torrentially unleashed in a Bethlehem manger. God forfeited Godhood to save us from the tragedy and travesty of perfection having gone terribly awry by our own hand. He abandoned all that was rightfully His in the endeavor, having every right to walk away from a creation that walked away from Him. God became man and in the becoming, still allowed man to reject His offer of salvation and redemption. Love without conditions. Such actions ooze with the stuff of authentic love.

## A Thought
- Do I hold to a cheap love that promises the escape from pain, a promise that it can't deliver?
- If I am honest with myself, do I in reality prefer the shallowness of cheap love to the rigors of real love?
- Am I willing to submit myself to a love that will not save me from pain but will fully support me in that pain in order that I might grow into Christ-likeness?
- If not, am I willing to live a marginalized life that will miss all that God has intended for me?

**CHAPTER 2**

# THE POOL
## Embracing Our Handicaps

*"That is why, for Christ's sake, I delight in weaknesses, in insults, in hardships, in persecutions, in difficulties. For when I am weak, then I am strong."*

2 Corinthians 12:10

*"Each handicap is like a hurdle in a steeplechase, and when you ride up to it, if you throw your heart over, the horse will go along, too."*

~ Lawrence Bixby

**I CAUGHT IT OUT OF** the corner of my eye, nearly missing it except for an accidental glance. It was something of life bursting onto the stage of life in silent subtlety, as do most things of grandeur. Happenstance or life, whatever it was, God was handing a precious moment to those with eyes keen enough or lucky enough to see past the gray mayhem of living to a miracle set as a bejeweled stone in the gold setting of life. Slight and unobtrusive, this miracle unfolded before me.

My mind leapt into the middle of it all and attempted to analyze the event sterile, as if logic can explain the miraculous or give us some sort of control over the miraculous. Rabindranath Tagore said, "A mind all logic is like a knife all blade. It makes the hand bleed that uses it." Mercifully, my heart wretched it away from logic, stopped the bleeding, and simply let a miracle be a miracle. The tender threads of a magnificently marred tapestry were being intricately woven right in front of me, and I almost killed it.

It was a small parking lot and a patch of grass away, a short distance for healthy legs but a vast expanse for tiny useless appendages. He was dressed for church as any six-year-old boy, a dress shirt giving him an air of pending adulthood yet years away. Black dress shoes were scuffed at the toes and sides. A shiny black belt girded navy blue dress pants that were slightly worn at both knees. His frame was tiny and slight, suggesting both a fragile body and a fragile heart. On his knees, peering out the double glass door at the front of the church, he sat a small parking lot and a patch of grass away. Longing and foreboding were swirling through a six-year-old heart whose legs were unresponsive in delivering him to that for which he longed.

The object of his rapt attention was our dog. All ninety-eight pounds bundled up in love, licks, and affection sat in our front yard. She was a furry invitation to love and be loved. This six-year-old boy's tender heart yearned to come and play with her. Ursula K. LeGuin wrote, "It is good to have an end to journey towards; but it is the journey that matters in the end." Dustin's journey would matter more than he would ever realize.

Spina bifida refused to let his legs carry him across a small parking lot and a patch of grass. They refused to carry him anywhere, rendering his legs limp appendages that had forsaken their role and robbed a little boy of his boyhood. And so Dustin sat yearning on a cold tile floor behind a double glass door until the yearning was too much. A small parking lot and a patch of grass away were all it was and everything that it was. It was then I caught it, and I will never forget it.

A fragile, six-year-old frame filled with passion to love and be loved pushed open imposing doors, scissored a limp body out between them, and dragged unresponsive legs across the parking lot. Atrophied pencil-thin, his legs trailed behind him as useless limbs that had just as soon chosen not to take this journey. They seemed to ardently rebel against the journey, being dragged along against their will. Planting thin arms in front of himself, he would draw his tiny body ahead a few precarious inches. Again, putting palms to concrete, he would lift his torso and slide forward yet another few inches. His eyes were fixed on our dog. Determination was indelibly etched across a young brow. Lips were pursed and tight in the throes of terrific physical exertion. He was remarkably persistent and defiant. The few who witnessed the great effort found themselves stymied in admiration and ashamed at the fragility of their own efforts at life and living.

The monumental effort unfolding in front of me was the manifestation of the unquenchable commitment of a young life to live despite the handicap that threw an insurmountable barrier across the path to living. Forcing himself into life in lieu of the resources that would have naturally taken him there, Dustin refused to be relegated to the fringes of society and the sparse borderlands of living.

But he was six. The number of his surgeries was the same ... six: one for each year of his life. None of them had put him on his feet or put his feet under him. And yet he remained ecstatically alive, infused with all the energy of a little boy, yet lacking the legs to seize that energy and race off into life. The gravity of it struck me as he set out to drag himself to us, a small parking lot and a patch of grass away.

But it is not always this way for so many of us. I watched him, fearing that he may eventually succumb to the hopelessness that engulfs so many, thereby relegating themselves to the very borderlands that he, by virtue of his efforts at that precise moment, was trying to avoid. Refusing to be beaten, he dragged himself forward. And then, another thought abruptly rammed itself into my mind. His handicap is clear and obvious. My handicaps are just as inhibiting, but they are hidden. However, they are just as devastating as his.

### How Large a Small Distance

The clamor can be heard rising from the temple complex. The commotion and noise of it all spilled over the temple wall in waves of jubilation, the soft bleating of sheep, the thick lowing of cattle, the chants of ancient hymns, the squeals of running children, and the cooing of doves from lofty marbled precipices. There was the heaving and jostling of the masses in worship and celebration. The rotund bellow of the ram's horn sent a deep summons, its thick call washing over the wall and rolling out into the countryside, quickly becoming thin as a vapor of sound, eventually dispelling on rolling hills and deep in lonely olive groves. Smoke rose, drifted, and listlessly floated from the sacred bowels of the temple, becoming diluted into thinning wisps by a passive breeze. A thin haze hung over the temple, slowly dissipating at its own edges.

The road south from Jericho was clogged with a continual flow of the faithful. Caravans weighed down with provisions lumbered along. Flocks of sheep pressed tightly in a woolen flow, coursing toward the Sheep Gate, being portents of the sacrifices to be made. Cages burst with the wild fluttering of confined wings that sought release. The velvet cooing of doves rubbed the day soft.

Lumbering cattle lazily grazed on sporadic clumps of grass with the tight snap of leather whips being only a minor irritant. Muscular flanks of oxen pulled tight and lean, rolling heaving carts forward. Sturdy hooves pounded the ground, drawing carts loaded high with supplies and goods. Already hawking their wares, sellers worked the arriving crowd, exhibiting theatrically broad gestures while proclaiming the supposed value of the product. Once-in-a-lifetime deals were being offered with the flagrant passion of a mesmerizing charlatan. The human spectacle added a hint of drama to the growing energy engulfing the city. And for days, the scene along the road goes.

But the paralytic was not part of it, not even a little bit. We can be close to something and yet be alienated from it and invisible to it. For thirty-eight years, he had been both alien and invisible. He had watched it come and go from a distant place of immobility and isolation. Many times, he had allowed his mind to become unencumbered through the liberating wings of his imagination, sending his mind out there to walk the streets, smell the smoky sweet aroma of the sacrifices, gaze up at the smooth marbled walls that challenged the sky for supremacy, and mingle with the throbbing crowd. In his imagination, he stood there as the ram's horn bellowed fat and deep, sending pigeons bursting into the sky and the massive crowd below into a reverenced silence. Prayers were murmured, psalms were uttered in ancient chants, the weak eyes of the old were cast upward, and the fresh eyes of the young strained to understand. He would be at peace, but only momentarily, until imagination clashed with reality and found itself with wings clipped, once again shackled to a handicapped body lying helpless by a listless pool.

North of the temple wall laid the pool of Bethesda. Little more than a stone's throw away from the wall, he was in reality a world away, locked in a place brimming with the collective accumulation of defective humanity. The handicapped were sequestered and tucked away in that gray place, thereby conveniently whitewashing the face of the culture by putting the less desirable elements out of view. They had been relegated to the borderlands of life and living. Thomas Carlyle said, "Isolation is the sum total of wretchedness to a man." Here human wretchedness had coalesced and mingled, wallowing in the collective depravity of their condition.

The communal sound of the festival filtered through the colonnades just enough to remind the outcasts of the world they were not a part of. Weakened by the distance that divided the two worlds, the combined sounds drifted diminished over the pool. They lingered only long enough to extend a teasing invitation that could never be accepted. There was nothing festive about the colonnades and the pool that they encircled. They served only as a taunting reminder of how impossibly large a terribly small distance can be when one is handicapped. Here, there was only pain, suffering, and unfathomable hopelessness.

Why Jesus goes to the pool, we do not know. Why He went—apparently without the company of His disciples—to be in the company of the outcast is likewise unknown. Scripture leaves His decision for the stuff of conjecture and pondering. But it's likely that love drew Him. It's God walking among the wounded and finding a home among the handicapped. It is God watching the larger spectacle and realizing that larger life does not reside in the larger spectacles, so He heads to where real life resides. Jesus is not drawn to pomp but to poverty, as somehow the heart of God is able to beat the fullest in the lowest places.

And so, He went. The mood, the atmosphere, and the tenor at the pool lent no trace of the festivities at all. There was no hint of celebration there. The sounds of merriment and celebration that drifted out to the pool found no correlation there. They were completely otherworldly. Celebration was abjectly absent at the pool … utterly so, providing a stunning and emotionally reeling contrast.

Jesus stepped through the colonnades and paused, drinking in the scene of human wreckage strewn around the pool. The depravity washed away any festive notion whatsoever. All hints of gaiety vanished as if they had never been. Celebration evaporated entirely. God was in the carnage and not in the celebration, choosing instead to walk among the filth rather than engage in the festivities. He was not in the drama, but in the dregs. He was not at the portico. He was at the pool.

## THE HANDICAPS

Jesus skirted the colonnades and watched, peering across the vestiges of discarded humanity. Cavernous sockets both dark and deep sought out light and found none. Eyelids edged with a crusty film attempted to trace sound and probe silence, following voices with tilted heads. Catching shards of sound, the deaf pieced them together in an attempt to apprehend a world without sight, creating a mosaic of the clamor and clatter of the world as they had painted it across blind minds.

But it was no substitute for the real thing. It was the cruel reality of that fact that fostered deep discouragement and festered a profound longing all at once. Yearning for what they could not see brought no sight. Hope was held right up to exhaustion where it could be held no longer, forcing the blind to die desperately desiring what they could not comprehend. And so they clustered around the pool, and they waited.

Palsied limbs were truncated, stubby, and atrophied. Joints protruded in gangly knobs where bone was tightly covered in weathered skin. Appendages lay twisted in gross contortions that had a ghastly aura about them. Crawling and grasping, they attempted to embrace some semblance of living with a debilitating handicap, all the while lying weighed with the terrible shame over that which they had no control. They were filled with minds desirous of living but manacled to bodies that callously refused that wish. And so they clustered around the pool ... and they waited.

Paralysis demanded that a body refuse to respond to the commands of the mind, rendering the body entirely unsympathetic to the deep hope of the heart. The distinction of the mind as separate from the body was no clearer than here, in these lives strewn around the colonnades. Few things divide the inner man as much as a mind that passionately desires to thrive and a body that will not permit it.

Milky white saliva traced thin lines down assorted chins and dripped off beards. Sopping clothing was bathed in mucus. Words were slurred to the point that they were entirely incomprehensible and seemed more like guttural moans. Sometimes life leaves us with nothing left to say, so all we can speak into it are the rasping sounds of a soul in pain.

The paralytics lay drawn up in atrophied bundles of twisted flesh that lay littered throughout the cold colonnades. It was the barest existence, which in reality may be no existence at all. And so they clustered around the pool and they waited.

The colonnades cut the morning sun, carving long shadows that threw themselves across the court and dipped deeply into the murky green waters of the pool. Moans of discomfort arose in a sporadic chorus of pain and babbling incoherence that gave full voice to the futility of their conditions. Cries of pain rose and then drew down into silence. Birds flitted among the structures, oblivious to the wreckage below. Their songs were somehow misplaced, being very much out of sorts there. And Jesus scanned this place and this pool.

There was a profound poignancy to one of the discarded lives that lay strewn there. The severity of his condition was deepened by the duration of the condition. Scripture says that "he had been in this condition for a long time" (John 5:6), paralysis enfolding in upon itself repeatedly in a morbid kind of free fall. The agonizing question in many of our lives often is "how far can we fall?" In asking the question, we tend not to fear the fall; rather, we fear how far we will fall. In those most desperate moments, our question is "will we ever stop falling?"

Multiplied misery increasingly layered itself upon itself, being terribly punctuated and made bitterly stale with time. Jesus knelt beside him and scanned the fleshly wreckage, drawing in each imperfection and every distortion that fitfully bespoke of what the man was created to be but was not. Brushing away the circling flies in a gentle sweeping motion, He pulled a tattered garment over an exposed shoulder, ran gentle fingers down a twisted trunk, and then tenderly cupped an atrophied head in a broad hand. Forcing this intimate collision of man and God, He directed His stare into the man's weary eyes and forcefully voiced the greatest question ever ... the only question ... "Do you want to get well?" (John 5:6).

The perfect invitation was extended. It was prompted entirely without a request. The question was directed to one in dire need of the question who may have forgotten how to ask the question at all. Sometimes we forget that there is something other than the sickly colonnades and contaminated pools that we lie around helplessly. However, the contemplation of healing had been so long in duration that the paralytic's mind was reduced to a single possibility, one option, one way to be healed. And that had become his focus for thirty-eight years. His mind, like his body, was in paralysis of a different sort. He said, "I have no one to help me into the pool when the water is stirred" (John 5:7). The paralytic held the paralyzing belief that being dipped into pool at the stirring of the waters was the single option available to heal his paralysis. What he forgot, or maybe never knew, was that the miraculous is never confined to options.

### Myopic Vision and My Plan

Gross tunnel vision: I have it, I live in it, and I respond to my world out of it. God is welcome to intersect my life; in fact, He is passionately invited to do so. But I relegate His work to a well-defined box, forcing Him to function within the tightly finite parameters etched out by my myopic thinking. That thinking has evolved entirely within the limits of my handicaps. There is no room for the miraculous. Instead, I attempt to calculate how the impossible might transpire, trying to outline the footsteps of the infinite before He shows up. When God comes, I have the obvious solution ready for Him. I think that I possess the only real possibility that effectively addresses my need and my handicap. In the ignorance spawned by my pride, I am brash enough to instruct God Almighty.

There's no surrender in this, nor is there any hint of the created holding the Creator in breathless awe. I have already predetermined the path to my healing and have likewise determined what it will take to get there. I have decided the course of action that is necessary. The only thing that God needs to do is implement what I have already ascertained as bringing healing in my life. So all I need Him to do is to show up and be ready to go.

Am I blind? Or am I ignorant? Am I brash, or am I arrogant? Do I deem myself so acquainted with my handicap that this familiarity has given me the expertise to devise the solution? Am I really that good? My mentality would seem to be a mix of it all. God does not bring the miraculous into my life. He simply provides the vehicle to get me to my predetermined destination. A little push into the pool is all that I need. A slight nudge in the right direction will do sufficiently. It's terribly rudimentary at best and exceptionally stupid at worst. God is demoted to some sort of menial assistant.

### THE FUTILITY OF OUR PLANS

It was not to be. The paralytic would never dip himself in the pool. His healing did not lie there, in those waters. His healing would have nothing to do with any execution of any plan he had devised. Actually and oddly, it was much simpler than that. There was no need for something external such as the waters of a pool. It was not about an obedient God that only had to follow the man's direction in order to bring about his healing. It was not about a plan; it was not the myths of mythology, the utilization of any array of finite resources, the establishment of an effective strategy, or the combined mental fortitude of man. It was about encountering God, one-on-one in an encounter that was as simple as it was powerful.

Jesus' voice was calm but sure. "Get up! Pick up your mat and walk" (John 5:8), He says. Thirty-eight years of disability vanished in the span of eight simple words. Limbs instantaneously became firm and straight. Atrophied muscles were suddenly ripped strong. Misshapen joints were drawn and twisted perfect. A wholly unfamiliar vitality rose through his trunk and leapt out through his limbs, warming and igniting every tendon and every shred of muscle.

And then, for the first time in thirty-eight long, abysmal years, he stood cautiously to uncertain feet. Overwhelmed by the alien nature of the experience, he found himself doing that of which he dreamt a thousand times and more. Sometimes we've longed for something for so long that when God hands it to us, it still seems a product our longing and not the reality that it now is. Eyes widened in disbelief. There was tentative step that was followed by another and yet another. He found himself engulfed in the wonder of actually walking instead of dreaming about walking. Confidence mounted with each step until he was dancing, spinning, and leaping. He stood wonderfully aghast, unable to absorb the remotest sense of what had happened.

In the miraculous mayhem of it all, he paused, knelt on new legs, and tenderly picked up his mat, folding it into rolls of reflection. It was time to move on. It was time to let imagination become reality. He stood and scanned the pool, slowly realizing that this was no longer where he belonged. In an instant, his life had been dislocated and relocated. Turning to Jesus, who by now had drawn back and watched the manifestation of life restored, he uttered a simple thanks crammed full with thirty-eight years of incalculable pain. Setting out, he walked past a column, ran a contemplative hand across its cool marbled surface, and sporadically paused to extend an emotional farewell to several of those who had shared his journey. After one final turn, he glanced back at thirty-eight years of life. Pausing for only a moment, he then walked out of the colonnades into the city, leaving behind him a pool he never needed.

### HIS PRESCRIPTION FOR MY PARALYSIS

How foolish I am to write my own prescription. I never need pools. I am so enamored with myself that I should think to know the course to my own healing. How arrogant to think I know the prescription, much less that I can actually write it. So often, I am so stupidly foolish. I am intensely grateful that God does not attend to my methodologies or my strategies. His love shapes His directness, and I am so grateful that He is direct.

Whenever I slip into my own sense of self-sufficiency, I am anything but submitted to God. And here I am in danger from my own devices and my fabricated solutions. The things I have devised that I am convinced will help me are most often the very things that will harm me and send me deeper into whatever it is that I'm attempting to escape. I am so often the architect of my own pain and the engineer of my own failures. So many times, I design my own destruction.

At these places, I need God to step in and say, "Take up your mat." When it comes to mats, I have many of them. I need Him to level me with His directness, bypassing all my constructs, all the pools I think so necessary, and to thrust me up and out to the healing that I so desperately need in just the way that I desperately need Him to do it. I desperately need God to get me out of my own way and out of His. Forget the pool. Just get up and walk! For this, I praise Him and love Him.

### Dustin's Victory

And then, the six-year-old boy is there, having navigated the small parking lot and that patch of lonely grass, dragging those useless appendages that would demand he not live. He had arrived. A crowd of observers had slowly gathered and had watched it unfold, seeing in him the tenacity of a young heart unwilling to let a handicap dictate his life. For Dustin, overcoming was not an option; it was lifestyle. Caught up in the wonder and love of my ninety-eight pound dog, they melded into one another. Held in the furry embrace of love and licks, he looked up and said, "God don't want me to live by my handicap! He helped me crawl right over here."

He did not have a preconceived idea of what God needed to do in his life. He was not consumed by his own notions of how God should intersect His handicap. He did not sit off on the fringes of life and yearn for life. He was open to whatever God was going to do at whatever moment He was going to do it. At the moment, this six-year-old took up his mat and walked. So must I.

**PONDERING POINT**

We all have our handicaps. Some are apparent and some not. But we all have them. And in some way, they relegate us to the pools in life, the fringes and borderlands of life and living. Here we apply our own solutions. In time, their inadequacy fails us, and we succumb to the handicap, whatever that might be for us. Having succumbed to them, we stay in those places, those places that are a small parking lot and a patch of grass away from real living.

**A THOUGHT**

- What are my handicaps?
- How have I attempted to solve them?
- Am I ready to admit that my plans have failed?
- And am I ready to allow God to apply the right prescription?

**CHAPTER 3**

# DARREN AND A PLASTIC FISH
## How Far Have I Drifted?

*"Come, follow me," Jesus said, "and I will send you out to fish for people."*

Matthew 4:19

*"Life is just a mirror, and what you see out there, you must first see inside of you."*

~ Wally "Famous" Amos

**DARREN AND A CHEAP PLASTIC** fish—it was a dollar store bin filler indelibly stamped with "made in China" that bordered on being junk. There were numerous needs in Darren's life, so numerous that he himself was lost in them. They were pathetic and endless, or so it seemed anyway. A plastic fish was little more than a cheap toy that momentarily anesthetized a childlike mind trapped in the deterioration of a thirty-five-year-old body. It was a mere trinket, a point of focus upon which to forget the realities that had bent him and ultimately broken him. It served as a pathetic distraction from all that had cut thick furrows across his head and heart far too early and far too prematurely. It was a cheap, plastic fish.

The years had stooped his gait and lined his hair with lighter shades of premature gray, cutting deep fissures across his brow and thickening young skin. His gait had been reduced to a shallow shuffle, dragging thick shoes across coarse pavement. He wore the soles thin on the outsides edges, further canting his gait. His soul was much the same, deeply worn along the outside edges as well, throwing into a precarious imbalance the cadence of an already distorted life. Darren found himself limping through a world that placed ultimate premiums on that which is new, believing that any value is inherent only in the degree of newness any object possesses. The world viewed his worn edges as old, used up, and spent. He was evaluated unfairly as discarded humanity and rendered invisible to the eye of a world too busy.

Baggy pants were threadbare at the knees and frayed at the pockets with stitching pulled and strained at variant seams. An oversized shirt bespoke of his desperate efforts to fit in life. Like his shirt, it never happened. Stained and limp, a faded handkerchief hung from a weary pocket. A mouthful of decay filled each smile and poured out in each conversation. Chapped lips were edged thick by coarse stubble sprouting from a grimy bed of mottled skin. The expanse of his squared jaw and sunken cheeks were covered with a bumper crop of inattention. His words were primitive and slurred, rolling off his tongue in seamless bursts that made comprehension nearly impossible. Shoulders were drawn down by the weight life had exerted on him, pulling him forward in a Neanderthal sort of cadence that was long and slothful. And he wanted to show me his plastic fish.

"Kind of like the disciples, huh? They caught fish. They were fishermen!" he said. A broad smile of decay anticipated a hearty response from me. Darren was thirty-five, yet he was enamored with a dollar store plastic fish. "Like the disciples, huh?" His persistence accelerated my desire to talk to a real adult. Church was over, and there were many candidates milling about. My momentary objective was to determine how to terminate this infantile conversation and find someone with some shred of intelligence to talk to. I moved to close the conversation with Darren and did so quite deftly, I thought. He would have no idea that I had just ditched him.

"A box without hinges, key, or lid, yet golden treasure inside is hid," wrote J. R. R. Tolkien. Simple things contain great treasures. As I stepped away from Darren, he held the plastic fish in his weathered hands as if it were a precious treasure and muttered softly to himself, "I was a sinner, now I'm a fisher of men too."

### God Strikes

There are unexpected moments in life when God sends simplicity as a blinding light that is far more pure and infinitely more superior than all the intellectual musings I could ever hope to devise. Darren's words... "sinner" and now "fisher of men," though soft, backlit my soul in blinding light and thundered through the very core of my egocentric spirit. They rocked me, simultaneously illuminating my flagrant sense of superiority as paper thin and backlighting my egotistical self against something far greater and far grander. It was a collision of the most revealing sort.

A light both brilliant and revealing was thrown onto something I had unknowingly lost in the dark pool of piousness and shallow Christianity that I had cultivated. "Sinner" and "fisher of men" represented two opposite ends of life. One was represented by sin sheathed in death and thrust into my life on one end, and that of salvation and the humanly unexplainable privilege of salvation handed to me on the other. He had seized something spiritually authentic that was indefinably powerful because of its innocent simplicity.

His words drew me down as my soul seemed to melt into repentant puddles on the pavement, pooling around Darren's feet. And in my heart, a stark thought abruptly shot through my brain. It seized my heart and surged through my soul as the light exposed the grotesqueness of my immaturity ... "go away from me, Lord, for I am a sinful man!" (Luke 5:9). I had rarely felt so abjectly ugly and so starkly far from God. I was sickened by myself and had nowhere to run in order to get away from myself. Darren had brilliantly backlit my life with a handful of simple words, a plastic fish, and an innocent life. I was repulsed by what I saw in the blinding light.

## FISH AND LIGHT

The cool of the night aimlessly drifted by; time drifted listlessly with it. Waves gently lapped the weathered wooden hull as if the night was completely pacified with simply existing. Sails flapped passively, rolling in a dance with an occasional listless breeze that floated out from somewhere deep in the night. The timbered creaking of shifting weight was soft against the darkness. Oars dipped deep and silently, spinning tiny whirlpools of water that softly gurgled in the thin veil of satin moonlight. The damp scent of water gathered in a thin layer of mist that skirted the water's surface. The night was intermittently rendered musty with the odors of nets wet with nothing but water. A distant heron called hauntingly into the night from a far shore, seemingly wading in lonely waters on the distant edge of the watery bastion. Muffled voices and the lights of other boats drifted listlessly across the water.

Nets were cast in a perfectly spinning arch, pirouetting to the rhythm of the night as they were launched by thick arms sure with experience. Slapping the water, they were given a moment to sink into the night of the lake. The keel of the boat became smaller in the submersion. The chalky white moonlight was shattered into a million moving shards of milky light on the underside of the waves, fading as the depths were listlessly plumbed. The water cooled, darkened, and was stirred by soft currents. All was listless in a dreamlike descent.

And then there was a massive tug initiated by the same sure arms of experience. The net reeled and folded in upon itself, instantly enfolding everything within it. A series of firm tugs followed in a different kind of rhythm that was much less peaceful and more intentional. Lunging toward the surface, the net broke the liquid plane and was hauled into the coarse belly of the boat.

Again, it was the same. There was nothing in the nets embrace but weeds, water, and disappointment. A gruff remark, and then a curse edged rough with the abrasion of frustration cut the night and oozed the pus of anger into the boat's belly. Frustration was manifest and coarsely expelled into the night by exasperated fishermen whose finest skills could not coerce the deep waters to offer up their bounty. The waters stubbornly chose to withhold their living treasures. The net was hurriedly prepared by frustrated hands and launched again, and again, and again. Frustration layered upon frustration until nothing other than frustration defined the whole of the night. As Peter Shaffer put it, "I was an accomplice in my own frustration." The fishing boat was rapidly becoming filled with a horde of accomplices.

The moon slowly descended to sleep behind the horizon. The multitude of stars drifted across the expanse of the velvet blackness, moving in unison with the turn of the universe and the winds of heaven nudging them to the same horizon. Night would soon drift into day. The nets remained empty. Soon the sun stirred with the first tentative band of pastel thin light on a yawning horizon, softly illuminating empty boats. So went the night.

This was Simon Peter's world, that of his father and his grandfather. His was a lineage of weary boats, hemp nets, flapping fish glinting in flashes of silver, sails, and storms. He was isolated within the world of trolling by night as the fish rose to cooler waters and sleeping by day. Lost in this world of his, he was so engrossed in its demands that he was defined by that world, having standardizing everything else by its shape and form. This world of nighttime fishing and the life that goes with it dictated the shape, tenor, and tone of his life. It was so familiar and natural that becoming this world, for Simon Peter, was being nothing less than who he was and where he needed to be.

There was little thought of anything else for he knew nothing else. No other world other than the methodical frustration of sparse nets, contrary winds, too few fish to market leaving purses thin with coinage, long nights followed by exhausted days with the only promise being more of the same … nothing other had backlit his life enough to see anything any different.

### In His World

There was an unexpected intrusion in Simon Peter's tiny world. A carpenter turned prophet found His way to this place of nets, nights, and weary men. Word had spread carrying rumors of miracles that had long drifted across the lake, having reached the shoreline and lapped against the wooden hulls of the docked boats. It was likely that many of the fishermen had gotten wind of Jesus as their sails might have caught a slight breeze.

But it was of little import. Rather, it was really more of an inconvenience. Like too many nights, the night had been long and fruitless. The nets had yielded nothing more than water, weeds, and weariness. There were no fish to market that day. The lake and the night had joined forces to deny these hunters of the deep any trophy. The coming night would be pressed with the need to make up for a night lost. It was time for sleep, troubled sleep at best, but sleep nonetheless. Yet, despite the need for sleep, there was an intrusion … of all days.

The crowd grew, giving some degree of credibility or celebrity to whoever this was. These frustrated fishermen picked up a few words here and there, discerning pieces that remained only pieces within the fatigue that enshrouded their minds. Religion won't catch fish and nice words won't mend nets. Sweeping platitudes won't feed hungry families, and brazen prophecies won't raise wily fish from elusive depths.

Edgar Allan Poe wrote, "Experience has shown, and a true philosophy will always show, that a vast, perhaps the larger portion of the truth arises from the seemingly irrelevant." Jesus seemed breathtakingly irrelevant to exhausted fisherman. The shattering reality of His poignant relevance was about to play itself out in a weather boat on stingy lake.

Simon Peter had seen what the winds of rumor had only blown. A mother-in-law had been healed by this itinerant Jesus person. The crippled walked pensively but surely on unfamiliar legs with crutches joyously abandoned at their feet as a necessity that was instantly rendered unnecessary. The blind stumbled in the attempt to align faces with voices for the first time, turning to drink in deep blue skies and finding themselves hopelessly enamored by mounds of brilliant wildflowers. The pallor of death was swept from the faces of catatonic infants with tiny arms and thin legs instantly washed alive with vitality that had no explanation, except ... He had seen it.

Simon Peter had attempted to correlate these astonishing miracles with his world of boats, frayed nets, canvas sails, and fish. The experience and the exposure had not changed him yet. It was only an anomaly because his world had not been directly intersected. What he had observed was wonderment, but wonderment that had taken place some distance outside the parameters of his tiny and predictable world of wooden boats and hemp nets. It had yet to manifest itself dead center in that world and to render everything entirely less than predictable.

However it happened, Jesus was suddenly in Simon Peter's boat; dead center in Simon's world ... ground zero. Suddenly his boat was turned into a podium and a fisherman was turned into a water-borne chauffeur. From the bow of this tired fishing vessel, the words of Jesus droned on. It's not that they weren't compelling. It's just that they fell upon a mind dulled with fatigue and deluged with both empty nets and empty pockets. Sometimes the greatest messages are missed because the human mind is occupied with a miniscule net of fish drawn from some tiny puddle when the Fisher of Men is standing right in their boats casting a net into the whole ocean of men.

Scripture does not indicate what Jesus said that struck Simon; it's what He did. And then, the command came. The nets had already been mended, cleaned, and stowed. Weary sails had been drawn tight and tied. Arms were weak and heads were fuzzy. The fish had undoubtedly descended to cooler waters, far beyond the reach of their nets and all of their accumulated skills. And yet this Jesus wanted to go fishing. The logical argument was of no use. A lifetime of experience was discarded and discounted by this Teacher. He was confidently insistent. We must remember that the requests of the divine are not held hostage to the logic of our minds. And so, wearily Peter mumbles, "But because you say so, I will let down the nets" (Luke 5:5). And he does.

Oars are lowered by weary fishermen who exchanged glances washed in confusion, anger and a slight flush of stupidity for agreeing to this idiotic venture. Plunged into cool waters, awakened oars create spiraling eddies in their wake. The morning sun was now full, having already lifted itself off the horizon of a new day, spilling a cascade of gold that broke into sparkling flecks of yellow glitter on gentle waves. Oars were drawn in with glistening droplets falling from their weathered edges, ever so quickly catching a slight fleck of sunlight before becoming lost in the waters below. Arms of experience grasped the nets, spread them, and deftly launched them in perfect flight. Again, they slapped the surface of the water as they had a hundred times the night before. A thousand times maybe. This time however, it was different.

## BACKLIGHTING

Instantly there was a slight tug. Then, the nets were seized and sent wildly convulsing. The pull was overwhelming, catching the strength and experience of even the most seasoned fisherman entirely off guard. Strained arms were etched with protruding veins. Faces were flushed red. The boat listed under the weight as nets were hoisted to the surface. Drawing against the collective resistance, the surface was broken in an explosive torrent of foaming water and flailing fish. The morning sun caught and threw the first silver glint of hundreds of thrashing fish reflected riotously in the churning waters. The water was agitated, surging white and frothy with the multitude of the catch.

Simon Peter was astounded, his mind gaping with the inability to correlate what he saw with what he knew. God makes the irreconcilable reconcilable. When that happens, we're left using logic to parse it all in order to force some reconciliation in our own heads or else simply embrace by faith that which will always defy the confines of logic.

A sudden panicked call went out to other boats. A small wooden fleet scurried and cast off in pell-mell and chaotic fashion; experienced fisherman completely inexperienced with netting the impossible. Oars plunged deep and hard, frantically pulling against morning's water. A small army of boats surged forward, creating panicked wakes. The catch spilt as a silver torrent into other hulls. Boats creaked, listed, and then dropped to the water line, rolling fat with the bulky weight of the catch.

Simon Peter was caught in the breech of trying to draw in nets that were fraying and snapping while correlating the event in his own mind. For him, it was irreconcilable. It did not match his world or his experience. He was thrust beyond his limited sphere by an event that had occurred in his world, in the very center of it, right in the middle of who he was and what he did.

It was entirely otherworldly, smacking of something supernatural even. Every sense and sensation of the miracle was inserted into the very center of his life to blow him beyond that center. His life was now held in sharp and poignant relief against something incomprehensibly greater and immeasurably grander than he. He was no longer compared solely to his world, a comparison that once gave him permission to inhabit that world without thought. Now, instantly, he was held up against something infinitely beyond his world. And there, in the stark and contradictory contrast of a miracle happening in his boat, on his lake, with his net and his hands, he saw himself. Here, he was backlit.

Starkly backlit by God, his life was thrust into keen and crippling perspective. The blinding light revealed the thin veneers of his life so much so that he was exposed beyond his ability to comprehend the exposure, much less deal with it. The din of the activity faded as Simon was drawn down, face to face with his revealed self. The sea, the boats, the commotion of fellow fishermen ... they all disappeared as he devolved deep into himself. Simon Peter was fraught with himself, finding himself grappling with the reality of his person as he had never seen it before, or been willing to see it.

Herodotus said, "Illness strikes men when they are exposed to change." I find myself taking issue with that statement, as it would seem that when God brings change, it exposes the illnesses that we already have. Our response to God showing up in the middle of our lives is not based on the fact that He showed up or that He's initiating change of some sort. Rather, our response is based on what His showing up reveals about us.

Peter turned, stepped, and lunged to the front of the boat. Here, Jesus had watched the miracle unfold; God incarnate enjoying the provision of the fish, the message in the provision, and lives about to be changed by the provision. Simon Peter dropped before Jesus, a proclamation of utter transparency leaping from his lips in stammering honesty. Starkly set against the activity around him, he shouted, "Go away from me, Lord, for I am a sinful man!" (Luke 5:9).

God had invaded the core of Peter's being, and he had been illuminated against it. Here he saw the real self. He acknowledged what had been exposed as far too much to comprehend and far too big to allow him to recalibrate it all into something that made sense. He could not embrace it, so vast and staggering was the exposure. So, he had to get away from the light and get it away from him. Yet, he would ultimately find that entirely impossible. Soon, the disciples would be named by Jesus, and this fisherman's name would be the first called in a list of many names. It was no wonder, as being backlit is often the precursor to being called.

### My World Defining Me

And so I am lulled into the ebb and flow of my life, into the circumstances that swirl in changing pools around me, the eddies and rippling waters that reflect back to me more of what they are than who I really am. I blindly accept those reflections as being me, allowing myself to become impoverished in the surrender of acceptance. It is when God steps into the middle of my world that what I took for God I find not to be God or of God. It is when He seats himself dead center, squarely at ground zero, that I am inoperably exposed. It is here that something vastly superior is held up against who I have defined myself to be and what I have settled for.

Too often my own light is borrowed, reflected off of varying events around me, much like the moon borrows its light from the sun and reflects back what does not belong to itself. My life is backlit by weak imitations that reflect things that are not their own, backlighting my life by anemic events that reflect a light so washed out that the landscape of my life is hardly perceptible. This I eventually take for light with the eyes of my soul having become so unaccustomed to real light that its absence is no longer comprehended. I then settle and sell out to vagueness as this kind of light provides little more than that. All the while, the profound challenges and wild passions lay a silent captive to the deep shadows that such a light casts, shadows that never surrender their contents to whatever light I bring to them until my life is backlit and the shadows are forced to surrender.

## THE HOPEFUL SHOCK

The shock of being backlit by Jesus rests in the instantaneous awareness that it brings. The sudden illumination of everything makes everything vividly stark and painfully clear. Such is the penetrating nature of this light, that the light itself brazenly outlines and defines every sordid aspect of who I am, leaving no room to ponder or stew over them myself. Neither does it give me room to manipulate what has been revealed, because the clarity is so pure that it's cognitively impenetrable and completely indefensible. Otherwise, the moment would be robbed, becoming something less than wholly divine in the thievery.

To be backlit by Jesus is to fully see and fully comprehend everything at once. All that is left for me to do is to embrace the truth so vividly set before me or squander the moment in a futile attempt at denial. More times than I can explain, I have rushed to the front of the boat, prostrated myself before Him, and begged him leave because I am faced with the horror of myself.

At those times, my disgust with myself clearly bars my relationship with Him. Inevitably, every time, He looks beyond what I cannot. He sees who I am versus what I have become, delineating the difference in a starkness so clear that I cannot stand before myself. He reminds me of His grace that makes my grotesqueness the raw material from which He weaves His glory. And then, bedeviled and helpless by what I see in me, He calls the authentic me to works beyond my comprehension when the only thing I want is for Him to leave. And it is in the angst of desperately wanting to flee and break His hold on me that I am held against myself and am drawn kicking and screaming into phenomenal growth.

## MAKING A HABIT OF THE LIGHT

And so I go fishing with Jesus every day. Fishing for men? Yes. But also that kind of fishing that repeatedly backlights my life against the majesty of God. It is placing myself in His presence while fighting every urge not to do so, readying me for the poignant realization that I am not what I presume to be; being with Jesus will highlight that every time. It is not His disappointments in me, for His grace will always temper that. It is my own disappointment in myself. I want to avoid Him because I want to avoid the pain of personal honesty. But I find an incongruent passion that causes me to leap into the boat because I know the joy of being honest before Jesus and what He does with that. I am constantly, repeatedly, and forever changed.

## Darren and a Plastic Fish

People continued to mill about me, but they had vanished amid deep thought and emotional turmoil beset within me. I turned back to Darren, who was meandering off to some unknown destination. I reached out and touched his shoulder. He stopped and staggered a bit as he turned to look at me, his body long worn beyond grace and dexterity of movement. Sparkling eyes set deep in worn sockets met mine, shocking me into the realization that I did not have that sparkle at all.

I paused. "Can I see your fish?" I stammered. Although a rare treasure, he instantly placed it in my hands without hesitation or forethought. He unabashedly shared the wealth of his life in a simple gesture, freely giving to a soul that needed what he had found, handing to me what he had grasped. I desperately needed the authenticity of his faith and the deep conviction in whose light my own pathetic belief system shrank and ran sour.

Such treasures often come in simple packages, like Darren. Their simplicity is in their security, as few would look there. Few look there because few lend their eyes to simplicity because simplicity suggests vacancy and emptiness. Those who do look there find the opposite—they find treasure. Those who genuinely look are not out to rob or pillage the treasure but rather seek it as a precious gift that no one can hoard or hold individually. Simplicity is bigger than one individual and is made to pass to and through all individuals, so it passes much more simply through simple people like Darren. Simplicity does not cloud truth, so truth shines unabated where the complicated things in life seem to diminish its light sometimes to the point where there is no light at all.

This light found in simplicity is to be savored, drawn fully into oneself and then left to enrich the next passerby. Hidden away in the Darrens of the world, God has deposited His light, set to explode into any life that is daring enough and desperate enough to engage the light in simple places.

I held his plastic fish, turning it this way and that, drawing down into its plastic and paint as had Darren, trying to draw out of it what he had.

"I'm going to hang it in my house," he blurted. "I don't have anything on one wall. It's all white. Just white, that's all. And I'm going to hang it right in the middle," he said.

A barren wall; like his life. His faith was hung right in the middle of his own bareness. And I thought, how very appropriate and how absolutely wonderful.

I handed the plastic fish back to him. "I'm going to go home right now and hang it up!" he said with electric excitement. As he turned to shuffle away, I called after him and said, "Thanks, Darren." There was no response. He hadn't heard me. He was engulfed in the symbol of his faith, a captive to his mad love affair with his God and his fish. Other people still mingled about me, but I no longer desired what they offered. As Darren stepped into the passenger seat of a waiting car, I realized that I wanted what he had. I wanted a plastic fish. I wanted a vibrant faith. I wanted to be consumed with God, as was this disheveled man, to have all of that hanging in the center of my life. This simple man of polyester shirts and worn shoes had backlit my life in such a way to show me the terrible deficits that I had.

I can still see that fish in my mind. It is a clear and vivid reminder of my faith, of following Jesus, of that to which He calls me. Being reminded of that by an event that backlit my life so that I could see my life. And so, Darren, if someday you are to read this, I simply want to say what you didn't hear that day … "thank you!"

**PONDERING POINT**

It is easy to become engulfed and enamored by our worlds, allowing them to shape us, lowering us to a sense of inferiority or raising us to a sense of superiority. Either way, we lose the authenticity of a relationship with Jesus Christ. In these places, we need some event in our lives that will hold us up against Him, allowing us in that encounter to see our true selves as we are backlit against Him. Raising us, or crushing us, whatever we might need; either way, bringing us back to authenticity in Christ.

**A THOUGHT**
- How far have I drifted from Jesus?
- Has there been an event that backlit my life, and if so, what did it illustrate?
- If I have not had one, am I willing to ask God to give me one?
- What have I done with the insights of that event?

**CHAPTER 4**

# A LEATHER BELT AND A THREE-DOLLAR BUCKLE
## What Defines My Life?

*"There is no fear in love. But perfect love drives out fear, because fear has to do with punishment. The one who fears is not made perfect in love."*

I John 4:18

*"The unexamined life is not worth living."*

~ Socrates

**GANGLY AND PIMPLE-FACED, JONATHON STOOD** pensively on the arriving cusp of adolescence. Staring down a long corridor of his life, the path wound from uncertainty to uncertainty. His movements were cumbersome and terribly awkward, having been set to the chaotic cadence of abuse. Stumbling and uncoordinated, he tripped across a life script measured out and metered in notes of deep pain. Long, pencil-thin limbs that, despite enduring effort, found little ability to flow and function in unison. Deftly uncoordinated, he bumbled through life. Wiry glasses were set canted across a thin face of confusion, pain, and fear. Worn polyester pants and thin cotton shirts were the stuff of thrift stores and secondhand shops. His was indeed a secondhand life.

Fingers inept and fearful pensively reached out to the world around him. He desperately tried to be right and do right in order to have that world nod in agreement at some success, despite how minor. Each effort was slapped with the thick rod of ridicule and beaten with words dipped deep in the slurry of caustic criticism. Inevitably, he would crawl away into dark corners of his bedroom and his life where he drew up into deep shadows, wincing and crying. His heart and his body were strewn with senseless lacerations that knew no solace except isolation. He was alone, desperately so.

Jonathon was barely twelve years of age and already an outcast. He was relegated out beyond the fringes of society by parents who birthed and then rejected him. Parents who beat a helpless baby, who abused an infant whose tiny eyes pooled with the desire for acceptance in the very midst of rejection. Parents seized and satiated with incomprehensible evil, who extinguished cigarettes on his tender skin and snuffed out hope in his confused heart, who dropped him on his head for personal amusement and levity. Repeatedly, they had forced him naked into the backyard with welts swelling across his back from the sharp snap of Dad's thick leather belt. There were relentless beatings for trifling mistakes—most times, for no mistakes at all. Many nights, they left him outside to sleep with the dog while the rest of world slept inside.

Sexual abuse would follow, rendering him a helpless party to the most putrid of human depravity, culminating in the violation of a life too small to protect itself, much less comprehend any need to do so. A life too tender and too innocent to understand the abuse perpetrated upon it. He found himself peering back, a face of innocence pressed against the glass from outside the world, longing to belong. There was a simple and unsullied yearning to have the world invite him back in. For it to create a place that would tell him that he mattered, that he had value, and that he counted for something more than nothing.

Jonathon was a reject in likely the most complete form I have ever encountered: a discarded piece of emotionally maimed humanity wrapped in a twelve-year-old body. His pain had deeply marinated throughout a tender twelve-year-old soul, injecting a toxicity that poisoned the very essence of his humanity. His was a life sopped and seeping in the blood of a soul martyred for the amusement of troubled parents. His was a heart mutilated for merriment, a life sacrificed for the sick sexual pleasure of others. A depository of deviance, his life was depleted at twelve. And when he was no longer of value to those who had used him, the drama was raised to a crescendo of accumulated cruelty … he was discarded.

He was abandoned on a desolate road that stretched into a desert of nothingness with little more than cactus, brittle sage, and an endless ribbon of simmering asphalt. Waves of shimmering heat rippled the arid landscape and sucked the desert dry. He felt exactly the same inside. Eventually, a kind deputy sheriff found him wandering and dehydrated. And it was here in the psychiatric hospital that I met the remnant of this little boy—the pieces that were left of whatever he once was, if he was ever anything.

I could only presuppose what Jonathon would have been like had he not lived those twelve years of hell. What could he have been, what would he have been? Deep under layers of stratified emotional chaos that marked the epochs of his life, there laid a glint of something profound, something precious. It was there, and it was real despite the magnitude of his outbursts, the innumerable moments when the accumulated carnage of his life would erupt to the surface in the molten magma of rage, rendering him a seething vegetable of the abuses of others. Even then, there was something remarkable about him, something flagrantly rich and wonderful that even his most outrageous moment could not hide.

Victor Hugo wrote, "To love beauty is to see light." It may be that we don't see beauty because we've spurned it and not permitted enough of its light into our lives in order to see it in the first place. Within Jonathon, there were flecks of diamonds amid his detonations. He was a gifted child, beaten and abused into human oblivion; a wonderment, grossly misshapen by cruel hands into an oddity, a freak. But it was still there, something precious; gross in its deformity, but there. And I saw it with whatever light I had.

## **Belts and Abuse**

Jonathon refused to wear belts. Many of the beatings he had incurred involved a thick leather belt deftly used by his father. Seasoned and supple by countless beatings, it had been cinched tightly around his hands to hold him while the sexual excesses of others were perpetrated upon him. Drawn tight around his neck, it had coerced obedience from horror. It was anything but a fashion accessory. Rather, it was an instrument of horror and a tool of terror—an implement of undiluted evil.

When his father's belt was confiscated by the authorities, it was found to have traces of blood splattered across its leather surface. Bits of skin were found embedded in crevices, a testament to brutality. Jonathon would not wear a belt. No wonder. The sight of a belt would traumatize him, rendering him a fleshy, infantile pile of trembling humanity that whimpered in the labyrinth of a million horrid memories of abuse, each screaming at the top of its lungs, callously throwing their sordid pictures vividly across the forefront of a panicked mind. The torrential deluge of years inundated a brutalized heart that had no more defense against the memories than he had when they were originally seared into his brain and branded on his heart. Seizing him in the clutches of memory that seemed as real as the original moment, Jonathon was an unwitting prisoner shackled to the horror of his past. I often cried for him. So did others. Sometimes, I still do.

Belts. I would never wear mine around Jonathon. The symbolism was so stringent and overpowering for him that he could not see beyond the belt to the person. His mind halted at the specter. Its symbolism was so deeply entrenched by the welts and blood that its presence was consuming. He would melt and utterly disintegrate at the sight of one. And so I never wore one. Ever.

**It Rules Us**

"What do you want with us?" (Luke 4:34). Confused and disoriented, the man heard caustic words leap out of his own mouth that were not his own. These mysterious utterances were oddly brazen yet somehow tentative, sounding like nothing that would represent who he was. The experience was dreamlike and inescapably surreal. This bewildered man valiantly struggled against whatever this was that seemed to have commandeered his voice. The words and the sadistic inflections within which they were encased were fired and then detonated among the listeners, sending satanic shrapnel throughout the temple and the pressing crowd gathered there.

There was the terminally sick feeling that something cold and wholly destitute of any shred of humanity had fully invaded and conquered him, setting up a stalwart stronghold with unassailable ramparts. Wrestle as the man might against whatever it was that held him, he was effortlessly subdued by it and found himself some sort of helpless marionette in a rancid, fiendish drama, watching the crowd gasp in horror at something that he could not control. If our denial and insensibilities grant us some leeway, we realize that there are times when we find ourselves held captive in just the same morbid way.

The voice was bold, flagrant, and narcissistically flamboyant. It projected itself as pompous, cynical, emotionally taunting, and powerful. Controlling the hapless man, the words that were vomited out from within him seemed to slither about the room, filled with venom, striking here and then there, shaking the congregants who had gathered in that most holy place.

The contemptuous attitude of Satan remained obviously unchanged since he was cast from heaven with his minions. Satanic evil has no means of redemption because it will not permit itself any. Evil is not an option for Satan; it is his very character and core essence. And so it remains unchanged, as change would cause him to cease to exist, a thought that likely enrages him.

Raw and fiendish, the demon who had abducted the soul of this man delivered a razor-sharp taunt and issued an arrogant challenge. Unabated evil can become so enamored by the frenzy of its own blackness that it counts itself invincible, even when facing the Messiah.

The demon spun the man around to look at Jesus. Listing the man's head and staring through slanted eyes, it snarled, "Have you come to destroy us?"

Whatever the spirit was, it was blatant and arrogant as it tested the resolve of God by overstating his strength as that of many. An intimate collision was set to occur that was but a portent of a cataclysmic battle that stood not far away on the horizon of time staked with three crosses.

Suddenly, the demon executed an audacious maneuver, an attempt to exercise power by naming the adversary.

"I know who you are—the Holy One of God!" (Luke 4:34).

The vying for the power of this single life in this single place commenced with an agenda for every life precisely and even intimately mirrored in this single life. The enemy had infiltrated a soul and had infiltrated the very house of God. Indeed, it was a deft and cunning act. By doing so, he had shown his deceptive ability as profound ... marvelous even. Here was full-blown evil walking among God's people, in God's house, entirely unnoticed by the crowd gathered there until it blatantly unveiled itself. Too often, full-blown evil walks among us unnoticed. Too often, full-blown evil works within us unnoticed.

The worst of all evil may be invisible evil. I am reminded that evil can insert itself in the very places where I would naturally assume its absence and therefore miss its presence. To evil, nothing is sacred. The demon's contempt for God corresponded to the raw evil that defined him—evil resident even in belts.

The battle was then engaged. Jesus had seen this before. There was at one time a great battle in heaven where evil took excessive stock of itself, arrogantly regaled itself as superior, betrayed God, and was vanquished with the betrayer cast to the earth wrapped in the rage of his own defeat. The result is that he now roams that domain with a single intent to which his allegiance is nothing but militant ... the destruction of mankind. If he cannot destroy God, he will destroy that which bears His image; he will attempt to destroy us. And sadly, he has performed that task with great flair and appalling efficiency. He was performing it here, yet again, right in front of Jesus himself.

A decisive countermove is made by Jesus. "Be quiet ... come out of him" (Luke 4:35), He says. The two things that lead to freedom were pronounced: the silencing of that which haunts us, and then its removal. We are terribly inept at performing those tasks, and so we errantly assume that it's really rather impotent and more the stuff of whimsy. But when God speaks these things, things change forever.

The words of Jesus fell, and there was a sudden internal wrenching in the man that was not of the man, but the colliding and engaging of two opposing forces fighting for the supremacy of the man. Tearing at the man's core, they met in lethal combat on the battlefield of his soul, seeking that soul as a timeless trophy. In the savagery of the spiritual skirmish, the man was thrown and flung helplessly to the floor, heaving a state of deep panic and perpetrating confusion throughout the crowded room.

The two opposing forces vying for his life were infinitely superior to the sum total of his own energies. He was a physical manifestation of a titanic inward clash where irreconcilable forces sought to occupy the same space and make the same claim. As soon as it had begun, it was over. The battlefield was cleared of the enemy. The diabolical forces that had stood arrayed across the landscape of his life were suddenly, inexplicably silent and then absent. The landscape suddenly transitioned from being a torn and ravaged battlefield to a topography that was listlessly placid, hushed with silence, verdantly lush and sufficiently fertile for birthing a new life. All was now still and quiet, which was likely something that had become entirely unfamiliar to the man ravaged by evil.

Cognizance wistfully stirred within the man, tentatively at first and then with greater force. The caustic fog of possession thinned, drifted, and then dissipated. "Where am I?" might have been the first question rising from a groggy mind peering around the corner of a cell door now opened, freed to ask that question and a million others as well. In what place had the demonic force left him at that moment? At what place in his life? Wherever that might be, was there any hope that he could go anywhere from wherever here was?

He may have been unsure of who he was, much less where he was, his identity having long been stolen by an occupying force bent on thievery. That identity was now restored by a liberating force that swept away the occupying force—the holy and passionate blitzkrieg of God unleashed, scourging every trace of evil from his life. The lock was smashed, the prison door was flung open, and now there were nothing but unhindered horizons at his feet. Too often, we have forgotten what horizons look like because prison walls block our view of them.

Freedom was an unfamiliar and alien feeling to him. His recollections of freedom were too dim and too frail to recall with any clarity. Freedom demanded that he must now initiate, he must decide, he must determine what to do next in the massive void of decisions no longer being dictated by an occupying enemy. There were no walls, only horizons. There were no chains, only chances. There were no fetters, only freedom.

Freedom brings the privilege to make decisions and the need to learn once again how to rightly make them. Maxwell Anderson said, "This liberty will look easy by and by when nobody dies to get it." Our responsibility in our freedom is to recognize the astronomical price Jesus paid for that freedom. Out of that understanding, we must always respect our freedom as both undeserved and priceless. For the man, it was a strange and unfamiliar place to be. And so he lay on the floor, paralyzed by freedom.

His eyes slowly cleared and sharpened as the seconds ticked by. A broad, callused hand rested gently on a dazed shoulder; it was the hand of a carpenter, seasoned by constructing lives and hardened for the pending rigor of saving them. The face behind the hand was firm, but warm; intentional, but unexplainably relaxed. The silence of irrefutable victory marked His features as well as the stirring confidence to bring victory, a calm of unarguable confidence that defined Jesus' eyes as something more than eyes.

Deep in the chiseled face, there bespoke authority, but of a far different kind that was wholly trustworthy and entirely indisputable—the kind of authority that you can rest in without any forethought as to its ability to perfectly hold you. An authority inexplicably superior to that which had ruled the man, so vastly superior that it can ill be defined even when all the definitions of mankind itself are gathered and brought to bear upon it. It's the power of authentic freedom that both begs and invites one onward to wild liberation, the ecstatic ecstasy of all the assorted shackles and fetters of enslavement having dropped powerless to the floor of one's life. All the barriers to restoration and to the making of one complete had both been vanquished and had vanished. The authority to restore his assets and his course in life to its original intent had now decisively acted. He was himself … himself restored.

## WHAT POSSESSES ME DEFINES ME

I am a muddled compilation of many things that define me. Things that lay their claim to my life, exercise control over it, and proclaim by virtue of these things that I am this or that. The agreements that I have made with these things do indeed allow them to define me. The manner in which I allow them to convince me that what they say about me is true leaves me a fool and a subservient buffoon. I empower them when I surrender by agreeing that I am what they have defined me to be. If there is ever a point where I question the things that have attempted to define me, I've so lost myself in them that I don't know enough of who I am to question them in the first place. Therefore, I default to their definitions, as I have no other definition to base my life upon.

However, there is on occasion that voice that shouts, "I am other than this!" There is that voice that is hauntingly distant and nearly indiscernible yet a truer part of myself than anything else. Despite the whispered nature of it, it screams truth that renders its whisper a thundering shout. Truth even in the most whispered tones will always roar.

Because of that simple voice, there is then a momentary wrestling and contending with what controls me. My own past and the things that elicit that past are much like the demon that possessed the man and much like a leather belt that possessed Jonathon. These things are vastly stronger, and I am haplessly subdued by them in the wrestling. I eventually surrender to something less than authentic. I surrender to a tragically marginalized self that is set against the real self. Even when I choose to fight against that marginalized self, I find myself subdued by it anyway. Far too often, I have no power to break it, and I am therefore doomed to surrender who I authentically am again and again. I am doomed to being trapped by the thing that imprisons me.

Yet, this possessed man was on the floor before Jesus, and that which possessed him was utterly broken. An alien and unfamiliar sense of some authentic self rushed in and flooded the very concourses of his life with something genuine. It deluged the corridors of his soul and inundated him with himself, with everything that made him uniquely him, despite the fact that he was an alien to himself. It was all terribly unfamiliar but perfectly familiar all at once. He was, in essence, freed to be born again. On the floor, the birth had begun.

The murmur of the congregants, bound by awe, finally found their voices. The sound of awestruck humanity drew the man back to consciousness. This indescribable Jesus was now kneeling before him, His eyes intent, both knowing the birth and watching it transpire, this man being created again for the second time. This prophet, this Jesus drew in the wonder of it all over again.

Jesus is relentlessly fascinated by new birth, as it is never diminished or dissipated for Him. Love creates out of love and because of love. Love can do nothing else. If love is not creating, it is not loving; therefore, it must always be about the business of creating. If love possesses a point of weakness that renders it vulnerable in order that it may be complete, this is it. Jesus loves, and here a soul was created yet again.

Scripture records no words exchanged between Jesus and the man. The speculation of conversation is left to the lost pages of history. But birth needs no explanation because there is nothing else like it. It is the manifest love of God expressing its infinite fullness in a finite package. It is God funneling His infinite characteristics into a human form so terribly limited, but created with limitations so vast that God finds ample room to manifest Himself in it. It's marvelous yet mysterious, and no effort of man—no matter how elegant or purposeful—can explain that.

I am no different. I too am possessed. Maybe differently with other things, but it is possession nonetheless. These things claim me, they control me, they strip me of the infinite characteristics embedded by God in my truest self, and they give me a diminished, dismembered, and marred identity at which I am frequently aghast. Worse yet is to accept this identity in the defeat of self; I doubt there are few things as horrible as accepting that we are less than what God created us to be. Indeed, it is God who can wrench those things out of my life. It is God who can sweep clean the battlefield of my soul and deluge me with the unique characteristics that define the work of the Master in me.

And so, the man reached up and clasped the hand of his liberator. The grip was firm as it always is and always will be. He was about to step into his new life. The power of Jesus' grasp was so sure and so strong that the man was hoisted to his feet. Jesus' hand, callused, thick, and broad, rested its weight on his teetering shoulder. The assembled congregants were lost in the emotional catacombs of unbelief, astonishment, and euphoric emotional trauma. They were immobilized by the impossible and stunned by the spectacular. One more look deep into His eyes and the two parted ways. He had met his Maker, and in that meeting, his Maker remade him.

## Another Belt

There is a tap on my shoulder. By now, I had developed a relationship with Jonathon; so had several others. Trust had been nurtured in the rich loam of consistent love, its seeds having been cradled in the tepid warmth of time spent. Soft waters of gentle affirmation had been tenderly applied to numerous wounds and had soaked through rough husks and softened parched seeds. Their heads were now pressing above the surface, and now, a tap on my shoulder.

I turned. It was Jonathon. And in his hand was something most remarkable. In feeble hands, he held a leather belt. But much more, it was a leather belt that he had made and shaped and crafted himself, with his own hands. He had set his hands and his heart to the very thing that struck such terror in his heart, and it was intricate and ornate, crafted to perfection by hands that were beaten and tied by just such an object. He had stained it to beautiful brown hues. And then, a brass buckle deeply polished so that light would effortlessly dance with abandon on its nearly glassy surface.

"It cost me three dollars," he said. On the buckle … my name: *Craig*. "I'm not afraid anymore," Jonathon said. "See, I'm not afraid anymore!"

The world stopped. All went quiet around me and dissipated into that belt and the gangly twelve-year-old who held it out to me. A broad smile of success was drawn from one side of his thin face clear to the other. Relishing in his victory, he was born again, a second birth. Maybe for Jonathon, it was his first. I don't know. And then the words that forced me to catch myself as their weight fell: "It's for you. I made it for you."

I took in my hands the very thing that had imprisoned this marvelous young man, the very thing from which he was now liberated. He had lived its messages. He had been held captive to their assorted horrors. His life had been dictated by them, and now he was free.

His thin arms were outstretched with the belt lying draped across tender hands. He handed me a symbol of the very thing that had held him. We hugged and we cried. When I replay those moments in my mind yet today, wherever Jonathon is, in my mind I hug him and still cry.

Some thirty years later, I still have that belt. I always will. For it is a reminder of what held Jonathon and defined his life. But far greater and far grander, it is evidence that we need not be held by that which holds us; we all can be remade.

### Pondering Point

There is something in every life that holds us and defines us. Something that so shapes us that we come to believe that we are that thing or that event or that piece or part of our history. We become helplessly defined in ways that are other than who and what we really are. We are held captive to a life that is not that for which we were crafted and created.

It is no small thing to realize this. And it is a marvelous thing to break from it. It is about realizing that Jesus frees us from that which we can't liberate ourselves. He frees us when we are completely blind to our own captivity and when we have confused imprisonment with freedom. When we embrace the reality of that which binds us, and we hold fast to the belief that the choice to be freed from it is ours to make, we can strip it of its power, hold it in our hands without fear, and shout to the world, "I'm not afraid anymore!"

## A Thought
- What defines my life and defines me?
- Where do those definitions come from?
- What have I lost in embracing them as defining who I truly am?
- Am I willing to break from them and be who God created me to be?

## CHAPTER 5

# CONVERGING WITH MY LOSS
## Do I Want the Dead Raised?

*"The blind receive sight, the lame walk, those who have leprosy are cleansed, the deaf hear, the dead are raised, and the good news is proclaimed to the poor."*
Matthew 11:5

*"We do not die because we have to die; we die because one day, and not so long ago, our consciousness was forced to deem it necessary."*
~ Antonin Artaud

**LIFE INTERSECTS US AT TIMES** in such ways that there is no rationale. Events unwind inexplicably, sometimes bringing with them a level of devastation that infuses us with a crippling paralysis. Many of us walk with a forever limp because devastation of this type has befallen us. Futility arises within us at times like this because we can't see any good in it; it seems that anything redemptive is impenitently absent. The travesty of it all is reinforced repeatedly by our inability to perceive even the thinnest apparition of good in these difficult events.

We squint intently with the eyes of our hearts and our souls, attempting to discern some shred of good that gives the bad even the smallest rationale for having befallen us. We desperately seek evidence that life is more than random circumstance that is given free rein to victimize our souls at its own whim. We panic at the thought of being that vulnerable. And if we are that vulnerable, isn't there something even remotely redeeming in the events that make the vulnerability justifiable or worthwhile?

Yet, often we're unable to detect even the most subtle rhyme or reason; we hope frantically for some rationale that would give meaning to the pit we're in, that would give us something to hold onto in the funnel cloud of anarchy that has ripped up the landscape of our lives. We are desperate for some "thing" that would allow us to scan the senseless devastation that lays strewn out to the very horizons of our lives and be able to say with confidence that there is a purpose to it all. We need to know that chaos is not the final determiner or irrevocable end of our existence. We need to have something that would suggest the goodness of God in circumstances that screams both the absence of Him and the absence of His goodness. In those most terrible of moments, these are things we are utterly desperate for. Such was her journey.

### THREE LOSSES FOR AMY

A young adult bruised far too prematurely, Amy had come seeking counseling. Hers was a triple loss: not one or two, but three losses in some horrific parade of malevolent evil. Her life was seemingly ravaged beyond even the thinnest hope of repair. Sometimes life is cruel with a cruelty that lashes us raw. Such was Amy's life.

Hurricanes of horror had slammed their enraged centers into the shore of her life three times in succession. The horrors now having passed and drifted inland, the wreckage of her life lay strewn and pulverized, extending out farther than she could bear to look. The splintered debris lapped the shorelines of her life on incessant waves of grief. She had been laid waste by the fury of life unleashed without restriction, restraint, or remorse. The landscape of her life lay utterly unrecognizable.

Amy sat on my sofa as a mass of devastated humanity, emotionally buckled and limp. Torrents of tears were absorbed in a handful of tissues clutched in trembling hands. Deep, guttural sobbing represented the last and only thing that she knew to do or could do. Teetering on the black abyss of suicide, she had peered down into its dark chasm, and as impossible as she would have ever thought it to be, she found its dark rift preferable to the landscape of wreckage that lay around her.

Suicide would be a journey from which life is irrevocably snuffed and from which no return is possible. It is the decisive and desperate action to take control when no other effort to take control has worked. It's the final prescription for interminable pain. And therein lay the compelling incentive to step into the chasm … it would all be mercifully ended. Leaning precariously into the pull of the abyss, she had sought me for counseling before allowing its black gravity to send her into a full free fall. Amy came for hope, for some flicker of something. Immediately, I realized the holocaust that sat before me.

## Two of Three Losses

The shots had come out of a hopeless night cloaked in darkness and held fast by mental illness. A toxic stew of mental illness, life lethargy, and prolonged marital conflict blended with alcohol and a loaded revolver set the stage for tragedy. Police reports indicated that her stepfather shot his wife—Amy's mother. One bullet was carefully placed in her head to insure the efficiency and permanency of the slug. It was decisive, exactly as it was meant to be. Sometimes hopelessness is decisive. Apparently, Amy's stepfather wasted no time turning the very same weapon on himself, firing a second time just as efficiently and just as accurately. The horrific drama of two lives blown into oblivion was over in less than thirty seconds, but it would reverberate down the concourse of Amy's life forever.

## A Third Loss

There are those times when life has dealt us such a cruel blow that it could not possibly be followed by anything else. We sense that there should be some sort of reprieve or some morsel of mercy tossed our way. Justice and fairness has been placed so far at bay that further injustice seems unjust beyond anything life could possibly think to do to us. Martin Luther King stated, "Injustice anywhere is a threat to justice everywhere." Therefore, we live in a panicked kind of hope that there must be some kindness in life, some small gesture of grace that would cause life to relent, cease the brutality, and end the injustices. If not, injustice will reign unjustly.

But there was another suicide of sorts. Not an immediate suicide like the one that had leapt out of a hopeless night and dissipated just as quickly into its stealthy darkness. Those kinds of suicides are easily identifiable because of their immediacy. This one was a slow suicide, like the types so many of us live out, not even knowing we're living them out. This kind of suicide ends in death just the same. It is designed to kill us; it simply takes longer to get the job done and so we dub it "living" when it's the very same process that occurred in that hopeless night.

Out of the pain of a murder/suicide, Amy would search for a father who had long abandoned her. She decided to turn to him in an attempt to elicit some morsel of solace. Surely, if anything would open a door long closed, this would be it. Compassion and empathy would certainly find enough rootage in such tragedy to span the vast gulf of decades lost and cut through the soupy fog of alcoholism. Believing that good could not help but show up in so much mindless tragedy, she began a frighteningly desperate search for a father who was more a stranger than anything else.

After a painfully rigorous search, she eventually found him. She discovered him abjectly lost in a disintegrating cultural morass of alcohol and drugs. He was a hapless recluse engulfed in senseless, self-perpetuated destruction. His instrument of suicide was not a gun. His death would not be the result of the pull of a trigger, the action of a firing pin, the sudden muzzle velocity that followed it all, and an instant death. The slower death of variant substances, both legal and illegal, did what that single slug had, only slowly enough so that each of death's morbid stages was grotesquely drawn out in a manner missed in the immediacy of a shot to the head. Her father was physically alive, but dead in every other respect. Amy turned to him, cautiously reaching for a sustaining arm in the gale force winds that raged around her.

With trembling fingers, she placed a telephone call to a father who was likewise a stranger living out a distant existence a thousand miles away, both geographically and emotionally. Having stumbled dazed, bloodied, and maimed out of the savagery of the suicidal storm that had swept down the shoreline of her life, she thought he might, for once, pity her and be the father he never was. Even if he were to be a father for only the briefest of moments, simply saying a few things that had even the most minute bits of fatherhood scattered within them, it would be enough.

The phone rang, he answered, and within the achingly short span of a handful of sentences, his words went caustic. She was met with words slurred by alcohol, leaving only the barest recognition of a voice from a very distant past. She strained to correlate the incoherence with the father whose well-worn memories lay in a distant past rendered foggy by time. Barely had the conversation taken shape before a drunken rebuff erupted on the other end. A history thought to be long gone and forever relegated to the annals of the past leapt into the present.

His words were callous and vile, wrapping his rejection of her in toxic trappings. Crushing feelings of abandonment surged out from her past in the form of a slammed receiver, immediately dropping her to the floor under its weight. Holding a phone gone dead, drowning in an empty dial tone that seemed to mock her hopes for a father, she collapsed into a heaving heap on the floor of her apartment and sobbed for two dark hours. She was torrentially engulfed in a third loss.

Now this bedraggled and hopeless young woman sat in my office. She was desperately attempting to string together the events in a way that would allow her to somehow still believe that God was good and that God had a plan of some sort, that the insanity had some redeeming thread hidden away somewhere in the ravaging folds of its black fabric. Any sense of justice or goodness was entirely gone, leaving her desperately searching the folds of her mind, plumbing the depths of her soul, and frantically praying down the halls of heaven itself to find it. Her pain was steeped in her inability to do exactly that. She was dying. There would be a fourth death if I failed. There would be a fourth if God didn't show up.

## Another Loss

Two crowds moved toward a healing collision. One headed south from coastal Capernaum with the Son of God amid a swirling mass of mesmerized admirers. Another one headed north, spilling out through the chalky white basalt arches of a city gate bleached by an unrelenting sun, scoured by gritty winds and stuccoed rough with pain.

A funeral bier and a grieving mother set a cadence slogged in the mire of despair. Death had come as the indomitable thief, and it had pillaged freely. Its thirst had not been satiated the first time, so it had returned to take the widow's son after it had taken her husband. She was bent twice by death.

Napoleon Bonaparte wrote, "Death is nothing, but to live defeated and inglorious is to die daily." This woman had died daily for so many years that living a life of death was her lot. Sometimes death is wholly confused with life, incarcerating us in a penitentiary of death until death does us a courtesy by actually coming to steal us away. It is a most horrid existence, and she was living it. Stumbling and then collapsing, she fell faint into the sturdy arms of those who escorted her in a sullen procession punctuated by the plaintive wails of the grieving that accentuate the silence of death and called its work out into the open. She herself was living death.

Off in the distance, just beyond the edge of a horizon now shimmering in the heat of a day, there walked a prophet. His cadence was set and measured by the defeat of death, creating a very different tempo. He had just vied with death in the dying body of an obscure servant of a centurion and had won. So powerful is He, that death had been thwarted from a distance. This Jesus could reach across chasms of space and time and quell death even from those remote places. This woman's situation was quite different. To the contrary, despite pleadings long into the dark night of the soul, this woman had surrendered a son to death. She had not won either time.

Jesus and this woman were set to meet standing on the opposite ends of life, closing in from opposite directions on the hard-packed dust of a thin road that would direct the two to each other. Two fluid masses were set to merge in an historical convergence; one desperately needing what the other possessed, not knowing that a convergence of God's power was about to offset death's power. Flowing, they came together along the dusty road of grief that wound through a mother's heart.

An only son and a widow—the sting of death had struck twice. First, a husband's funeral with a cold bier, a grieving crowd, and an unredeemable loss just like this one. The very same road of dust and death was being walked ... again. She found herself passing the same bleached basalt arches that she had passed once before, their chalky whiteness mimicking the pallor of death and chiding her. The footprints of that journey were still fresh across the dusty expanse of her heart. Her son had assumed the vacated headship, providing financially and representing the family in the social and religious life of the community. He likely postponed marriage out of his obligation to the family. And now he passed as well. It was one death but a multiple loss: a son, a provider, a spokesman for the family, a seed for a next generation that would never be was lost all in one single blow. This woman of loss was inconsolable, and she was drowning when the two waves met.

Word filtered back to Jesus about the approach. Death, ever persistent, was about its dark business with its black handiwork laid out in full view in an approaching funeral bier. Jesus had thwarted it only days earlier in the life of a menial servant. Recoiling in the rage of that defeat, death had raced ahead of Him, seizing a life once and a family twice as if to exact revenge and retribution on this Messiah. Now, it flagrantly waved its work in His face.

Jesus was told, "She is a widow." He paused and recalled with vivid clarity the furrowed lines of pain etched across his own mother's face at the death of Joseph, His father. He remembered the spastic convulsion of grief that wrenched his mother at death's visitation to His own family. He recalled her face awash in tears. Burying her head in His chest, she murmured the repeated and plaintive "why?" that echoed the crippling disorientation and abrupt finality of death. His own tears had likely joined hers, as sin begets death and death always seizes the heart of God.

Somehow, because of that, He was closer to the widow's grief. This was the eldest son, as was He. The provider for this family, as Jesus was to His. He saw His own past in the widow's face, His life in her story and, in the oddity of their shared humanity, He saw His future in the funeral bier. His heart went out to her long before He had reached her, as God's heart went out to each of us infinite eons before He ever breathed life into us. Jesus' choice to become one of the very humans that He had created allowed Him to identify deeply with His own creation by becoming that creation. He is both God and His creation simultaneously. He quickened His pace, and the waves converged.

## My Funeral Biers

Funeral biers frequently tread the thin, dusty roads of my heart. Sometimes their contents are clear, known, and understandable. Yet, known or unknown, they thread that thin, dusty road with far more frequency than I would like.

The trembling fingers of my heart draw across the coarse boards of those biers, hoping for the slightest pulse or the most subtle semblance of warmth that would refute what I know to be true. Denial of death does nothing to offset death, despite the desperate desire I have that somehow that might happen. These funeral biers are familiar—too familiar. When they come, my life clouds with thunderheads of grief, my heart groans, my spirit wails in deep convulsions at yet another death that seems nothing more than another cruel act that gives life some sort of morbid pleasure. It seems that life seeks some form of sadistic entertainment at my expense and finds levity in my pain. And when life has had its fill, when it's gorged itself on my desperation and is finally content, it will then allow this devastation, whatever it has been, to destroy me. In the macabre spectacle, I have been expended in the provision of the entertainment.

Often I cry at the senselessness of it all. Sometimes I am inconsolable. Often I am desperate. Incapacitated, I stumble alongside the bier, holding whatever part of my life that has died this time, wondering when all these deaths will eventually kill me. Wondering how I will survive this loss in light of all the other losses. Paralyzed by the fear of what loss might be next. How soon will I again walk this dusty road? How many other funeral biers will there be? Will I survive another? When will I myself be the thing in the bier?

## AMY AND HER BIER

I saw that in Amy. Her eyes softly bespoke exactly that. She had walked that road not once, not twice, but three grueling times. She was spent. Her heart screamed it, and I felt it, its power thrusting me back into my chair and sending my clinician mind spinning for some answer to that which sometimes has no answer. Often there is no answer to death, only a response based in forced surrender. She was spent in supplying the morbid entertainment and so she plummeted, wholly depleted from the ghastly expenditure she had endured.

## LIFE FROM DEATH

But there is a convergence, coming along this very road, this same road that seems so intolerable. A road of resignation that blows only the dust of defeat in parched swirling eddies across graves where hope is interred and forever entombed. There is a convergence set for this woman's road, coming toward her, toward me and toward you, a meeting with a "man of sorrows ... familiar with suffering" (Isaiah 53:3).

Jesus was coming, closing, constantly drawing nearer when we would suspect nothing on this terribly desolate road other than pain. Word filtered to Him. Our pain resonates with His, rendering Him a true companion and not a distant spectator. He has experienced our pain, but perfectly so. He has walked beside the biers, but He has also been laid in them. The difference is that He rose out of them with the futility of every bier resting in the astounding reality that every one of them has now been undermined in His resurrection. His heart goes out to you, to me, to Amy, and to all the other Amys stumbling through all their grief as they trod the roads of death and broken hearts.

He quickened His pace, and the crowds merged. In the middle of the human congestion, He finds her, turns to her, and in the interior of death's apparent victory and life's displayed cruelty, he says, "Don't cry" (Luke 7:13). The widow has had every reason to cry, as do we.

Crying is what's left when nothing is left. So she's crying and for good reason. Now, she had every reason not to cry, but she doesn't know that yet. Both crowds momentarily converged, blending into a single solid mass drawn around a solitary funeral bier. Stillness settled, and the crowd became hushed.

No miracle had been requested. Perhaps it was not known that one was possible. Perhaps loss can be so scorching that restoration is inconceivable. Maybe the thought of a miracle seems so ridiculously incomprehensible that it's shoved into an emotional abyss of fanciful thinking. Perhaps loss can be bigger than our ability to comprehend it and therefore vaster than our ability to conceptualize a solution to it. Perhaps.

Jesus paused and stared into the vacant eyes of a worn woman left hollow from the incomprehensible nature of loss, the thievery having stolen the spark that sets mankind apart from all else in creation. The precious spark of life was gone from the soul of her eyes, and Jesus was grieved by the dimness He saw there. He turned from the widow, eyed the bier, and squinted in soft determination. Coarse boards, hardly the gilded chest that should carry the treasure of one of God's created beings. It was more the symbol of surrender carrying the thing surrendered, representing the utter helplessness of mankind to redeem loss. It screamed the inability that we often have to choose something other than surrender. It bowed to death as if it felt it had no other recourse.

Then, a squared grimace of determination mixed with a slight smile of pending liberation set itself in His features. Eyes glinting, Jesus moved toward the coffin. The crowd parted in His advance. Confidence marked each determined step. He halted barely a step away from the bier. Without hesitation, He reached out and deliberately touched the bier, gently running His fingers across its embalmed coarseness. Oblivious to the pallbearers and to the crowd, His heart was determined and His focus concise. With words firm, confident, and yet soft, He drew a breath and with an intonation of impeccable authority said, "Young man, I say to you, get up!" (Luke 7:14).

In loss, most often our underlying expectation is that we adjust to the loss. Loss is rarely about reclamation. Rather, loss is about burying what we've lost as deep as we can possibly bury it and moving on. So when Jesus speaks to us about abandoning the burial in some sort of living reversal, we find ourselves taken aback, sometimes in confusion and at other times in anger because of such an audacious action on Jesus' part. Sometimes, the greatest intrusions are when Jesus steps in to resurrect the very thing we've determined to bury. In our terrible shortsightedness, we can't see life, so we demand that death be left to be death. And it's here that Jesus angers us when, in reality, He has come redeem us. It's likely that many of those in that gathered pool of humanity that day felt some of those very feelings.

Yet, Jesus proceeds because the desire of God to restore His creation is always greater than our lack of faith in His ability to do so. And so, a slight, shallow breath was drawn by the dead son on the heels of the breath drawn by Jesus to utter the command of life. There was a pause in the son's body as if what was seen was a mirage, a projection of a corporate hope embraced by everyone gathered there but being nothing more than a projection. And then the next breath came deeper and more robust; then another pause. Then, unbelievably, another breath raised a dead chest.

Ashen gray skin was slowly rubbed warm with a complexion deepening into soft fleshy tones. The body faintly stirred. Muscles drew a stiff arm across the rising chest. The body shifted slightly as if stretching itself awake from sleep. Pallbearers, suddenly balancing the shifting weight of life in motion were lost in an emotional abyss. Their minds became frozen in the grip of the impossible being made possible. The funeral bier was now transformed from a carrier of death to a deliverer of birth.

A hand rose and clasped the coarse boards. Securing a tight grip with fingers wrapped in burial cloth, the body was pulled upright.

It sat for a moment as if coming to terms with life coming from death. A gasp raced wildly through the crowd, followed quickly on its heels by the electrifying reality of what was transpiring. Grave clothes listlessly unraveled, their loosed ends softly fluttering as they were caught by a gentle breeze. The pallbearers anxiously dropped the bier and backed away, as miracles of the most divine sort seem an odd mix of the miraculous and fear.

The man's hand traced a tremulous path up the side of his head until he found the end of the cloth. He then peeled the wraps off his face in sweeping circular motions that became increasingly ecstatic with each rotation. The last wrap fell away, and a gasp rippled through the crowd, themselves pulling away. The man shaded both of his eyes from the surge of blinding sunlight and with squinted intensity, he scanned the crowd. A murmuring swell surged across the throng. His eyes then landed on Jesus. Ever intent, Jesus smiled, held out a hand and escorted the man up from his bier and out to life.

Immediately the young man was conversant, possibly recounting the glories of heaven to Jesus or perhaps recognizing Jesus as the visiting God descended from that place. Likely amazed at his own return, he gave praise to God. Turning in the midst of his praise, he caught sight of his joy-stricken mother. Stretching out reinvigorated and longing arms, he shouted, "Mother, Mother!"

We do not know exactly what he said. The text does not say. It's possible that such a moment of intimacy was far too private and far too glorious to be diminished by penning it into mere words. But he talked and laughed and likely shouted. We can be assured that coming back from death leaves a lifetime of things to talk about.

The funeral was over, but the crowd had not grasped that yet, not entirely. Nonetheless, it was indeed over. The text states that Jesus "gave him back to his mother" (Luke 7:15). The terminology is reminiscent of the return of a prisoner of war or a captive released from imprisonment. It speaks of the place of captivity having been invaded by a superior force and the prisoner abducted to freedom. Released, returned, and fully restored, he was free.

The response of the mother is unrecorded. She was likely hysterical, as would be most of us. It is probable that she touched him with pensive hands, hugged him deeply, drew back to look with amazement, to verify, then touched and seized him yet again. A mix of wild joy was likely wed with a sense of sheer impossibility that told her that what she knew to be true could not be true. In the wild gyrations of death upturned, she likely had to allow her senses ample time to take in the unfathomable reality before her in order to know it to be true, and based on its truth to begin the joyous task of recalibrating her life based on a risen life.

The bier was now empty, except for the memory of death robbed and life retrieved. A dead man stood on a dusty road outside of basalt gates now rendered a warm mauve from a sun leaning toward a western horizon. Pallbearers stood beside an empty bier turned on its side as if it had spilled its contents, for it had. A book of life once slammed closed was now thrown open with ample empty pages upon which to pen a life-long novel. Hope was reclaimed from the abyss. The dead man was standing in a pile of unraveling grave clothes with the brazen confidence of death unraveling all around him.

The crowd condensed toward the center and closed in around the young man, each person anxious to verify the truth of what had been witnessed. The sun, still bright and vibrant in its westward descent, warmed the landscape. The crowd eventually turned toward home. There would be no burial today. The gravesite would be backfilled with nothing but dirt. Mourning was turned to celebration. Jesus did what He came to do without those for whom He did it being able to fathom the full majesty of what had just happened. The Son of God moved on, headed toward His own funeral bier.

## COMING TO OUR BIERS

And so He comes to our coffins. When we see no recourse to yet another loss in our lives, He comes down that hopeless road and looks at us with a compassion of eternal proportions. He says to us, "Don't cry." There's a squared grimace of determination mixed with a slight smile of pending liberation. Eyes glinting, Jesus moves toward our many coffins. Confidence marks each step. He halts. Without hesitation, He touches our funeral biers; gently He runs His fingers across their coarseness, oblivious to the frigid distractions that death brings with it. His heart is determined and His focus concise. With words firm, confident but soft, He says, "I say to you, get up!" (Luke 7:14). And life is restored. Our lives … yours and mine and anyone who would risk hope.

The funeral is indeed over, and often we don't really realize it. What has been stolen is given back to us, and we stand in utter amazement, sometimes hysterical that what was lost to us has been given back. Eventually, we turn toward home. There will be no burial today. Mourning is turned to celebration. Jesus does what He came to do without us being able to fathom the majesty of what has happened. And we are stunned by His work in our lives.

## AMY'S RESTORATION

Sometimes we don't know we're dead until we're made alive again. Sometimes things in our lives have to die so that we, by holding ourselves up against the loss, can see our own deadness. We sometimes need to see that, in the grander scheme of things, it is not necessarily about the return of that which has died. Rather, it is about seeing how that which has died highlights our lack of living. Often, the first step in our own resurrection is realizing how dead we really are. And sometimes it's the death of things in our lives that highlight how little we're really alive in the first place.

Oddly enough, in the end it was Amy in those biers. Not her mother, her stepfather, or her father. All three of them were dysfunctional and had deeply scarred her life. She was the accumulation of their sordid actions and self-centered choices that had been spilled out upon her and had drowned her for year after devastating year. Heartless neglect and sadistic abuse had merged in an acidic mix that had dissolved her soul, rendering her life a zombie-like apparition. She thought herself to be living, but she was thoroughly dead. Any spark of life had long been extinguished by these three people before she was old enough to know what that spark was. Their actions had put her in a bier decades ago. Their deaths made way for her resurrection.

Therapy would be long and arduous. The bier and the funeral procession would traverse the dusty roads of her soul for quite some time. Sometimes life's journey is not about the miraculous as much as it's about Jesus working out the miraculous along the long, dusty road of the mundane. In time, however, there was a convergence along her road. She realized that the death of that which was gone from her life gave her the opportunity to live. It was more about something being removed than something being lost. And in their removal, she rose.

Unexpectedly and shockingly, she drew her first real breath, sat up for the first time, groped to unfurl the grave clothes, and squinted into the light of life and the face of Jesus. At twenty-six, she is alive for the first time. Today, her bier is finally empty.

## Pondering Point

Things die in us and around us. We relegate ourselves to the losses, sometimes railing against them. They cause us to raise questions about life, about God, and about the validity of life and living. We presume that death implies burial. Burial assumes the permanence of loss. We relegate that part of ourselves or life as forever vanquished to thievery, with the resultant diminishment of our lives beyond our ability to control. Stolen hopes and pilfered promises fall upon our lives like a sudden summer cloudburst. However, Jesus is the Master at seizing what is dead and resurrecting the loss. He is the unchallenged Master at bringing something immeasurably grander into our lives than that which was lost. He stands ready to walk beside your biers, whatever they might be, whenever they might be.

## A Thought
- What are my biers?
- Have I become so comfortable with them that I am hesitant to rid myself of them?
- How many have I relegated to the past that I might be able to reclaim through Jesus?
- Am I willing to invite Him to my biers, knowing that my life will be radically different because I made that choice?

CHAPTER 6

# JUDGING IN THE COURTYARD
## Stripping Away Appearances

*"Woe to you, teachers of the law and Pharisees, you hypocrites! You are like whitewashed tombs, which look beautiful on the outside but on the inside are full of the bones of the dead and everything unclean."*
Matthew 23:27

*"One's real life is so often the life that one does not lead."*
~ Oscar Wilde

**FILTH DESCRIBED SUSAN VERY WELL.** While it was an apt depiction, it failed to embrace the fullest description of what she was. Some lives seem to be nothing more than a brutal manifestation of the accumulated slag and scum that is leftover in the wake of some departed tragedy. These people become the thing that life has done to them, being so irreparably identified with their own tragedies that they themselves are a living manifestation of those assorted tragedies. Hers was a life that was already an abysmal collection of untold catastrophes that resulted in nearly indescribable filth. She was only fourteen.

Susan was of little note as she stepped off the bus that first day of summer camp. She was one of over one hundred campers swirling in an arriving mass of anticipation. Gathering tattered bags and a tattered spirit, her eyes were set hollow with the effects of a life lived in hatred. Filth and a pervading stench separated her from the rest almost instantly. Her soul seemed to reek with a putrid odor that handily eclipsed the smell emanating from her skin and clothing. There was about her an inner ugliness that permeated everything else about her, that had consumed her and had digested whatever shred of good there might have been. It all seemed to have effectively left the fragrance of any human goodness now consumed in the sludge of whatever it was that defined her.

Her defense mechanism was so refined that she immediately repelled anyone who drew near, thrusting others so far away that she guaranteed her own isolation. Her own woundedness was so complete that the poison of the pain she felt spewed in venomous rage at anyone who approached. Her self-hatred was effectively projected outward onto anyone who dared draw near physically or emotionally. She seemed as something less than human, something abominable, something terribly horrifying within which any shred of humanity was consumed and utterly lost.

The following week of camp was to be marred by ugly confrontations. She devolved into assorted rages that were wild, brutish, entirely unprovoked, and profuse. She refused to shower. Ferocious outbursts were filled with anger distilled into lethal poison that devastated other hearts, young and old. Physical assaults and violent rages had an insane wildness and a touch of insanity about them. There emerged at times something animalistic about her, something very primal that raged unrestrained by either reason or rationale. At times, the line between that of a visceral animal and a human being was blurred and ill-defined.

In the end, Susan was isolated in a lone cabin. Her parents refused to come and get her. Her pastor was unwilling and unable to deal with her rages, as her life did not fit neatly into some clean theological rubric that he could manage. The camp staff gathering to pray for her but found their prayers to be ineffective. Some sort of spiritual possession was questioned, and rightly so. She was a monster—a raging, pathetic monster that we waited to relieve ourselves of at the close of camp. Such was our judgment of her.

## JUDGING FROM FEAR

Judging is, I think, a manifestation of our own fears. We judge so that we might have some sense of control and some feeling of superiority. If we judge that which is before us, we assume we will not become whatever it is that we are rendering judgment upon. We set ourselves apart as distinct from that thing or that person, with that distinction somehow convincing us that we are different. Judging places us above that which we judge, meaning that we will not succumb to it from our supposedly elevated position.

We judge because we fear, and because we fear, we are not prone to look deeply into the person that we're judging. For if we look deeply, we might see ourselves. We might be forced to surrender to the reality that that which we are rendering judgment upon is as much a part of that person as it is a part of us. Superficial judgment allows us to bypass our own humanity and live in the lie of superiority. The person whom we judge is then sacrificed to our thin, self-serving judgments. Whatever it is that God wanted to do in our lives through that person is tragically lost.

## JUDGMENT REVEALED

It was to be that final night of camp. The next morning, a mass of buses and cars would invade the gravel parking lot, snatching up sunburnt campers filled with the wild tales of a week's adventures. But that would be tomorrow. For now, night had fallen, drawing up a warm blanket of thick summer air across the camp and out beyond the wooded expanse, tucking the world in at each horizon.

Crickets sang in a chorus of the night from the deep woods, lulling the day to slumber with their mesmerizing notes. Frogs bellowed thick from a stream that meandered through a wooded ravine down a slight ridge. Their chorus hauntingly rolled up the rise and across the small meadow. Lightning bugs cast dancing pinpoint pigments of yellow across the shadowy landscape and deep into the tall stands of sleepy timber. The moon had only shaken a sliver of itself awake, mingling with the starry minions. It was a divine night, soft and subtle. God's creation was melding into perfection.

With the campers bedded down for that final night, I strolled down to the chapel now bathed in the soft shadows of night. A few moments with God at the end of a long week seemed so right. Drawn, I descended the winding dirt and gravel path with the soft crunch of each step muffled by night's thick softness. Slight shadows cut from the thin pastel light of a sleepy moon seemed to whisper something about reverence and what it is to be alone with God.

Another person had thought the same. The outdoor chapel was framed by a wall of river rock that extended muscular granite arms around an expansive gravel floor. Across the gravel expanse there stood a rock and timber altar with a muscular, rough-hewn cross as a shadowy sentry. Thick timbers supported a vaulted wooden roof spread with broad knotty pine boards. The woods beyond were alive with the night. And Susan was there.

A shadowy figure knelt at the altar. Her aloneness was poignant, an isolated life kneeling before an altar in a desperate hope of somehow breaking that isolation. The crying was soft and indistinct, muted by her fear of vulnerability. The moment was a manifestation of a broken heart and deeply wounded spirit that had somehow collided with God enough to strike a spark of hope. She was kneeling there, her fingers embedded in the rock altar, hoping that this hope would not fail her as had everything else.

We had all seen her as ugly, despicable, the slimy scum of humanity that teetered on the savagery of a wild animal. We wanted nothing more than to see the sun break on the final day of camp and watch her leave both the camp and our lives. We could not wait to be rid of her, to relegate this vermin back to the hole from which she had crawled. To say we hated Susan was likely excessive. To say we despised her was likely true. And yet, here she was, broken. The wounded humanity she so vehemently lashed out from was pouring out across that rock and timber altar. Her core was exposed and for the first time, I saw a slight glimpse of her humanity. I had errantly judged it not to be there for fear that I would recognize it in myself. Now I saw her brokenness and in it, I recognized my own.

I feared her, not knowing in that moment what to do, not wanting to do anything out of the fear of behaviors I'd observed and the hatred I'd seen spew from her. But I found myself walking toward her anyway. Having made no conscious decision to do anything, I stepped, my footsteps dictated by something wholly other than me. Suddenly, I was beside her in the thick dark, in the thick of night—in the thick of her night. Without a word spoken, she reached up, took my hand, and drew me down to her side with a force that buckled my knees. Putting a trembling arm around me as if the whole of her spirit was leaning its weight on me, I felt for that brief instant the intolerable hell of her life. And in that moment, I understood why she was what she was.

Her words were to silence the night that surrounded us. Nature drew down into the moment, stood on tiptoe, so it seemed, as God reached out from the expanse of that starry night and changed a life through a most remarkable collision.

Her next words set me back, instantly slicing through all the things that had caused me to judge her so harshly and revealing who this really was. She said, "Would you pray with me?" Without a word from me, her heart ruptured open in prayer. I never uttered a sound. There was no need, as such an action would have been only an intrusion in that transforming moment. Massive floodgates surged open, and an enormous reservoir of pain that had accumulated over the incalculable expanse of years and events deluged the darkened chapel. I knelt ... stunned. I had arrogantly diminished her in my judgments, and I experienced my own cleansing in hers. It was a marvelous and privileged moment.

In the end, we spent over an hour kneeling in the gravel, cloaked in a deep summer's night. Her prayers, a lifetime tidal wave of events and circumstances, kept coming—of abuse and neglect and drugs. The assorted maladies such as hunger, too few clothes, empty birthdays, numerous evictions, and the rejection of society that abject poverty brings to a young life. There was a devastating abortion and a fathomless litany of other terrifying choices that had shredded her soul. A father's alcoholism, a brother's suicide, and a mother's continual marital unfaithfulness layered in it all. Things that I could have never have comprehended. Hers was a devastated life beyond description: a human holocaust.

And it all poured into the night, across the rock and timber altar, down the gravel floor, out into the deep woods, and into the expanses of heaven itself. When it was done, she was free and her core was cleansed. Likewise, I was free. In that chapel, God gave me far more than I had ever expected as I had trod the dirt and gravel path earlier that night. I saw bits of me in her, and they were likewise swept away in her own release.

The next sunrise may have actually been her very first sunrise, the day dawning over a new life. With the sun barely warming the eastern horizon, she went to the shower. Her clothes were deposited in the washer. She combed her hair into long, translucent waves, brushed her teeth bright, and put on fresh, clean clothes. A touch of borrowed makeup and a slight spritz of perfume rounded out the transformation. Arranging herself in the mirror, she gently primped herself to perfection.

Susan walked into the cafeteria for that final breakfast wholly new. Silence fell over one hundred campers. Its power was deafening. All of our superficial judgments had defined her for all of us. So complete were they that we all sat there trying to make them fit this new person for, sadly, we knew no other way to define her. The old judgments of a monster melted away in the light of their gross insufficiency, and a fresh understanding of this remarkable young woman seized the room. A litany of miracles walked in with her.

At that final breakfast, she went from table to table to table. Asking for forgiveness from those she'd hurt. Weeping with those whose lives she'd scarred. Holding the faces of so many in her hands, looking intently into their eyes and telling them how sorry she was. Hugging and holding and crying with an endless array of campers and counselors. No one ate breakfast that morning; sometimes life becomes bigger than food and larger than any agenda. Sometimes life intersects us so powerfully that the only thing we can give attention to is that which intersects us. And Susan intersected us all.

A revival broke in that cafeteria. Clusters of young lives gave themselves to God over eggs, bacon, and a radically changed life. Busses and arriving cars were asked to wait until the surge of one life changed had fully raced and run through the hundreds of other hurting lives that morning. The vast gulf between what we were and what we could be was searingly highlighted in Susan. And in the end, God ravaged the work of Satan and the deep pain of innumerable adolescents through the life of a single young lady who chose to see her core and live differently because of it. It was the most remarkable thing I have ever seen. A wretched and putrid life detested by those around her changing the very lives that had hated her, thereby leaving a legacy of life with them.

## An Errant Judgment

The rocks had dropped one by one. Each thud stirred a slight wisp of talcum-like dust that quickly settled. With it, a slight wisp of hope and of life spun gentle eddies in her heart. Garbled whispering rose from the gathered cluster of angered religious leaders. Cutting glances rendered razor sharp with hatred were slung across the courtyard toward her. Righteous indignation wrapped itself like a robe around pious bodies. And then, a slow dispersing of those gathered in their robes and finery, with the old leaving first. The sound of feet on departing gravel built and then gradually lessened as the courtyard was emptied.

Soon, silence drifted in, leaving the scene littered still with lifeless rocks to attest to hatred halted and judgment deferred. The only thing left was a prostitute and the Son of God. What remained was a broken human groveling in the acidic guilt of promiscuity … and Jesus. Hollowness and wholeness stood one to one.

Half naked, the hours had been truncated with deception, discovery, detainment, and deliberation. She had been deep in an illicit sexual embrace, and eyes were watching it all happen, peering past slightly parted curtains. A door stood slightly ajar. Shooing away curious passersby, they collected visual evidence as to the unfolding offense under the guise of a righteous action while hiding the feeding of their own sensate passion by vicariously engaging in the heat of passion themselves. Then the trap was sprung. She was seized, a few loose garments were thrown around her naked body, heckles of debauchery were hurled at her, and she was dragged away. Her partner somehow vanished; his purpose was fulfilled. But that was earlier.

The religious leaders had now departed. Jesus slowly stood. His gaze, contemplative and soft, shifted from the marks scrawled in the dirt and was drawn across the empty courtyard. It is painful that people condemn in others that which they cannot accept in themselves. That somehow the act of condemning some sordid vice or caustic behavior in others supposedly frees those rendering judgment from those very same failings. They had in some way proven themselves invincible to whatever they were confronting because they had identified it and confronted it in another. In doing so, they somehow viewed themselves as insulated from that same thing.

In the oddity of facing our own filth, judging is most often not a necessary action, but an action initiated out of the fear that those judging might themselves engage in such horrific actions. Judging is too often a self-centered act designed to free the one judging from the belief that they will ever be consumed or controlled by that which they are judging. The sense of love that one might possess for another human being succumbs to the fear of what oneself might actually do and the narcissism of self-preservation that arises out of that fear. It had all resulted in their judgment of this woman. The rocks that littered the courtyard yelled it loudly, long after those who had dropped them had exited.

Jesus drew a slight breath, paused, and then turned. Before Him there now knelt a hollow human being. Few turn to the profession of prostitution unless there is wounding emptiness. There are few people in life who are so relentlessly hollow and hold such an unyielding self-hatred as those who ply her trade. She had likely arrived at this moment in time empty and numb, in desperate need of a touch, of some slight affirmation. Receiving even a morsel of someone's heart and life might have been just enough to pull her up and out of the life that she lived. Empathy instead of judgment; compassion instead of condemnation; love instead of legalism; someone who might look just a bit beyond the putrid exterior to see the wounded and bleeding person inside.

Men had used her, violating her for a few scant coins. They saw her only as an object upon which to release their sexual tensions and live out their distorted fantasies. They had been unwilling to see the person who died a little more after each illicit rendezvous. They didn't care to see. They had judged her too, but they judged her differently. They had judged how she might be used by them and how the assets she possessed could be abducted in the vandalism of another human being.

Then there was the disgust of other men that was thrown out in taunts and heckling as she made her way through tight streets. Vendors refused to sell her goods. Still other men wanted to stone her, to kill her, to rid the world of her without understanding why she was who she was. Each of them rendered their sordid judgments, each colored by their place of proximity and point of orientation to her life. It was the very same thing I had done to Susan.

Yet, the man who now stood over her in an abandoned courtyard was a very different kind of man, the kind of man I would like to be. His example prompts and prods me to grapple with my inadequacies rather than judging those in the lives of others. His example convinces me that something human resides in even the most destitute of persons and that I must be diligent in seeking it out even when I can't see it. His eyes see past our actions and ground themselves decisively on our humanity, thereby utterly refusing to allow our frequently pathetic conduct to define us. I must do these things so that I might do the same as He did.

Jesus had no need to judge. He did not need to judge the prostitute in order to feel insulated against her atrocities. He had no need to elevate Himself over her to feel safe from that which had destroyed her. He was not concerned with advancing Himself or His interests at her expense. He simply saw her humanity, He asserted it through His actions, He shielded it, and then He allowed it to be released rather than condemned by the rendering some sort of self-serving judgment.

Jesus stood in the breech and turned the condemnation away. "Woman, where are they? Has no one condemned you?" (John 8:10), he said to her. A life of condemnation was suddenly still and hauntingly absent. It would be reasonable to assume that she was painfully aware of the legal consequences of her trade. In the social circles within which she navigated, there were likely other prostitutes who had fallen prey to such judgment and had summarily been stoned to death. Certainly, the stories of these morbid executions and all their grisly details had found their way to her, whether it had been some distant stranger living on the periphery of her life, or someone she knew well. Death by stoning was not an alien concept to this woman.

That day, her world had suddenly spun in a gyrating blur of deceit, confusion, panic, and morbid fear. When it finally cleared, she found herself kneeling in the talcum dirt of a courtyard, living out the very gruesome moment that she had likely played out hundreds of times in her own head. The saga that she had played out over and over in her mind always ended in a death so horribly gruesome that her own imagination was insufficient to write the script adequately. Yet, here she was, and the script was being vehemently written out for her.

However, suddenly she found herself entirely free of the condemnation that had satiated her life and shackled her heart. It didn't end as it was supposed to, as she had rehearsed it so many arduous times on so many lonely nights. It was an odd and alien experience for her. She was no longer suppressed by the judgments of others that were designed to elevate them. She was not sacrificed out of the need of someone else to feel superior. She was not used so that someone else was satisfied in the using. She was freed to be different and to do different.

Often, God intervenes in ways that are outside our realm of experience. Often, the very thing we need, we cannot imagine. Often, the scripts that we write that foretell our doom are completely contrary to the scripts that God has written for us. But Jesus intervenes from outside our realm of experience, meeting needs we couldn't identify and handing us a script that we could never have imagined. And in the perfect freedom of these kinds of moments, we find ourselves frozen. This prostitute was frozen and unable to look up. Her silence makes it clear. This man had turned away the wrath that had followed her all her life. The stones of judgment lay still in the dust.

Their voices had been muted, and she had no idea what to do in a relationship that granted her life because she would not be judged based on the shallowness and hidden fears of others.

Caught in the void, she attempted to understand what had happened. In her mind, she was dead. Yet, she wasn't. She floundered in this unexpected freedom because freedom is the place where judgment is absent. She was free to be who it is she truly was without the proclaimed judgments of others forcing her to remain who she was or die being who she was. She stammered with the words forming in the midst of mental groping and said, "No one, sir" (John 8:11). It was just the two of them. Face to face with this man, she was alone in the courtyard of her life.

## Our Courtyards

"Then neither do I condemn you. Go now and leave your life of sin" (John 8:11). It is not about judgment or punishment. There was no recitation of sins. No lengthy exposé on the spiritual and psychological implications of sexual sin was recited to this woman. There was no need. All that stuff was clear. It was known. Her choices were not the point of discourse for they were only the manifestation of pain, not the pain itself. The lacerated core of this woman that had been heartlessly bludgeoned by so many others is what defined her. Not the outward appearances, as they are only a product of those wounds. Not the manifestation of behaviors. Not her acts of sexual promiscuity. But the terrified and bloodied inner self that intentionally repulses all others at all costs so that wounded self will not incur further damage.

It's about refusing to judge, as judgment only sentences others to that which we're judging them for. It reviles them based on our insecurities; it condemns them based on our rules, and it shackles them to the cold iron of our limited notions. Paulo Coelho said, "It's one thing to feel that you are on the right path, but it's another to think that yours is the only path." We need to take a wholly different tact and attempt to see past the behavior to the person behind the behavior so that we can release them from the wounds that bind them so tightly.

## OUR COURTYARDS

Likewise, I have stood in many of my life's own courtyards. There, in those places, inherent in me is the undeniable knowledge regarding my own nature and the manifest actions of that nature. My own sludge and slime is quite apparent. Yet, I often pretend that is not the case, rummaging forward through the accumulated filth of my life, pretending not to know the reason for its accumulation or altogether denying its accumulation. Playing dumb. Feigning ignorance. I find myself expertly utilizing the assorted tools of denial, justification, rationalization, and blame-placing to extract myself from the muck and mire of my own existence. I judge others ruthlessly so that I think myself superior and insulated from being what they are, thereby escaping accountability and the possibility of their fate. But I know. I know full well, and I stand condemned as much as anyone else.

But, those who condemn me have departed. The rightful punishment that I deserve is suspended. Justice as I perceive it has been placated and postponed. Everything that should be happening to me is not. And in the absence of judgment is freedom. God renders all judgment void because the cross consumes every rock, pebble, and grain of it so that nothing is left to stone us with. The distractions, demands, and declarations of the world as it rails against my sin are rendered silent. Any judgments are unable to shackle me to my sin because judgment has been suspended. Everything that would urge me to defend defenseless actions is absent for there is no judgment against which I must defend myself. Every voice that would legitimately and rightly describe the repercussions of my behaviors has fallen silent. Justice is suspended in silence. And it is only God—my sin and God and the freedom to be different.

## A Choice Freed from Judgment

What was her choice after Jesus turned and left? She stood there, aghast and in paralysis. The sunrise would likewise dawn an entirely new day for her. In the months and years ahead, she would wash Jesus' feet with her tears. She would attend to Him, push through the crowds that hailed Him and then condemned Him, and follow Him through the pressing mobs and winding streets of Jerusalem to Golgotha. She would endure the eternity that seemed those three and a half hours on the cross. She would watch Him die, wait through that Saturday with angst indescribable, and be the first in all of time to see Him risen. Her life would be radically new in ways incomprehensible to her, being wrenched out of the bed of prostitution and propelled to partnership with the Messiah. All because Someone refused to bind her with His judgments and, instead, sought her freedom.

## The End Product

The bus had rumbled up the long gravel road of the camp, dust and diesel leaving a path attesting to its journey. The dust and diesel was now dissipating and thinning in a slight summer breeze. Clusters of birds raised a cacophony of song in the dense foliage of the surrounding woods. Golden sunshine rained from a generous sky of blue. Hundreds of sunburnt campers with suitcases, duffle bags, and rich memories gathered in clusters around of the many cars, busses, and vans that inundated the parking lot. In the departing mayhem, there was a tug on my shoulder. A transformed face greeted me. This was not the girl who came off this same bus six days ago. Instantly, I was in the grip of a hug dripping with the love of a grateful heart. Long and rich, the hug was one of life and living. In the midst of the embrace, she whispered, "Thanks so much. I'll never be the same again."

Her bus rolled off down that driveway, leaving a trail of dust and diesel as it had when it had arrived. On board was a miracle. God had gotten to the core of her courtyard and suspended judgment. There, she seized the second chance. And it changed her forever.

**PONDERING POINT**

We judge based on externals. It's easy that way. Seizing and evaluating the obvious is easy, convenient, and simple. It allows us to render rapid judgment and avoid encountering a life at the core of that life. It's cheap living that's superficial and thin. We do the same with ourselves. We are distant from our own cores. That, however, is precisely where Jesus meets us. Here, at the core of our courtyards, we are afforded two things: genuine repentance centered in the acknowledgment of our core, and then the chance to do something radically different. From there, the way is opened for a wonderfully wild departure into the fullness of life and the fullness of God.

**A THOUGHT**
- Am I willing to see myself at the core of myself with the absence of appearances and fronts?
- Will I dare that kind of honesty, being aware of what I lose?
- Am I willing to do that for others?
- And am I willing to respond to that revelation by choosing a radically different course for my life that may touch the entirety of my life?

**CHAPTER 7**

# ASIDE WITH GOD
## What Am I Hearing?

*"Hear this, you foolish and senseless people, who have eyes but do not see, who have ears but do not hear ..."*
                                                            Jeremiah 5:21


*"Half of us are blind, few of us feel, and we are all deaf."*
                                                            ~ William Osler


**DEAN WAS DEAF. IT WAS** that simple, but it was inordinately complex at the same time. Deafness brusquely sets us apart. There are things in life that tend to draw lines in sharp relief that distinctly set us apart from everyone else. Sometimes those lines represent little more than shadowy nuances and tritely trivial differences that might alienate us a bit. However, those kinds of disparities are so slightly different that they're cordially categorized as "unique," and therefore they serve to compliment who we are.

And then there are those more monumental dissimilarities that drive us so far apart from everything around us that we are no longer a part of those surroundings. These are the kinds of aspects or attributes that are so blatantly divergent that they brazenly define us as unlike everyone else. These differences create a yawning chasm of dissimilarity so vast that it simply can't be bridged. The result is a decisive alienation where we are summarily rejected and blithely cast off to the roadside of life, indelibly stamped as something far too different than everything else that traverses the road. R. D. Laing said, "Alienation as our present destiny is achieved only by outrageous violence perpetrated by human beings on human beings." Since the road of life demands conformity, part of that violence is finding a place to put those whose lives fall outside of our acceptable parameters. One of those places is the roadside of life.

Dean was deaf. As if that didn't create enough dissimilarity between himself and the world around him, he was mentally retarded as well. Individually, either of those was sufficient to alienate him from his community. Each one would have been more than capable of aptly thrusting him to the roadside of life. Yet together, they placed him so far afield from everyone else that he was abjectly thrown to the gravel strewn roadside of life, condemned to live out his days prostrate on the roadside as some pathetic freak who would be either pitied or ridiculed as the world incessantly rushed by on its way to other things.

He had never mastered his deafness. Some lean into their disability and shape it to serve them. He never leaned into it, so he served it. Some work to compensate for their handicaps by strengthening the things that are not handicaps. He never compensated and was depleted by them. Surrender to misfortune is likely the greatest misfortune. Out of his surrender, he decompensated down into a silent oblivion where he sat hunched and utterly alone as the world paraded by him on its ill-defined journey to other ill-defined places.

Sign language and lip reading never broke him out of the deafness that had tossed him to the roadside, that place so isolated and yet so close to a world afoot that it constantly left him with a mind-numbing paradox that bred disappointment of the greatest sort. Dean was held outside, off the beaten path with no hope of ever setting foot upon it in order to take even a single step. In time, he embraced the roadside as the place to which he had been exiled, drawing away from the road altogether and making his home on the gravel shoulder of a road that he soon forgot existed. Dean withdrew to a place where there were no destinations from which one has come or to which one might go. He was left with the miserly crumbs of a landlocked present.

### A Conviction of Greatness

Life sometimes entices us to believe that there is so much more to something or some person even though it escapes our vision. We engage that thing or that person with a staunchly certain but entirely misty conviction that there lies within him or her something profound despite the fact that it's completely hidden from both the individual as well as us. It seems that we walk curious circles around them, looking and probing for some crack or tear that will grant us a slight peek inside. We look for some chink to wriggle through or a knob that we can wrestle with long enough until some hidden door opens and grants us entrance to the cloaked and hidden riches within. There emerges a dogged persistence about it all because we dare not bypass what lies within the person, even though it's held away from us. By far, the best place to find these most remarkable people are on the roadsides of life.

That was Dean. He was a kid that I simply could not let go of, though there was nothing tangible to hold onto. His mild mental retardation placed him even further away, a young man of riches unearthed that doggedly provoked me back to him. He was maddeningly frustrating and painfully abrasive at times, unable to break through the soundless wall of his own deafness and reach out from the roadside to engage that which was outside of himself. His coarse and caustically rash behaviors seemed to be an expression of his deeply engrained trepidation of the world combined with his own frustration of having chosen to seclude himself from that same world.

Somehow, he found solace in thinking he controlled his choice to live on the sequestered roadside because it gave him a sense he could move out onto the road should he so choose. Despite the self-induced allusion that he could do so, he couldn't.

It was not a choice to be relentless in my frequently frustrated pursuit of this deaf, roadside young man. I had no choice but to be relentless. Sometimes what you see in another is far too gripping and too terribly fascinating to let go of, even when you're met with nothing more than rejection and ever-thickening walls. Indeed, there were colossal walls that were thick, tediously fortified, and towering. I found myself relentless in pursuit and then disappointed into withdrawal, only to do it all over again simply because this kid was too precious to leave behind as I journeyed down the winding stretches of my own road. We either walk past those people who are strewn on the roadside of life, pretending not to see them in our frantic hurry, or we recognize that they are simply treasures lost whose journey down this road is as important or likely more important than our own. I could not leave Dean.

## DEAF TO LIFE

Torrents of rejection and an avalanche of scorn were the sordid lot of the beggar. They were his lot due to the assumption of others that sin brought about his disability. In the minds of the various passersby, the pathetic reality of his situation could only be a natural consequence of some collection of putrid choices that were conceived by sin and birthed by selfishness. He was not judged for his handicap but what others presumed because of his handicap. Treasure that couldn't hear was left to rot by those who could hear but chose not to.

The world was deafeningly silent for him. The soul has no need of ears, for it is never deaf by handicap, only by choice. In the recesses of his soul, the man could hear that something was missing. However, he could not identify it because he had never known it. Far too often, what's missing in our lives originates in the blatantly flawed assumption that something doesn't exist so it's not there to be experienced. We explain and subsequently brush off the holes in our lives by viewing them as some natural part of who we are. This errant observation gives us self-inflicted permission to leave the holes empty, assuming that empty is what they are meant to be. We then forfeit the understanding that there's always something that fits those holes to form-fitting perfection, and whatever that is, it's certain to be masterful.

Life is indeed masterful. It's an orchestra full and complete, a tireless prodigy of a God who authors stanzas and pens measures that are absolute genius. But for the deaf man, it was absolutely silent. The musical pieces and masterful renditions for which life was created were soundless for him. Notes and scores that were casually written across the faces of friends, that were penned in the raucous flamboyance across bustling open-air markets, and that found subtle notation in droning bees gently drifting from blossom to awaiting blossom, each gave the faintest hints of the melodies they illustrated. But the sounds were never there for this man who could not hear. The sheet music ran in front of him in endless reams, but it didn't spawn a single sound.

The haunting call of numerous geese aloft, the pounding surf throwing itself against a forever beach, or the fingers of the wind rustling through listless treetops were silent for this man. The roll of a distant summer thunderstorm on a humid horizon or the raucous laughter of life rising from the soul of humanity itself was nothing more and nothing less than the sound of silence. Kahlil Gibran said that to love fully, one of the many desires we should possess would be "to melt and be like a running brook that sings its melody to the night." Yet, for this man, the brook of love was silent despite however listless or torrential it might run. Entombed in a vacuum of deafening silence, this orchestra had always played soundlessly for this deaf man—vigorously indeed, but vigorously silent. He was deaf, and he was starkly alone.

He strained in the failed attempt to interact and engage with the music and the melodies. He endeavored to hear out of the silent desperation of deafness, crafting imaginary sounds in his head as he assumed they might somehow sound. But to try to participate in a world you can't hear leaves you always outside of that world despite how hard you try to enter it. His lips were slow and drawn with words that were broken shards of ill-formed verbiage. He arduously attempted to wrap words around voice and syntax and intonation that he had never heard. He spent himself in perpetually frustrating efforts to do what he couldn't conceive and could much less imagine: putting sounds to words he'd never heard.

His words were slurred, distorted, verbally twisted, and linguistically bent, readily inviting and successfully garnering ridicule, mockery, and confusion from those who lived in the world of sound. His was a life forced out onto the fringes of life, exiled there in a lonely land where silence is a hated but forever companion. There was no breech in the wall to slip back through in order to touch humanity and belong to something other than the silence.

Rejection and silence were both isolating; the difference is that one is a choice rendered by others, the other is a chance dealt by the uncertainty of life. What they have in common is that the person upon whom both fall chooses neither. It is something like a full emasculation of everything it is to be human. This is what it was to be deaf and mute. And so the beggar's life went.

There was a rumor that had circulated like a persistent wind that ushers in spring despite winter's insistence that it not come. A distant murmuring unheard by deaf ears but caught by others said that Jesus was in the Decapolis. This prophet and miracle worker had come. He seemed more a mythical figure, the misty manifestation of some ingenious novelist, but fiction nonetheless. Yet, he had intriguingly transcended myth and became myth having been made man. The verdict as to who this Jesus was remained a point of discussion and debate. Some of that was quite heated, and some of it was really rather innocuous. Yet, He was coming, and the captivating idea that He was something more than a mortal man and that maybe He was myth-made-alive was compelling.

Had those around this deaf man tired of his dependency, these friends of his, or did they care for him? Was he little more than an object that could be used to entice a miracle from this prophet? Was their intent little more than a ploy for a cheap thrill? The text is unclear. Their motive is foggy and indistinct. But this Jesus arrives, and they shuffle the deaf mute off to this wandering, mythical prophet.

This course of events didn't appear to be an action of the deaf man's own accord; there is no hint of self-determination or self-initiation. There doesn't appear to be any inkling that the possibility of being ushered into the world of sound could occur. How can you possibly know what you're missing if you've never had it? How can you desire something if desire has no place to be cultivated and you've no idea that there's anything to be desired? Yet, most often the intimate collisions in our lives are a result of something entirely unknown colliding with us, because we'd be nothing but blind paupers if we went any further without it.

Yet, sometimes we see in and through others what we could not otherwise see because it's not within us to see. Sometimes we experience the passionate and vigorous pulse of desire vicariously through the heartbeat of others as we sense the pulse in them. Sometimes our vision of the possible is only possible because we see that vision reflected in the eyes of another, and we watch it dance about in their smile. Sometimes we actually end up dancing because others have caused us to believe in the dance and have ushered us out on the dance floor even when we can't hear the music ourselves. And in dancing, the music arises from within simply because each of us has a song that is meant to be sung in the larger chorus of life. Such were the deaf mute's friends.

And so, the rumor drew them to Jesus. Soon the embedded mass was found. Ushered by these friends, the deaf man engaged the periphery of the crowd and then pressed toward its center. The small entourage cut a swath through the fluid array of assorted humanity that swelled and eddied around Jesus. The clamor of a world of never-ending needs simultaneously sought relief. The world clamored around Jesus seeking some shred of hope and some healing that might arise from that shred of that very hope. The crowd swirled around this wandering prophet as if in the grip of the undertow of all creation, an irresistible current from which all other currents find their sole source. Passing through a cultural morass of assembled humanity, the deaf man was guided toward the center.

The aged, the stooped, and those aimlessly shuffling in the grip of long years wandered about in a cloudy curiosity. Children darted in and out. The blind walked about groping, stretching trembling arms outward, substituting touch for sight and sound for vision. Stumbling, they made their way to Jesus.

Crutches that were terribly crude and deeply weatherworn were nothing more than primitive prosthetics that sought a miracle for an absent leg. Off to one side, a cripple pulled himself toward Jesus, his fingers clawing the arid soil, dragging useless appendages and tattered garments that trailed in the talcum dirt behind him.

Farther down, limp in his mother's arms, an infant teetered on the chilling precipice of death, the pallor of death strangely awash across the face of newborn life that rendered his skin hues of suffocating purple. His mother stood on panicked tiptoe, stretching her neck to catch a glimpse of something, anxiously groping toward the center of the mass. It was all silence to the deaf mute. It was all wildly alive, vibrant, turbulent, and wonderfully riotous, but deathly silent. From his vantage point, the drama was only partly revealed.

Pressing onward and inward, it was more of the same. The scene was packed tight with shifting layers of broken humanity, the curious, the destitute, those maimed and horrifically bent, stalwart individuals draped in lavishing flowing garments, and others clutching threadbare wraps, exuberant adolescents and exhausted elderly. Desperate cries and guttural moans, cordial conversations and panicked voices, whispered tones and the yells of those frantically jockeying for position raised a chorus of mankind expressing the reality that sin has put every one of us on the roadside of life. In reality, we are all the deaf man.

Finally, the last layer of jostling, clamoring humanity parted like the parting of some glorious tapestry. A man of silent stature stood in the crowd, yet infinitely above it. He seemed myth made real in a way that surpassed reality itself. In some indefinable way, this Jesus embodied everything that was lost in mankind, creating an utterly mortifying sense of exactly how much we'd lost, and yet instilling an electrifying hope that all of it could be redeemed. It was mesmerizing and captivating.

The nucleus of the swirling mass of people and their needs was deafening in silence. Jesus' back was to them. Slightly stooped, His hands gently rested on the shoulders of an elderly, seemingly broken woman. The look of astonishment was set in her eyes and splashed across her face. A worn cane lay abandoned at her feet as she tiptoed from side to side and timidly bounced on rejuvenated legs. Something unusual had transpired. In His tender interactions with this woman, it was immediately clear that there was thick compassion in His touch, His stance, and His mannerisms. A parting word to the woman and He turned.

His gaze shifted and panned the crowd. Mussing the hair of a playful child, both smiled deeply and invaded the heart of the other in a superbly divine intersection. Another step and this Jesus was magnetically drawn to the outstretched arms of an ecstatic infant. He moved toward her, His face electrically alive with love and aflame with anticipation. To squeals of laughter, He took her, held her high, pulled her to His chest, ran His hand across a misshapen leg, and it was drawn straight. To complete the convergence of two souls, He drew her deeply to His face. And then He gently handed her back to an elated set of parents who now held a daughter who was wholly whole. All of it was too much for words; it was too inexplicable to embrace in the confining catacombs of human understanding. The only stammering question that one could formulate was "Who is this?"

Before the answer could be given, Jesus was drawn to the pleas of those who had brought the deaf mute, pleas the deaf man could not hear. The man, this Jesus stepped toward them, riveting His attention on those who had brought the man. He seemed discerning and listening with some sort of intuition and understanding that superseded anything they could comprehend.

He then turned intense eyes and fastened His gaze on the mute. His eyes were more than human, although they appeared to be something that was fully human at the same time. They were infinitely deep, profoundly thoughtful, and intensely focused. His soft but chiseled spirit enamored the crowd and drew the deaf man to Jesus. It was a terrible yet inviting contradiction of commanding power and gentle softness brought together without the diminishment of either. Jesus' eyes had the breath of infinity behind them.

Suddenly, there was a voice in the deaf man's soul that was not his own, indiscernible but a voice kind and magnetic. For the first time in his life, he had a completely wordless conversation that through some marvelous means transported the fullness of this Jesus into the fullness of this man. Suddenly, he was not alone on some desolate roadside but was fully engaged with Someone who creates roads. The deaf mute found himself becoming entirely lost in the spectacular collision of God with men until Jesus took his arm, gestured, and began to move out of the crowd. God was afoot, the Creator of the universe in intentional motion toward an intentional destination. It was all terrifying but exhilarating at the same time.

This fluid mass of humanity parted a second time, but from the inward out. Shifting layers of broken humanity sliced a swath to the edge of the mass. Jesus breeched the fringes of the crowd, walking with a man whose life had been lived on the fringes of life. Jesus was in the process of isolating a man who lived isolated in deafness, as it is often in isolation that isolation is broken. In a moment, the crowd was far behind them, their voices falling into a distant murmur. Those who advocated the deaf man's healing were absent, their role completed. Suddenly, inexplicably, this deaf mute was alone with God.

## Ears and Tongue

Ears and tongue: the world is drawn in through one and self is released through the other. They both engage in a partnership of exchange, drawing in and letting out. The ears draw in the world to process it, and then the tongue releases all of that back into the world with part of the person now attached. The whole, marvelous process adds to life, flavoring it, adding another entirely distinctive facet to life itself, affixing yet another unique note to the chorus of the ages. There, in the world of the deaf, this exchange was never initiated. The deaf man was isolated from the world and to the world.

Drawing the man along, Jesus sought isolation. It was within isolation that isolation would be broken, as often we break things in our lives by audaciously forging right into the middle of them. We venture into those places one-on-one, God and man in a relationship echoing back to a lost garden. The Creator and the created rectify lost creation through an act of intentional re-creation of walking smack-dab into the face of that which shattered that original relationship and therefore shattered us.

In this joint journey, Jesus and the deaf mute walked past the rancor and raucousness of an open-air market filled with bartering and bantering, scales, and sweeping gestures. They skirted around scurrying children and walked past stray dogs milling close to tables spread with red meats. A pair of centurions laden with weaponry strode past in the service of oppression, granting Jesus and the deaf mute no notice. Passing priests in ceremonial robes stepped in pompous cadence on errands of perceived righteousness.

And then, an unexpected turn into a vacant alley made up of basalt stones that cut a manmade canyon. In the basalt chasm, the sun found scant room to watch the making of a miracle. It cast angled rays, precariously canting itself to catch a glimpse of the pending phenomenon. The din of the open-air market and the jostling of the vendors were put at a sufficient distance, becoming gradually muted and fading soft and indistinct into the background.

Then, a miracle was wrought with gestures that were so familiar to the mute. Gestures were the very means of understanding and the way in which the deaf mute had navigated his world. Jesus was not a God interacting in mystery and inexplicable ritual, but rather in simple intimacy. There were no methods cloaked in indiscernible actions or unfamiliar formalities bred of stale tradition. Everything was simple, direct, and familiar: fingers in ears and a touch of the tongue. Saliva was a symbol of the fullest sharing of self as a participant in the miracle with the deaf mute.

Jesus engaged the man, not as a distant entity cloaked beyond recognition in some sort of misty immutability. Saliva was believed to have had a curative quality, a belief entirely fictional in nature but powerful culturally. The symbolism of the act provided a needed vehicle that outweighed the myth of the act itself. So, Jesus ingeniously chose to use myth as a vehicle for a miracle, a miracle done in the simple language of a deaf mute's isolated world to obliterate his isolation and blow his world open. Jesus is not the God of distant swirling galaxies, reaching out from light years behind them to touch us in some grandiose and diminishing manner. Instead, He is the God that walks down the vacant side streets of life to meet us alone in dark alleys of our loneliness.

And then there was something for Jesus Himself. Something the deaf man could not hear or participate in. Jesus looked up to heaven. There was a weighted sigh of a God whose love eliminates His ability not to feel. It was a reflection of both His heart and the heart of His Father. It seemed to be the private pain of a God grieving over the pain of His own creation. The reality of divine love outweighed divinity itself, rendering Jesus unable to escape the lethal weight of a fallen creation and the devastation of that fallen state for simple men like the deaf mute. Jesus' sighing was likely the plaintive moan of God once again embracing the awful reality of fallen mankind as manifest in this single, mute life. It seemed to be the expression of great angst that arose from an infinite understanding of how far this man's life was from God's original intent for him.

There, in the solitude of that alley, God would meet the need of one man. In a few days further up the road of Jesus' own journey, He would meet the need of thousands with a scant seven barley loaves and a few small fish. A few months beyond that, He would meet the need of all mankind on a barren hill, bloodied arms splayed wide and nailed firm. It would be a hill that would not be sandwiched between the walls of some abandoned alley, but between two crosses and two worlds, set out for all to see. However, there was the need of the moment.

"Be opened!" (Mark 8:34) this Jesus said. "Be opened!" Not just his ears but also his life, as no miracle is excluded or in any way restrained solely to the obvious. Miracles are far too big for that. "Be opened!" Be free to live fully, to hear in perfect pitch the richness of the notes and measures, the scores of life and living. Be opened to engage everything else in life that was open. Be opened so that being closed simply cannot be.

Jesus uttered the words, took a step back, and watched life unfold as the miracle reverberated far beyond the miracle, something like when a stone is dropped in a mirrored pool, sending ripples far beyond the point of impact. An alien experience transpired for which the man had no point of correlation. Sounds began to filter through. The orchestra gradually swelled and expanded. The void of silence filled to capacity with sounds he had only imagined. In reality, the sounds were exceedingly beyond anything he had ever dreamed even at those desperate moments when he had accessed the fullest of his imagination in order to try to hear something.

Suddenly, he heard the crunch of gravel beneath his feet. Shifting his weight again and again, he reproduced a sound that his stunned and hungry mind had never imagined. The barking of a dog floated in from afar. It was riveting, with the source of the sound and everything that defined it being entirely unknown but completely captivating. There was the bubbling stew of human voices that drifted in from the jostling open-air market at the distant end of the alley. Birds darted overhead in tangles of wild flight, cheeps and chirps synchronizing the feathered masses' journey. He was caught in the rapture of hearing his own breath and the whisper of a breeze teasing the folds of his robe.

And then words, the first he had ever heard, annunciated clearly, perfectly, and concisely. His own voice was suddenly drawn in through perfect ears. The sound cascaded across his brain as some sort of perfect melody of intonation and emotion, leaving him speechless once again, but in a very different manner. C. S. Lewis wrote, "Miracles are a retelling in small letters of the very same story which is written across the whole world in letters too large for some of us to see." The retelling had occurred. The letters were written in bold relief. The cycle was now marvelously complete.

Jesus stood silently, giving the man room and time to embrace the wonder of the moment. Miracles become freeing and claustrophobic at the same time, opening up entirely new venues that are often bigger than our ability to embrace. Time was needed to allow this astonished man to reorient to the miracle of a life restored. Maybe he needed time to believe that life could be restored and that the actual restoration created a conflict with his weak faith and doubting heart. Maybe we're so unaccustomed to God's original design for us that when it's restored, it's initially far too alien to simply embrace with any kind of ease. Maybe Jesus saw in this man, this deaf mute, the liberation that the cross would extend to billions.

It may be that the individual miracles, like this one, allowed Jesus to foresee in this single solitary face what the cross would do in a sea of faces across spans of time. Not the kinds of miracles that would eventually fall to the deterioration of frail bodies and the eventuality of death, but miracles that would be eternally fresh because they open up all of eternity to those who opt seize it. I wonder if moments such as this one gave Him the strength to endure the long moments on a lonely cross.

And then, the first words of another human being that the man ever heard. "Don't tell anyone," Jesus said. The first words seemed irrational and inexplicable. The world of sound brings with it responsibility to the world it unveils. Miracles bring with them accountability to both the Restorer and what has been restored. A relationship with God brings obedience, the responsibility to act on faith even when that action appears irrational, contrary, odd, or plainly wrong. "Don't tell anyone." But containment failed. The measure of the miracle was larger than the measure of the man to contain it. But that is what happens when an infinite God interacts within our finite frames. Thankfully, what God does is always bigger than we are and bigger than our ability to contain it. Our faith may be big enough to elicit a miracle, but our faith is seldom large enough to embrace it once it actually happens. Jesus took his arm, gestured, and began to move out of the alley and into life.

### Aside in an Alley

And so, Jesus pulls me aside at times and isolates me in my isolation. He places creation aside and draws me to a secluded place, away from the crowds that surround me and the world that has so often thrust me to its fringes. Often, I am terrified to be there with Him because I am confused and frightened to be one-on-one with God. I would much prefer to have Him heal me at a safe distance or intersect my life in the companionship of others, or touch me as part of something larger within which I can meld. But one-on-one in some alley in my life, secluded with God? Sequestered with the Creator? It is both terrible and wonderful.

And then, to have Him connect with me intimately in that place of isolation, the God of the ceaseless cosmos coming to me in my isolation? Not coming to some localized proximity or in distant earshot, but coming in my language and in the raw essence of my being. God steps into my isolation and speaks to me there. Not standing outside of my isolation and beckoning me out of it. But purposefully coming in, gently taking my arm, and gesturing me out of it. Partnering with me and in the partnering coming squarely into my isolation to commandeer me and rescue me. Cutting through the mass of tangled issues, convulsing pain, wretched self-absorption, wrenching history, and self-hatred that surrounds me and drawing me along with Him to a place where we stand face to face in utter isolation, and He heals me.

And there, in those isolated alleys of my life, He frees me. He relishes watching me come to life and then fumble with a life that's so new that I have no idea how to hold it. As some bemused child, He is just as amazed at watching me come to life as He was when He first formed Adam from the dust and "breathed into his nostrils the breath of life" (Genesis 2:7). It is just as poignant for Him, never being diminished for a God whose love for His creation rages undiminished. God is always reaffirming that creation can only exist if it is constantly creating. "He has done everything well ..." (Mark 7:37). Harkening to yet another statement, "and God saw that it was good" (Genesis 1:10). In that alley, God was creating all over again as He always does, doing everything well and good.

## DEAN'S ALLEY

It was experimental, but the doctors said that surgery might restore Dean's hearing. He was not enthusiastic. Dean walked through the process more like a laboratory rat that had no idea of what was happening or what the possible outcome might mean. He was lethargic through the whole process, as demure and distant as someone surrendered to subsisting outside the fringes of life.

The day following his surgery came lax and without expectation, much in the same way we limply anticipate most of our encounters with God will ultimately be. I turned, and there he stood, much like he always stood: distant and seemingly lost on the fringes of some thought. My first response was to say "hello" out of some prescribed routine, knowing that he wasn't reading my lips and that it really didn't matter. Sometimes rote and ritual turns life lifeless. It robs us of expectation and hope. I felt that way with Dean. But I said "hello" anyway.

He simply looked, tilted his head a bit, and registered something in those crystal blue eyes that I had never seen before. Sometimes we imagine something so much for so long that when it's ours, it's both wonderful and terribly different than we had ever imagined it being. I think that was the case for Dean. He had heard my voice. The surgery had actually worked. For the first time, he had taken in the tone and flavor of the single word that I had uttered and had found himself awed by the utterance. He smiled and seemed to wait for more.

I paused. "Can you hear me?" I asked tentatively, desperately hoping that he was no longer locked in and I locked out.

Instantly, he stepped forward, grabbed my arm, turned, and in the rush of wonder pulled me down the hall and into his room. Dragging me through the door, he stopped in the middle of that quaint room and pointed at the various objects around us in frantic gestures. It was all so new for me that I had no idea what he meant. He continued to point in a manner insistent and adamant, walking around the room in a rigid gait and pointing while staring a hole through me with those crystal blue eyes.

Finally, my own emotional deafness lifted, and I realized what he wanted: he wanted me to pronounce what the objects were, to speak their names, to say them so that he could hear their syntax for the first time. Picture, telephone, window, bed, floor, light, wall, cup, rug, Craig; Dean was a young man surging alive with an urgency that flooded the room with a terrific and wonderful energy. He was hearing syntax and syllables for the first time. He was so famished for sound that once he had expended all of the objects in his room, he dragged me outdoors, and we did the same thing again and again.

Sometimes you sense that you've been put in a place of inestimable privilege that you don't deserve. Life has its moments where you suddenly find yourself walking on hallowed ground, sensing in those moments that you are completely unworthy of standing in such sacred places. The most enthralling thing of all is the realization that such places do indeed exist and that on occasion we are invited into them. That's where I was that day. God came aside this young man through the hands of a caring doctor and an experimental surgery. Now I was privileged to stand beside him as well, inundated in a tsunami of wonderment and life.

It went on for days and days. I couldn't wait to see Dean. In indescribable awe, I watched a young man come alive in a way that makes coming alive worth all the pain and disappointment and deafness that we have to endure to get there. A miracle came to me through Dean. Deafness was abated in infinitely more ways than simply physical hearing. Dean reminds me of deafness and what it can do to a person and a life. Dean also reminds me of deafness abated when God comes alongside a single life and renders deafness deaf.

## Repeated Deafness

Unlike the deaf mute and unlike Dean, my deafness and my inability to speak to my world come often. Frequently, I need Jesus to put His fingers in my ears, touch my tongue, and banish my deafness. Sin, selfishness, and the persistent lure of the world render me deaf and ill suited to speak as I should. My condition is pitifully recurrent. More often than not, my deafness is something like a persistent state that renders me unfamiliar with anything else.

God's presence is likewise persistently recurrent. Daily I am in this alley with Him. While it exhausts me and I find myself sweltering in embarrassment, He never tires. He likes, it seems, these alley encounters. He relishes taking me aside. And I know that one day He will take me aside for that final time, that time when I will ascend to a place where deafness and speech deficits will simply not exist, and any talk of them will be met with quizzical looks. The memory of them will be entirely vanquished. And there, in that place, I will stand eternally before God in perfection with new worlds perpetually opening up to me. In that place, the layers will constantly part to reveal something new. His smile and the relish in His face will never be old, but always new.

### Pondering Point

The loud voices in life, those that clamor for our attention, are most often not the vital voices. The fact that they have to clamor for my attention suggests as much. It is the smaller voices that are weak, thin, and easily drowned out that are rich. It is these that tend to be the priceless voices, their worth easily lost in the pompous and presumptuous voices that say much but hold little. It is easy to become deaf. And when we do, we miss the precious voices whose worth is immutable.

### A Thought

- What am I hearing?
- Is what I'm hearing dictated by what I've chosen to listen to?
- Are these things loud enough to deafen me to other things?
- What is being drowned out? Is God being drown out?

CHAPTER 8

# ON THE ROADSIDE
## Do I Really Want to See?

*"The LORD will afflict you with madness, blindness and confusion of mind."*
Deuteronomy 28:28

*"I say to mankind, be not curious about God. For I, who am curious about each, am not curious about God — I hear and behold God in every object, yet understand God not in the least."*
~ Walt Whitman

**A CLEFT PALATE RENDERED HIS** words heavy with verbal edges missing from vowels and consonants, softening and muddling many words into verbal oblivion. He was razor-thin and slightly stooped. Coarse hair grew in dense thickets on anemic arms and tender hands. Flat feet slapped the pavement in an awkward rhythm set to the metronome of an irreparably broken gait. His feet were set tight in a panicked shuffle when he came to corners, teetering as he rounded them. A thin smear of saliva coated his chin and chapped broad lips. Arms and hands reached out to the world with constant tremors. His was a life both pensive and uncertain, the stuff of darkness.

The most enthralling and captivating thing about him was his eyes. They were vividly crystal and icy blue, intense and deep, sparkling as brilliant gemstones set blazing against thick lashes. Icy, they were yet incredibly warm and inviting, a combination that created an entirely mesmerizing contradiction. Sharp and vibrant, the hues in them were striking. His were the most beautiful eyes I have ever seen.

Yet, for all their stunning and unusual beauty, Doug was blind. He groped through his world with tremulous hands outstretched into an endlessly black abyss. Tenuous and pensive, his eyes wandered in nothingness—searching, it seemed, to see something in the nothingness. Doug seemed to be waiting for his eyes to do what they were supposed to do but couldn't and never would. Somehow, he seemed to deny his blindness in the irrational hope that a fleck of color or a streak of light might find a place where blindness forgot to set itself, and in the breech actually break through. It never happened.

And that is how I met him that first time. Lost in his crystalline eyes, he placed his hands on my face to discern my features, to paint a picture with his fingertips. He used his fingers to bring patterns to the blackness and to set against its loneliness something other than the blackness. It was in that first meeting that his fingers saw something in my face. His fingers somehow ascertained much more than his eyes could have. From that moment forward, Doug would be drawn to me. He would become a soul mate, a connection that was made in his blindness.

Doug was also mentally retarded, the victim of a cruel life that decided to strike twice. It seemed that life was not satisfied with a single theft where his vision was taken, but it set out to steal great expanses of his mind as well. The multiple thieveries left his life one that was pillaged with its margins pulled in and set unjustly tight. Yet, it had granted him beautiful eyes.

Others would gather as vultures around a carcass to steal whatever might be left of him. The road of his life up to the moment I met him was marked by physical abuse, sexual assault, and gross neglect. He had no means to defend himself or really even understand the need to do so. So, whatever little bit that he possessed was there for the taking. All of the assorted actions perpetrated upon him were deeds of weak people finding a point of advantage over another and seizing it for their own gratification. Many people had gorged themselves on the defenseless young man, and they satiated their sordid desires on innocence. Such was Doug's life.

The months passed, and I grew to know Doug more. He longed for companionship, but more than anything else, he longed to see. Standing in the courtyard of the facility within which he lived, drenched in the rich golden loam of morning sunshine he could not see, he would call my name. Every morning, he would call out from a life exiled deep in shadow and a soul displaced by rejection, over and over raising my name until I arrived.

Tremulous hands groped toward my voice as I called to him out of his enveloping darkness. Resting his hands on my chest, they would set a palsied-like course to my face and then trace the contours of my features … day after day. Taking my hand and staggering into the darkness of his day, he would pull me to some object or place, asking me to describe a multitude of things from flowers, to bricks, to candy wrappers, to umbrellas, remembering and recalling each description with uncanny and precise accuracy. He would build into the folds of his mind what his eyes would not deliver there. He was set upon painting dazzling colors onto a black canvas, therefore finding himself desperate for an image borrowed from the eyes of another in order to paint.

Helen Keller said, "My darkness has been filled with the light of intelligence, and behold, the outer day-lit world was stumbling and groping in social blindness." Sometimes blindness is not blindness at all, and vision has no sight. Yet, Doug's life was a life relegated to the roadside of life by his blindness. However, he refused to stay there.

## ANOTHER ON THE ROADSIDE

Sounds provided no hues or shades of pigment. They threw no shadows, and they splashed no color. Dimension was absent. Shape, form, and texture are too marvelous to be seized from language or snatched from sound. It could all be explained, but it could not be experienced. Words floated in as markers, giving some vague shape to something shapeless. Pieces of the world passed by and were grabbed in words, but never captured in sight. Sounds drifted in and were caught on the ears of blindness. His eyes were dead. He had no means by which to reach out and seize the world of light, color, shapes, and shadows. He was a pauper, left only to grasp the discarded pieces of the world thrown his way on the roadside of life.

Sounds and words were not eyes, and so the man sat on a dusty roadside, apprehending the passing world by dissecting sound and grasping at tidbits of the melody and the dissonance that played round about him. He took it all and pasted together a world based solely on sound, leaving his world alive with voices but absent of images, color, light, and the breathless majesty of depth as it's rendered by distant mountains or even more distant galaxies. He had no visual elements from which to comprehend it as someone seeing it might comprehend it. He sat tattered both in clothing and life, begging to see through sounds and garner a few scant coins from generous passersby.

Frayed wraps, sparse with dangling threads, flirted with an occasional breeze. His hair was a tangled mass that was oily and coarse. The chaotic and tussled mess framed a weatherworn face. His skin was leathery thick. Time had plowed deep furrows that were embedded with a gritty mixture of dirt and sticky sweat. His eyes were cavernous and hollow. They were open, but open to nothing but darkness. They traced the sounds that moved about him, shifting and following them as they drifted by. His head was up slightly, tilted just a bit and digesting every morsel of sound that the world threw his way.

A battered cup was held out to the passersby of the world. It was hope held out into the dark of darkness. He called into the darkness and pleaded his cause, spoke his fear, held out his hopelessness, and pronounced his pain, somehow hoping that the darkness would respond to some piece or part of that which he threw out into it. He hoped that it would yield something that would get him through the darkness of the day.

His cup faithfully followed the sounds that passed by, shadowing the footprints that came to him in the form of crunching gravel and muted conversation. He reached out to the sounds, hoping that somewhere in them was a crumb for his body and possibly a cure for his soul. A passerby paused, extracted a weathered pouch, rummaged through its sparse contents, and dropped a thin coin into the waiting cup. His fingers leapt, quickly scouring the inside of the cup and locating the coin. He fingered it quickly, determined its worth, and then tucked it deep in a secure fold in his robe. Immediately, the cup was extended again, and the pleading resumed.

This was his life. A meager existence begged on a roadside from a world that he could not see, a world that was so much more than he could comprehend or imagine, so very much more. Human imagination is far too confined to be able to rise sufficiently to imagine God or anything that He creates, regardless of how simple that might creation might be. And so, the blind man could only imagine, and in his musings fall irreparably short of the realities that lay around him. The cup was extended again and again. The cries of a beggar filled the air, and a morsel was hoped for.

## I Inhabit the Roadside

I live on the roadside. And I ... I too am blind. Sometimes more and sometimes less, but I'm blind. It's not visual blindness, as my eyes are sharp and clear. In reality, it's the darker spiritual blindness that

I have, a blindness that is far worse. Bereft of spiritual eyes, I think I see when I don't see at all. I am fooled into thinking I perceive when I perceive nothing. *Nothing,* I eventually take for *something,* and I'm left achingly poorer because of it. I hate the blindness. Its evidence becomes striking and painfully clear in the turmoil, pain, and trials in my life. Thinking that I see, God permits times of devastation, and I realize in the horror and distress of it all that I don't see at all. I am utterly and abjectly blind. I'm blind even to the fact that I am blind, which is the essence of true blindness.

There is so much more going by me on the road of life, but I sit at its edge, on the gravel fringes with my cup in hand, straining to hear, to know, and to see what's going by on that road. I sit there begging for some morsel to satisfy a bit of the hunger in life, realizing that only God can call me onto that road and give me sight to see it. And so, I am on the roadside, blind, cup in hand, calling out. We all are the blind beggar.

### JESUS AND BLINDNESS

It was humid and lush. The road wound downward, meandering below sea level into tropical Jericho. Jericho was an ancient city with a history five thousand years old even before Jesus set foot in it. His journey, however, is eternal, rendering its history a slight vapor quickly dissipated by the winds of time and eternity. The gates of Jericho lay ahead. Jerusalem was on the horizon, and Golgotha was just beyond that.

The crescendo of Jesus' earthly journey was rising. Forces both physical and spiritual were marshaling and assembling themselves against Him. All prepared for a horrendous clash that was drawing ever nearer. Jesus had just recounted to His disciples the events that were to come. The meaning of the coming events remained hidden from them because those events were simply too powerful, too consuming, and too awful to be digested by this handful of mismatched men cavorting through history with the Messiah. But for now, Jericho drew close in the distance.

For the blind beggar, the sounds were different now, very different. Sometimes things are different, and we can't ascertain why they are. Sometimes that which is the same is different only because we're not astute enough to know that subtleties can change everything. Such was the case for the blind beggar. The sounds this time were not reminiscent of the typical traffic that flowed in and out of the city, to which the eyes of his ears were so accustomed. The blind beggar lowered his cup, leaned forward, closed blind eyes, and strained to focus with intent. He reached out to grasp every slight wisp of sound that wafted down the road and brushed across his leathered face.

It was unlike anything else. If words have a flavor, the words floating around him seemed sweet, slightly tangy, and basted with flavor. There was a crowd, but there had been many crowds before. There was an unfamiliar electricity and tempo in the sounds. Something completely unusual was pressing up the road, winding his way, and then cresting a slight roll in the landscape. Now it seemed to crest some unseen ridge and descend directly toward him with a momentum that pressed against him. It was the sound of humanity alive and not the wandering sort of humanity that he was used to. It wasn't about any sort of business; it wasn't humanity off in a hurried rush to some hurried place. Whatever this was, it was not headed somewhere with a somewhere focus, but it was alive and vibrant right in the moment. Each stepped was marked with some sort of rigorous enthusiasm. Eyes are not needed to see God afoot.

He reached out, groped, and then yelled into the blackness, "Who is coming, who is this about to pass by?!" The tenor of his voice was alive with the excitement of anticipation, of wanting to join a world that he could not see. This time, he sensed that he couldn't let this pass by with himself left on the fringes. With an insistence borne of his blindness, he continued to shout. Annoyed by the beggar's determination, someone retorted, "Jesus of Nazareth is passing by"

(Luke 18:37). Instantly, it was clear, shockingly clear. It was impossible. Stories of Jesus had meandered down this road before—many stories, many times. He'd heard the tales spun that sounded wild but at the same time titillatingly plausible. But this, this was no story, and this was not a tale. This was the very man the stories were about.

The sounds of an energized crowd on foot grew in intensity. A multitude of voices in a linguistic stew melded with increasing volume. Words once muffled became clearer. Word spread, surged, and rolled up the road ahead of Jesus like an irrepressible tsunami. It was Jesus. Not some story about this Jesus, but Jesus in flesh and blood. In a moment, the entourage was upon the beggar. His mind raced, trying to decide what to do because he'd never done anything other than extend his cup.

This time, he extended words instead of a cup. He forced a collision of God and man on a simple road. The words blurted and leapt from his mouth—"Jesus, Son of David, have mercy on me" (Luke 18:38). His plea was thrust into the darkness and thrown out onto the road. Sound was all he knew; it was his only medium of communication, and so he shouted again. His words penetrated the edges of the crowd and rippled inward. Those on the periphery caught his words and rebuked him, shushing him back into obscurity. They attempted to thwart his efforts to reach into their world. But the world of sounds was his domain. So he shouted again, and his pleas penetrated the crowd, falling, finally, on the ears of Jesus. And then, the world stopped, and sound stopped with it.

There was no hesitation, for faith always catches the ear of God. "Bring him here," Jesus replied. It was an order. It was immediate, and it was firm. Several in the crowd stirred and headed for the man. He was suddenly raised to trembling feet by strange arms. Unsteady and stumbling, he caught his balance. His cup dropped and lay spilt on the roadside; its role in his life was finally concluded because begging would end here. Therefore, the vestiges of begging would be left on the roadside much as he had been left there for so many years.

Roadsides and cups ... in a moment, they would all be things of the past. He stepped away from them, his arms outstretched, held on both sides by strangers who drew him off the roadside and onto the road. Attempting to apprehend the sounds around him, he pierced the edges of the crowd and cut into the very bowels of gathered humanity.

And then, there was a voice that was clearly beyond it all and above it all. The beggar heard a voice that carried a commanding tone and that possessed a residue of power that he had never heard before. Every other sound retreated in the wake of this single, solitary voice. It was oddly soft for its power, but it was confident and commanding. The starkness of Jesus' authority was exhilarating and yet terribly frightening, richly warm but defiantly powerful all at once. He had never heard anything like it. It was humanity that was thoroughly punctuated with the divine and laced with the very same power.

"What do you want me to do for you?" (Luke 18: 41) was the question. The words leapt out both in their abruptness and their unquestioning ability to do whatever was asked of them. The words were strong enough to bear even a request of the impossible. The question left room for an innumerable array of answers. The blind man was left with the opportunity to ask for things that his cup could never have held. The crowd was deafly silent. There were now no sounds other than the shuffling of feet, the flapping of robes caught in the slight breeze, and the sound of a miracle waiting on tiptoe.

The blind man's mind raced through the back alleys of darkness, of groping and poverty, of a cup and a few scattered coins. In those places, there were only a few scant morsels of food, of life, and of hope, sitting hunched on roadsides but never being on the road. Never perceiving the road or what traveled it, he was doomed as a blind bystander. Counting on the generosity of the road and those that walked it, he was helpless. Nelson Mandela said, "It always seems impossible until it's done." But until it's done, we struggle with believing that it can be done. All of the wildly gyrating thoughts of the roadside, cups and the impossible coalesced in the blind man's mind and then the answer leapt to his lips. "Lord, I want to see" (Luke 18:41).

## THE CRY OF MY HEART

That's my cry. "Lord, I want to see!" Not *think* that I see. Not substitute my blind perception of sight for His, but to abandon my assumptions of sight and seeing altogether and to really see. To be deluged with eyes that see as God sees. To ask for something I can't even remotely comprehend. To ask for something I can't ask for of my own because it exceeds the depth and breadth of my experience, my knowledge, and my ability to conjure up even the most basic shape of it. I want to drop my many cups, leave them strewn on the roadside, get up, stumble into the crowd, fall at His feet, and plead the impossible … "Lord, I want to see!"

There was a pause. He was seeing before he even saw. There was a smile on the face of this Jesus. The blind man could clearly hear it. There was a joy exuding in restoring sight to the blind and life to the lifeless. Jesus drew a confident breath, gave Himself a moment to revel in a life about to be restored. Lightly he touched the man's shoulder and stared into eyes that could not stare back. Eyes void of light, he prepared for a double miracle: eyes that were about to see, but a soul that would actually see first. With a voice filled with love, He said, "Receive your sight, your faith has healed you" (Luke 18:42).

The blind man shuddered and stumbled backward. He held trembling hands over his eyes and cried out. Blinding light assaulted him in a sudden flash. An explosion of deep color detonated across an empty canvas. Rich hues, textures, shadows, and shapes deluged his world. A tidal wave coursed through eyes suddenly restored, hurling him to his knees and bending him forward. There were no words for this. He was paralyzed in his attempts to associate his world of sound with that of sight. It was impossible to do so. There was too much, and it was all too fast.

And so he resorted to the only thing that made sense, that gave him grounding. Something that provided him a familiar benchmark in a world turned upside down. He resorted to sounds, to words, to that which identified his world only moments earlier. He shouted praise to God, ceaselessly and tirelessly while attempting to visually digest a tidal wave of color and a torrential barrage of light. The lessons of his blindness were the fuel for his praise.

A gasp arose from the crowd that itself was now only grasping what had just transpired. It was an impossible attempt to digest the impossible. And suddenly, it was blindingly clear to the throng that God was among them. The crowd didn't rebuke the blind man this time. Rather, they joined the man once blind. They partnered with him on the road. Praise was raised and caught the wind, drifted across the road, floating throughout the countryside and across history. As John Newton penned many centuries later, "I was blind, but now I see." Sight had come to a single man and to all men.

### MY ENCOUNTER WITH SIGHT

When vision comes, I too am on my knees. There is no other place to be. There is nothing else appropriate. Seeing as God sees renders all else blindness. I'm faced with the striking reality that I had presumed my blindness to be sight, thinking that I possessed that which I did not possess. Real blindness is the absence of the knowledge that one is blind. And most of us are, in this sense, totally blind.

And then I see the road. I never see all of it, but I see it. And I can see the roadside as well as the cups strewn there. That pitifully narrow slice of life that I inhabited in my blindness and in my ignorance is now pathetically clear. I will travel with Jesus now. That travel is a journey of praise marked in footsteps of humility. I am ever close to the hem of His garment, always diligent about being in step with Him. I want to trace His every move and copy His every turn. Ever delighted by His smile and always captivated by His glance, I am forever lost in His presence along the road.

The mass moved and resumed the momentum of the journey toward the gates of Jericho. For Jesus, it was one step closer to Jerusalem and one stride nearer Golgotha. One minute closer to an empty tomb that would repeat this moment, this instant, in the lives of untold billions. And what a remarkable moment it would be.

### God's Eyes

One day, Doug sat on a park bench outside of his room. In trembling hands, he held a single flower: a bird of paradise. As I sat next to him, he said, "I know what this looks like." This blind, mentally retarded young man refused to sit along the roadside of life. Doug had gathered all of our assorted moments together where I had painted explanations of the wonders of life across the darkened canvas of his mind, drawing from the palette of words the colors and hues of the mind and painting them the best he knew how.

And so he described the flower in rich detail. Then, taking me by the hand, he pulled me across the courtyard, explaining object after object after object in the richest of detail. I was stunned. I could not fathom him as blind; such was the complexity, the passionate romance, and the sheer exhilaration that embodied each detailed description. He saw better than I did because the heart always discerns more sharply than the eyes. Doug refused not to see even when his eyes had refused.

Doug refused to live life on the roadside. His handicaps were easily enough to keep him there, but his indomitable spirit precluded them all. When my time with Doug came to an end, he was living more than most people I know. On my final day with Doug, he said, "You know, I can see now!" And in my parting hug, I said, "Maybe someday you can teach me to see too."

### Pondering Point

Most of us prefer blindness, for it gives us permission to keep sitting along the roadside of life. Even more than permission, our own blindness keeps us from realizing that we're tragically sitting on the roadside in the first place. In time, blindness is presumed as vision because it's the only thing we know and we're forced to assume it as such. And at that point, our blindness has become our understanding and definition of sight. With this errantly presumed sight, we no longer realize our blindness. Do we really want to see? Indeed, it can be transforming.

## A Thought

- Do I see? Or is what I see my perception of what real seeing is?
- Am I willing to admit that I'm blind and that what I've accumulated in my blindness is less than what's really real?
- Am I daring enough to really see, knowing that what I see may demand more of me?
- Am I courageous enough to see the real world that lies out beyond me, and then to set my feet to that road?

CHAPTER 9

# I AM THAT "ONE"- SHEEP IN THE CESSPOOL
## Am I More?

*"And he brought him to Jesus. And when Jesus beheld him, he said, Thou art Simon the son of Jona: thou shalt be called Cephas, which is by interpretation, a stone."*

John 1:42 (KJV)

*"The beginning of wisdom is to call things by their right names."*
~ Chinese Proverb

**TODAY, IT WAS A TRANSIENT.** It was a chance passing as I walked my dog that was nothing of chance and everything of divine appointment. Ashamedly, I tried to avoid the transient as he staggered down the street in erratic steps laced with the staleness of alcohol. He drew up his weathered pack, shifted its weight, and limped toward me. The concourse of my mind was racing with presumed pleas for money, a scattered discourse of his misfortunes, or any number of sordid stories or pleas I simply didn't want hear. Mother Teresa said, "Loneliness and the feeling of being unwanted is the most terrible poverty," and this transient was terribly impoverished on both fronts.

What I was to discover is that it was much simpler than what I had wrongly presumed. All he wanted to do was to pet my dog. That's all. It was an agenda borne of love and spurred by loneliness that might somehow be carried out to completion by petting my dog, nothing more. It was hopelessness manifesting itself out of some small shred of hope that the loneliness might be abated, even if for the briefest moment.

Bedraggled, his skin was weathered thick and dark. Deep creases were packed with sweaty grime. Oily hair, long, stringy, and wild, exploded in tangles from the edges of a perspiration-stained baseball cap. A beard, patchy and streaked with gray before its time, incompletely littered his face. Filth laid layered deep into his polyester pants and turned a white t-shirt shades of sweaty brown. Stitching frayed the fringes of tennis shoes worn thin by wandering. Fingernails were embedded with the dirt of desperation, clawing life's sparse soil for a morsel of sustenance. A mouthful of inattention sported teeth, rotted and black. And in the midst of his life's thin scantiness and thick loss, all he wanted was to pet my dog.

My first response was one of revulsion. My second, which quickly followed, was one of suspicion about his intent. These were followed by the audacious thought that, in reality, this simply might be an unbearably lonely human being starving for love more than anything else.

"What's her name?" he asked.

A small connection was established by a simple question. I moved toward him and let out the leash. His eyes were hollow and ringed with the starvation of human isolation.

"Aspen," I said. "She loves people." He dropped his aged pack, knelt, put his hands on both sides of her face, and said, "You're a pretty girl."

Then, with uncharacteristic compassion, he hugged her, wrapping his arms around her ninety-eight pound body and holding her close to himself. Both melded into each other for a moment, meeting a need in the life of each other. Innocence and acceptance merged, paving the way for intimacy that was bereft of risk and completely open to vulnerability. They did something I rarely see or do myself. They genuinely connected in something so pure and undiluted that days of contemplation left me with but the barest understanding of what had transpired. For a brief moment, the disheveled man was alive—vibrantly alive. And in his aliveness, I saw my deadness.

A moment passed. Then, he drew himself stiffly to his feet and said, "She's lucky to have you." He then paused and nodded to himself, absorbing the moment to be able to draw from it in any one of the innumerable lonely moments that were yet to be his. He drew up sagging pants, shouldered his pack, said thanks, and lumbered away. He asked nothing of me. He made no demands of me out of the innumerable demands that life had made of him. After he turned the corner, I never saw him again. This unexpected intimate collision was over as soon as it had begun, yet its astonishing effects hung heavy all about me.

I stood in the middle of the road in a deluge of shame, caught in the swirling stench of my judgmental attitude and putrid sense of superiority. I had been ignorantly bereft of the understanding that I was no different from the man who had only moments earlier turned that corner and walked out of my life. I was him. In that encounter, I was far less than he. I had the same needs that he did—only I demanded that life meet my needs. He made no such demand at all.

Impatient with my introspection, the dog pulled the leash, jostling me from my thoughts. I cinched the leash in my hand, and we resumed our walk. I focused with soulful scrutiny on the corner the man had just rounded, wondering about him. In those thoughts, my mind wandered.

## SHEEP IN THE CESSPOOL

The muck and manure of society churned in a macabre-like stew all around Jesus that day. Swirling sewage had collected along the waysides and fringes of society and had spilt down the gutter of the culture. Sometimes, we relegate the disadvantaged and outcasts as somehow being less human than we are. We see them as the cultural sewage—though we're typically not honest enough to admit to that. There were multitudes of them there that day, looking like an assortment of transient maggots that had gathered around a carcass. A bunch of wandering people of assorted stripes and colors found their way to that place. It was repelling.

People are associated as being whatever their behaviors are. Their actions are too often believed to define their character and decree their worth, the things about them etching both their value and their character in indelible ink. They are irrevocably tied to, branded by, and labeled within the scope of their actions. Such attitudes rob people of their most precious asset: their humanity. Those who were there that day were viewed as lost, irredeemably unsalvageable, entirely undesirable, and obviously irretrievable. They were the excrement of all that is evil and decadent.

They were tax collectors, prostitutes, assorted thieves, and inebriated drunkards. They were zealots, adulterers, and the wayward of every sort and color. Every one of them was drawn deep from the dregs of society. It was the cesspool of the culture, and in the middle of it all, Jesus stood knee deep … God in the cesspool. It was implausible. Holiness stood in filth when holiness should have no place in filth. But there stood Jesus. There might be some brilliant intentionality in it all, that holiness was created to stand in mankind's filth to lift mankind out of that very filth. Sometimes the things that appear completely irreconcilable and mutually exclusive serve a shared purpose that could not be achieved except through their contradiction.

Others of a different sort also scanned the crowd that day. Visually, they infiltrated the many wandering who were gathered in tight clusters to hear Jesus. The decadence was clear to Pharisaical eyes and those narrowed by the law. Over there, she wore the scandalous vestiges of a prostitute. She had been seen in closed, muted conversation with varied men on street corners and deep in the catacomb-like darkness of derelict alleys. Currency had been exchanged. It had been followed by covert slippage into nearby residences. Lustful embraces followed. Eroticism was exchanged for cash. And there she was. And there was Jesus right along with her.

Stretching pious necks, they scanned the crowd further. There they stood, having been seen at their tables far too often, collecting inflated taxes. Gouging the lives and harvesting the purses of kin and neighbors, they had grown interminably fat on the sweat of others. They lived to shower themselves with the dividends of lives stolen and hopes exonerated. Lavish living was sucked from the lifeblood of their own kind as itinerant leeches of an oppressive ruling nation. Garnished in costly robes, faces soft with expensive lotions, hands smoothed and skin scented with the stolen privileges of luxury, they sported both gold and silver decor. There they were. And there was Jesus.

Eyes scanned the crowd further. There, next to several others, stood another. Alcohol has the ruinous ability to swallow up decades of time in but a handful years, taking with it families, incomes, and entire lives. Yet, there were those that had been so taken by alcohol and so pillaged by it that they remained unsteady even when sober. The stench of stale liquor and vomit exuded a putrid aroma all around them. They were slaves to a liquid escape that had drawn their families, their reputations, their money, and their lives down to the dregs. The sum total of their existence had become drowned in a bottomless drink, subsisting solely on the hope of the next drink. There they stood. And there was Jesus.

Others gathered, mingled, and drew close to Him. The poor and destitute milled about in garments of destitution. Widows abandoned by the insensitive thief of death stood about. Those marked with the physical handicaps that bespoke the gravity of their presumed sins were there. The diseased and deformed mingled, each a walking testament to their transgressions and to God's judgment of their transgressions. An assortment of sin pooled in one place. It was a living, breathing cesspool of everything that makes humanity pathetic. A vortex of everything that is unrighteous distilled in one location. Wretched and putrid described them all. And there Jesus stood. It was incomprehensible.

The feelings about the situation were stated, and the behavior was soundly condemned by the religious leader who had gathered. "This man welcomes sinners and eats with them" (Luke 15:2) they shouted in a sharp spirit of condemnation. Do I think any differently? Really? I don't think so. Of course, I would rail against the audacity of their comments. But inwardly, my heart is theirs. Why? Because I refuse to see myself in the crowd, nor do I permit myself to see any correlation with them despite the obvious nature of that correlation. Thomas Jefferson wrote, "Experience demands that man is the only animal which devours his own kind, for I can apply no milder term to the general prey of the rich on the poor." I find myself fully and willingly participating in this morbid food chain. And so, I am the same as the cynics who had gathered there that day.

I willingly observe people such as these, but from a distance, detached and somehow better. I am adamant that I have not succumbed to the squalor as they have. I possess some overstated sense of worth that insulates me from the foulness of humanity. I am insistent that I am a different sort of person—as if there were degrees of humanity; I say that I am not a transient in whatever way that I am. I judge every one of them on nauseatingly false premises, just as I did the transient who stopped to pet my dog. Thoughts of pompous superiority keep me different from them, thoughts that are preposterous because I am there in the cesspool too. I am just the same as each and every one of them. I *am* one of them. No better; probably worse. All that I am is as much a part of the cesspool as any of them. And that is why Jesus loves me. That is why He looks for me and chases after me.

Jesus paused out of the timeless realization that those who presume righteousness are in far greater need than those who recognize their decadence. He understood that, too often, presumed righteousness presumed condemnation of everything else. And so He raised His voice and projected it further, drawing in His detractors by His intonation. "Suppose one of you has a hundred sheep and loses one of them. Does he not leave the ninety-nine in the open country and go after the lost sheep until he finds it?" (Luke 15:4).

It's all about God in a mad search for the one, in desperate pursuit of the solitary soul on its transient journey from place to place. It's God on a wildly divine manhunt of love where He seeks and draws out His creation. His is a heart infinitely too big to miss even one single life hopelessly lost in the tangled wilderness of living. Out in the wilds of life, the loss of one outweighs the safety of the many. So much so, that the cesspool is a must. In what other place could He possibly be? In what other place could love be lived out as it could in this kind of place? In what other place is love given a venue in which to have ample room to display everything that it's capable of doing like this place? God is unrelenting and unstoppable. He has to be there more than any other place because it's in this kind of place where majesty can be most majestically displayed.

And so, Jesus was standing in the midst of lost sheep, directly in the path of the lives of those who had wandered away. Some had wandered so far that the path back had been lost in the wandering. Many were in grave danger. None of them were able to find their way back, leaving many to believe that there was no way back. Each of them was hopelessly lost unless the Shepherd sought them out, searched for them, scratched through the caustic dust of their lives to find traces of them. Scouring the countryside and navigating treacherous paths; descending steep cliffs; ascending rocky precipices; risking His life in order to retrieve theirs, willingly giving His life to ensure their safe return. In time, this journey, this search would require that He give His life for these gathered around Him. It required His life for me.

### I Am the Lost Sheep

I am that lost sheep that He seeks. I am that person. I am one of those people and, in some sense, I am all of those people. I am wandering too. It's an abruptly stunning revelation that's really nothing of a revelation because, inherently, I've known it all along. Embracing it mercifully relegates me to some base authenticity that benevolently reminds me of who I really am so I might be truly found. It robs me of my attempt to feign that I am what I am not. In pretending to be superior, I subsequently forget who I truly am and become lost in a deluge of personal aggrandizement that's paper thin. In time, I construct and import the lie so effectively that I have fooled myself and therefore become entirely untrue to myself. And a simple transient, bedecked with his authenticity, exposed me.

When I fully embrace the idea that I am the transient and that I am a compilation of all the people that were with Jesus in that place that day, my acknowledged depravity forces me to ask an entirely different question: "What then is lost in my loss?" It feels that the filth of my depravity denigrates me to the point that I'm of little importance anyway. That filth—combined with my disobedience and my incessant bumbling, my foolish decisions and defiant behaviors, laced with my judgmental attitude that betrays the whole of it anyway—leaves nothing of value. And so, I become convinced that I am not worth the cost of being sought out. Therefore, being sought out by this relentless God creates the pinnacle in human contradiction where I abjectly hate the fact that He's looking for me, while I passionately desire that He look for me until He finds me.

And yet, I am too embarrassed to be found. My depravity is exposed in the finding, and I am ashamed by its vivid exposure. Shame is given terrifying release and granted devastating power when it's lain bare before others. And so, it's safer and so much more convenient to be lost. And so not only am I lost, I hide in order to intentionally perpetuate the lost-ness. Drawn sick and disgusted by my disobedience, I am unworthy of the search and wholly unworthy of discovery, so I hide.

Yet all of that is irrelevant in the face of divine love. He searches for me anyway, and He does so relentlessly. God pursues me on a divine manhunt, overcoming every obstacle in His mad quest to redeem me yet again. There is a lovingly divine wildness in His persistence to ferret me out and bring me home. And He does find me because His relentlessness will not settle for anything less. And for this, among so many other things, I love Him.

And then a final caveat to the whole search. It is a glimpse of what thrills heaven as anything that would have the command to thrill heaven must be stupendous. It's what sends thunderous euphoria through the halls of the infinite. "I tell you that in the same way there is more rejoicing in heaven over one who repents than over ninety-nine righteous persons who do not need to repent" (Luke 15:7). And so, heaven cheers. A raucous shout of exhilaration rises when He finds me, when He found those gathered around Him that day, even when He finds the ones who had criticized and ultimately betrayed Him for what He was doing. A sense of euphoria breaks and surges in a tidal wave of exuberant joy throughout heaven's colonnades. The foundations of heaven shake. Angels break in riotous applause. Waves course through the concourses of the infinite, shake the pillars of the universe, and rumble off to the edges of eternity. How terrible it is to be lost. How magnificent it is to be found!

The prostitute succumbed, repented, and prostrated her life. Heaven cheered, and angels applauded in thunderous ovation. Tax collectors bowed in abject remorse, faced with the skewed priorities that flew in the face of all that was good. The infinite was deluged. The drunkard sought living water instead of alcoholic inebriation, creating room to restore all that he had lost. The pillars of the universe were rocked. The blind, lame, diseased, and those with assorted maladies spiritual, emotional, and physical were found, and a shout of deafening joy rumbled off to the edges of space.

Because being lost is so horrible, being found is grand beyond imagination. It is unimaginable and splendid beyond comprehension. I can only grasp a thin shred of it, some frayed thread through which I feel some small vibration of a cosmos rocked. But that small movement ... even that is exhilarating.

The religious and legal eyes of those gathered nearby did not perceive it. The words of Jesus were direct. They painted a vivid picture. He spoke with clarity and a decisiveness that religious and legal eyes had to parse to their advantage; otherwise, they would collapse under His words. The parsing of truth kills the truth as it always does. The truth was readily apparent, but it's readily revealing as well. Sheep and a cesspool of dredged humanity did not resonate nor correlate with them. They only saw a cesspool; it was beyond their ability to see more. All the while, heaven was wildly boisterous with the thunder of lost sheep now found.

I had Pharisaical eyes that day. I saw the cesspool. I did not see the sheep even when the sheep was kneeling in front of me, petting my dog, and talking to me. It doesn't get any closer than that, and I missed it entirely. I am ashamed.

## All I See Is Cesspool

I miss it in my own life and in the lives around me. I miss the magnitude of my own deprivation and the degree of lost-ness to which it speaks, which is the very thing that relentlessly drives God's wild and unrelenting search to find me. I am lost on the road of life, and I lie about the fact that I'm lost. The contrast between my lost-ness and His love is too broad and too massive for me to fathom. The meeting of the two is thunderous. How can the event of finding me be so profound? How can others—the filthy, the walking wounded, the degenerate, the self-centered, the calloused—how can all these who are so much like me be of such importance? How can these, how can *we* be so valuable, so precious that heaven itself raises the roof of the cosmos in applause?

I don't understand it. I work to believe it, and I am profoundly appreciative for it. I want to see myself as terribly fallen as the rest of humanity and yet as worthy as He sees me. I want to see others in the same way. I want His eyes so I can see my filth as simply a lost sheep among many other lost sheep being about the business of being lost and in search of a Savior who in reality is in search of us. He is passionately searching for that one lost sheep with an infinite aggression. And when I pause and contemplate the wonder of it all, I swell with His love. I am saturated with a profound sense of inestimable worth and count myself lucky to be among those in the human cesspool whom God loves so dearly.

My pace quickens to round the corner and see if I might catch a glimpse of the transient as he meandered away. I arrive and he is gone, likely off to some unknown destination, his frayed shoes and gentle heart plodding life's highway. I pause for a lingering moment and shout "thank you" down the empty street. My voice dissipates, likely unable to reach the man who has now stepped beyond the reach of my voice. One more glance down the empty road out of a deep longing to see the one who helped me see. I turn and head home, my heart thanking him for letting me see who I am and how great God is.

**PONDERING POINT**

Too often, it's not that we can't see our depravity. For most of us, our depravity is readily apparent; our deficits and failures follow us and suffocate us in the following. We have our monsters that seize our lives and stifle any hope or promise of living. We are sheep imprisoned in failure, shackled to self-hatred, bound by an overwhelming sense of incompetence, stripped by a feeling of inferiority with the scars of horrific histories resulting in stinking self-disgust. More often than not, it is easy to see ourselves in the cesspool. The problem is that we can't visualize ourselves being anywhere else. We forget that Jesus stands in the cesspool right next to us. And He calls each of us out of that place. As frightening or impossible as it may seem, God has come in to take us out ... to take you out.

**A THOUGHT**
- Am I willing to risk exposure and to risk the possibility of success because of the exposure?
- Am I willing to acknowledge that I am in the cesspool in the first place?
- Has the cesspool defined me and held me captive because of that definition?
- Am I willing to dare to believe that I am infinitely more than I have come to believe myself to be?

CHAPTER 10

# SEVENTY CENTS OF SIMPLICITY
## Richness Through Developing Childlike Eyes

*Jesus said, "Let the little children come to me, and do not hinder them, for the kingdom of heaven belongs to such as these."*
                                                           Matthew 9:14

*"It is the childlike mind that finds the kingdom."*
                                                           ~ Charles Fillmore

**HE WAS FOUR YEARS OLD** ... barely. Boyish innocence was tightly stitched and held fast to a deep zest for living. He was a mosaic of the threads of a splendid tapestry whose fibers were being woven into a soft spirit that reveled in life. I love my son. I love him for what he is and what I see in him that I am not. He is innocence untainted and unsoiled, a young boy who catches the essence of living through windows of the soul yet unsullied by life. Splendidly exuberant, he draws in life's energy and expels it freely to anyone who will embrace its gift. He is both a repository of living and the embodiment of simplicity. One without the other would dramatically diminish him, as it would any of us.

"I have seventy cents," he said. Sitting at a red light, I had no idea as to the nature, purpose, or rationale of his comments, arising as it seemed from the incessant babbling and wonderful spontaneity that frequently marked him. "Dad, I have seventy cents!" Attending to the blur and bustle of the marauding traffic that rushed around me, I attempted to placate him, hoping that he would drift on to something else. "That's nice," I replied.

He was irritably insistent. My verbal pabulum was insufficient. "Dad, I have seventy cents!"

His voice was emphatic. I glanced in my rearview mirror and watched him squirming in his car seat, obviously possessing some agenda of great importance to him that was swallowed up in the supposedly greater agendas that dictated my day.

Catching my eyes in the mirror, he held out a clenched fist clutching seventy cents and with sordid determination said, "Dad, I have seventy cents!"

### What We Miss

I am occupied, attending to the congestion and the wide array of events around me. The traffic of my life is made up of frustrating red lights, a rare green one, and irritating yellows that flash across my many intersections. All of the congestion of commerce and career, the snarls of success, and the raucous rhythm of rush hour that I embrace as essential and necessary to achievement. Johann Wolfgang von Goethe said that "there is nothing more frightful than ignorance in action," and my errant focus and abject submission to life's demands renders me exactly that.

I am caught in the blindness of believing that living life means winning, being horrified that an opportunity missed is an unredeemable loss that creates a permanent setback and lifetime diminishment. I must master life by gouging and gorging myself on its complexities at every opportunity, without having time to savor the tender exquisiteness of its intricacies. Mine is a hoarding of life rather than a delicate sampling. In and through it all, I miss the minute details in the mayhem, the subtleties that are the very essence of the larger things that I gorge and feed upon. In essence, I miss simplicity. "I have seventy cents, Dad!" It was a statement of simplicity, and so I missed it.

Crystal blue eyes and romping blonde hair, and his small hands cradled two quarters and two precarious dimes. They were clenched so firmly that his tiny fingers turned shades of red and white as he held them valiantly with arms outstretched in front of him. His face was chiseled with a squared hint of boyish determination, the manifestation of four-year-old eyes apprehending the core of life and living when I could not see it. He perceived with a clear soul what really mattered when I saw only an annoying red light and thick traffic. "Dad, I have seventy cents!"

And then I saw it; belatedly, but I saw it. Quite accidently, it caught the barest edge of my mind when it should have occupied a more prominent place. Out of the corner of my eye, from the farthest fringes of my life, it stirred. The simple intruded upon my chosen world of complexities when it should have been a central part of it all to begin with. A solitary figure sat on the margins of my wild world, passing by me except for a four-year-old attuned to the wonder of simplicity, hoping that the din surrounding me might ebb just enough to catch a glimpse. I finally saw it.

Scrawled by an unsteady hand across a tattered piece of discarded cardboard, stained and bent, were a handful of words. The edges of cardboard were torn, frayed, and mutilated, much like the man who held it. Primitive letters etched out the silent plea of a lost life. He was no more than ten feet away, and I missed him. The sign read, "Need help, please." It was a collision that I needed to have so that I might be rocked out of my sterile tasks and reoriented to real life. It would have been tragically missed if it were not for my four-year-old son. "Dad, I have seventy cents!"

## SIMPLICITY MISSED AND RECLAIMED

"Don't push these children away." Jesus' voice was purposeful, highlighting an eternal principal violated by stumbling men who chased after life and missed living in the pursuit of living. "Don't ever get between them and me. These children are the very center of life in the kingdom" (Mark 10:14, The Message). Simplicity is central to the infinite, which is an odd and incomprehensible dichotomy. That which is complex beyond comprehension embraces simplicity at its core and derives all that it is from that core. The infinite invites us to simplicity as that which is of eternal value is best seen in that which is simple and uncluttered. It may be that that which is simple is that which is closest to perfection, and that simplicity is brainchild of a marvelously creative God.

Simplicity is the key that turns the tumblers to the door of the eternal. It is the single and sole passport to an audience with the infinite. We must suspect then that such a concept is built into the fabric of the finite as well. Simplicity is the essence of life and living from which everything else springs. Without it, complexity loses its roots; it has no grounding, no boundaries, and no identifiable point of departure that defines it and shapes it. And it is here, with the cluster of children swirling around Him in innocent admiration, that Jesus declares simplicity as simply central.

The Pharisees and their malicious attempts to trap Him were barely hours old, still resonating in His mind. God incarnate, the Creator of the universe, had been asked to justify Himself. It was indeed the absurdity that arises when simplicity is missed. The rich young ruler and the stench of materialism were only moments away. Face to face with God, the rich young man would prove himself unable to see Jesus in the tangled web woven of wealth and the complexity inherent in the sordid accumulation of power. He had too much of this world and too little of the next, all of which leaves no room for simplicity. The walk to Jerusalem, betrayal, spikes, a splintered beam, oozing blood, death ... all of that was only a mere handful of days away. Awash in the many manifestations of man's sin and on the threshold of abolishing it, Jesus "gathered the children up in His arms and He laid His hands of blessing on them" (Mark 10:16, The Message).

### SIMPLICITY LIVED

As you look at this picture of Jesus, do you see it? It too is sadly on the margins of our lives, rather than being in the center of our lives. Jesus is sitting, gingerly drawing an armful of giggling and squealing children into His lap. The thick hands of a carpenter run callused fingers through mounds of curls gracing a tiny head, drawing a smile out of a timid child with a playful and slightly bemused stare. He embraced their innocence and simplicity as so far removed from the world He faced, the world that He would die for.

He sees in their impish and innocent faces the simplicity that keeps the world from seeing Him. He is at the vortex of His earthly life. In a matter of days, the entire expanse of history will be rocked by His death. The universe will itself reel. Hell will fall. Satan will flee. The immensity of the powers of darkness will suffer complete and uncompromising defeat. He will defiantly tread the bowels of hell itself, and then He will rise and He will, in His resurrection, change the entire course of human history for the full course of human history. What He is about to do is monumental beyond anything that has ever transpired in the whole course of existence.

But here, at this moment, sandwiched between these cataclysmic events, He laughs with children who have no sense of who He is or what awaits Him. Innocent, they are. And so He plays for a moment. He tickles and is tickled. He tells a joke, and the air is filled with the squeal of childhood laughter. Eye to eye with gentle intensity, He tells them of their immense value and of the Father's love for each of them. He will die for them shortly, their innocence maybe making that sacrifice more bearable and more compelling.

It is the Creator connecting through simplicity with the created in a way that is entirely unabated and completely unobstructed. It's the treasure of the deep soul finding connection with the vast God through simplicity. The mayhem of life's traffic, all of the red and green and yellow lights that had dogged His ministry, were laid aside so that He could immerse Himself in life's real purpose.

### THE DOOR OF ACCESS

From this adoring pile of romping children, His gaze shifted, directing his words to the twelve disciples standing about the scene. It was not to be a lesson for children, but one from them. Tussling with their youthful energy, He says, "Unless you accept God's kingdom in the simplicity of a child, you'll never get in" (Mark 10:15, The Message). The contrast is numbing, even paralyzing. The key to complexity is simplicity? But how can simplicity ever hope to grasp complexity, much less manage it? Simplicity would suggest intentional ignorance through the abandonment of the acquisition of knowledge. Alexander Pope said, "There is a certain majesty in simplicity," and that vexing majesty was abounding all about Jesus. It was a stunning and completely puzzling reversal. It was just too simple, and so it was missed as we miss it.

The complexities of life and living, the minute intricacies of the Law and the sacrificial system, the unfathomable breadth of the cosmos and starry hosts that beg exploration and contemplation, the mysterious yet striking predictability of nature, the grandeur and the magnificent majesty of God as the incomprehensible "I AM" (Genesis 3:14) next to which all of creation fades and pales into oblivion is accessed through simplicity? Here, in the laughter and play of these children lay the incalculably priceless key to kingdom access and the sole passport to the infinite? It was simply too simple, so simple that grasping it was, in itself, complex.

Peals of laughter drew them back from contemplation, a sweet elixir to a sullen life. The children had the voices of those who had seized the keys to the kingdom through simplicity. It meant accepting as these children accepted, with innocence and simplicity, humility and obedience, through trust that never asks if there is anything else other than trust. Engaging in a raw embracing, a simple acceptance free of attempts to determine how to shape one's life so that it might find a shred of acceptability before God. It was about freely accepting the unconditional as exactly that: unconditional. And so it was in the children.

Jesus stood, the lesson now having been taught by example and by word. He stooped, placed His hands on the children for a brief final moment, and blessed them, extending into their simplicity the blessing of God. He was able to do so because of the massive and free-roaming space created in and by their simplicity. Access to the kingdom was granted to such as these, its evidence seen in the blessing Jesus bestowed upon them. It was all so simple, yet so magnificently transforming. Lives have expended lifetimes trying to achieve what these children achieved in but a moment via the vehicle of innocence and simplicity.

A final hug, a parting embrace, and the children dispersed, running into the arms of waiting parents. A pair of them skipped off holding hands. Sticks trailed curlicue designs in the gritty dirt. Several ran around parents in errant circles of delight and innocent mischief. A small cluster of them gathered mounds of wildflowers, pressing their nectared petals deep into their faces, inhaling their perfumed ecstasy. The sound of laughter faded and then dissipated on the soft winds of the day. The bevy of children scurried off to the next adventure, not realizing that they had just had the greatest adventure of all. But simplicity embraces all life as an adventure.

## GETTING BACK

A honking horn exploded into the moment. The light was green. I instinctively punched the accelerator and drove off.

"But, Dad, I have seventy cents!"

How our hearts are drawn to simplicity, yet how quick we are to discount it and therefore relegate it to childish imaginations and base immaturity. How dreadfully painful it is when we cannot respond to it. Life caused me to drive by the transient, and to this day, I am irritated by the shallowness of my choice and the pathetic action that followed. Corey and I talked about that man, and we talked about how we could help someone with his seventy cents, his seventy cents of simplicity. Could I please have seventy cents of simplicity? Enough to see my world as Corey does. Oh, God, could you please grant me seventy cents of simplicity?

## How Do I Find Seventy Cents of Simplicity?

How do I balance complexity with simplicity? How do I rectify the God of the universe playing with children and incorporate that principle into my world? How do I correlate the melding of the infinite with simplicity? Where is that common ground where I can embrace simplicity with a relentless vigor and yet live in a world of complexity?

It is not the absence of complexity, for creation is woven of it, and it is the embodiment of God Himself. It is the example of the infinitely complex God playing and romping with simple children that we must seize, hold fast to, and draw from. The key is the full embodiment of both simplicity and complexity, where neither is lost or sacrificed at the expense of the other, but where the complete embrace of both brings fullness and balance to life. The challenge is to hold to both equally.

We assume that complexity is the absence of simplicity. Rather, is complexity not the very thing that highlights simplicity and makes it so obvious and so deeply cherished? Is it not in the holding of simplicity that complexity has a point of origin and a benchmark that dictates its shape, tenor, and tone? Is not simplicity that thing that keeps complexity centered at the very times when it might stray and keeps it balanced when the weight of complexity might shift? And is not the fullest embrace of the two, with each holding the other in balance, the very thing that maximizes life and living?

We need to live with seventy cents of simplicity, clutching it in our fists and refusing to let it go. We need to allow it to hold and ground our exploration, acquisition, and understanding of life's complexities. It is our task to gain an understanding of the world God has put us in but likewise to maintain eyes of simplicity that keep us centered on that which is central to all of life. Complexity that is not continually grounded in simplicity is apt to be errant, causing us to be consumed in the complexity itself. For that brief moment, following a confrontation with the Pharisees, a pending confrontation with a rich young ruler, and only days away from death, Jesus centered Himself in simplicity. So should we.

**PONDERING POINT**

"I came so they can have real and eternal life, more and better life than they ever dreamed of" (John 10:10, The Message). Could it be that this "more and better life" is in part the ability to embrace complexity while holding tenaciously to simplicity, allowing simplicity to ground us and center us in the complicated and detailed facets of life, each providing a balancing effect for the other, thereby allowing us to embrace the fullness of life without sacrificing anything that a single focus would cause us to miss? And is such a balance the work of God in our lives, His grace and power allowing us to achieve this dual embrace? Indeed, I think it is.

## A Thought
- Which have I embraced: simplicity or complexity?
- Can I embrace simplicity, or do I feel that doing so is dangerous and frighteningly naïve?
- How diminished is my life in the imbalance?
- How can I seek God in childlike simplicity this day?

CHAPTER 11

# HOW VERY MANY YEARS
## Rejecting the Pain of the Past

*"Then he went out to the spring and threw the salt into it, saying, 'this is what the LORD says: I have healed this water. Never again will it cause death or make the land unproductive.'"*
2 Kings 2:21

*"To regret one's own experiences is to arrest one's own development. To deny one's own experiences is to put a lie into the lips of one's life. It is no less than a denial of the soul."*
~ Oscar Wilde

**PEARL HARBOR WAS YET TO** be strewn twisted with steel and bloody memories. The bombs would fall only seven months later, listing the U.S.S. Arizona and littering the glistening Pacific harbor with wreckage of both metal and flesh. Tommy Dorsey and Glenn Miller were setting the cadence for a golden generation that was about to draw itself up from the commitment to isolationism and hurl itself against beaches from Guam to Normandy. The Depression was itself dwindling as fixed eyes still burning from the acrid smoke of Pearl Harbor scanned both Europe and the South Pacific.

In May of 1941, my grandfather passed out of life long before I passed in. I was told that there was no loss in his passing. Such a statement was horribly sad, even though I never knew the man except for two scant photos that gave but the barest hint of who he might have been. Family should have a bond of blood and spirit that transcends time and difficulties. There should be such an intricate intimacy of soul and heart that a statement like that one would be entirely alien, completely unwelcomed, and altogether unknown. Yet such statements are made.

The sordid stories that had drifted down the foggy decades revealed my grandfather as a man of rage, alcohol, and smoky pool halls. He apparently craved a lifestyle he could ill-afford as a brick mason, happily succumbing to those cravings and blatantly choosing to live the life despite the cost. They said that he made self-centered purchases and self-aggrandizing choices that he could not afford, relegating his wife and children to impoverishment during the poverty of the Great Depression. He flagrantly lived by amassing staggering debts that tallied out on registers that were financial, relational, and emotional in nature.

He had been a saxophone player with an artistic soul gradually suffocated by life and drowned in the liquid abyss of alcohol. Over time, the notes had soured in the bottom of shot glasses and empty bottles. His heart had stopped long before the heart attack. His shadow had vanished from the doorpost when my father was a tender six, leaving a wife and four children to face the destitution of the soup lines, raging unemployment, and a nation adrift in the Great Depression.

For my father, the loss was inexplicable, slicing a boy's soul to the core. A young heart that desperately yearned for a father in the very vacancy created by his father irresistibly drew six-year-old feet in worn shoes down dusty alleys to the derelict pool hall that his father had traded for his family. Peering through glass smeared by filth and yellowed by smoke, his eyes cautiously searched the vagrant mix of alcoholics and wayward men who sat about in smoky stupors. The sharp crack of billiard balls, muffled conversation, and clanking of glasses drifted through dense layers of smoke that permeated the room.

A six-year-old heart searched the sordid array of drifting humanity, hoping to catch a fleeting glance of a father who would never come home. Eventually catching a glimpse of this errant child, his father would glance over furrowed brows and callously shout, "What do want ... boy?" The snickers of assorted pool hall vagrants in the throes of inebriation added its own caustic smoke to the thick air surrounding six-year-old innocence. A bloodied heart pressing hopeful eyes against a derelict pool hall window would find itself re-wounded yet again by a callous father.

The need to run would seize him, even though the pain was so overwhelming that determining where to run was, at that moment, impossible. Sometimes, running away leaves no room to determine what or where we're running to. So, sometimes in life we just run out of a panicked sense that in the act of running we'll get away from whatever has inflicted pain. We run pell-mell despite the fact that what we're running to hasn't been defined. Worse yet, maybe we've determined a destination as entirely irrelevant, which leaves our running full of fleeing but completely empty of resolution.

Such was that moment. His six-year-old tears were profuse and blinding; wet and at the same time searing, they fell without restraint. Wiping them with worn sleeves as he dashed around dusty corners of vacant streets, he would finally scurry under the weatherworn front porch where he would attempt to seek solace that no porch could ever afford him. Carrie P. Meeks wrote, "You can't put abandonment and alienation under arrest." However, we would be wholly justified to do so if we could. My father was a little boy in a deep depression in the Great Depression.

However, time passed. The death of his father arrived prematurely. A sullen burial simultaneously embraced both pleasure and relief that he was gone but was likewise weighed with the grief that any hope of a restored father was now likewise dashed. His father had long abandoned the family to poverty. However, we still hold out some faint hope that life might pity us sufficiently to grant us a miracle. Death brings the hope of a miracle to a sudden and jolting halt. And so, while my father buried his father, he also buried hope.

Seven brief months after his death, Pearl Harbor erupted and men marched off to war. At nineteen, my father went off to serve in the Air Force. Eventually, the Axis fell and America got back to the business of home and hearth. The decades rolled by in a blur of marriage, children, family, work, and the innumerable array of threads from which the tapestry of life is woven. As it is with life, 1999 rushed onto the stage, leaving us wondering where the other years had gone.

My grandfather was an anomaly to me. A few tokens and shards of various stories were mere pieces of a scant puzzle that when put together provided only the vaguest representation of whomever it was that he was. Two black and white photographs, stained and discolored by time and framed by mottled edges, added mystery to the mysterious. They had been taken before his own innocence and giftedness were offered up to the gods of alcohol and narcissism. His face was filled with promise not yet stolen. He stood erect and confident. All the things he could have been were still there to be realized. But that was a photo snapped before his strength was sapped. There are no photos of him afterwards.

There was his pocket watch, gold and bejeweled. It was in many ways what he was but was never to be. Then, there were the other stories: abuse, drunken rages, and litanies of caustic verbal barrages that sent emotional shrapnel ripping through whomever they were directed at. The recollections were shadowy, coming to me out of the haunting grayness of an era now long gone. It was all a misty appendage of my history that possessed too little firmness to take hold of. It was the heritage from which I descended.

And so it was in 1999 that I visited home. My father was seventy-six. The death of his father loomed fifty-eight years deep in the past. Yet, inside my father was a six-year-old boy who carried the pain of smoky pool halls and the cobweb-strewn underside of creaky front porches. He had never visited his father's grave since the funeral back in 1941. There was yet a mixture of pain, simply finding himself unable to draw up enough compassion to nudge himself there to face the granite edifice that marked the place, that place where he had stood as his father was lowered into the soft spring soil seven months before a December bombing half a world away, the place from which he would depart into World War II … and then life. "I want to go see Grandpa," I said.

At my request, my father paused and then leaned back into folds of the recliner. Passively, he eyed me and then cast wandering glances across the floor and out through the adjacent dining room. Sometimes, you can hear pain in total silence, and I heard it. "You don't have to go," I said. "But I want to ask your permission to go. I don't want to resurrect any pain for you, but I'd like to see the grave."

For a moment, he went back for the briefest of moments. The assorted memories drew themselves up from across the misty decades etched in his soul and raced, it seemed, across the forefront of his mind. A kaleidoscope of emotions reintroduced themselves to him in the blur of a handful of seconds and thrust him back into his chair. Pictures and snapshots taken by a six-year-old heart flashed across a seventy-six-year-old mind, instantly coalescing into that place and that time. For a moment, the decades vanished, and he was back there in pool halls and under front porches. I grieved that I had broached the subject in the first place. His pain was far in excess of any selfish need that I had to piece together my past. I wished I could have retracted the request, to have pulled the words right out of the air and let it all lie as it had since 1941. Quietly, he leaned forward, collected a few words, and once collected, turned and said, "I think it's time I went."

### A Cemetery Five Decades Later

Fifty-eight years changes things. The cemetery looked different, far different from that day in May of 1941. Several circuitous drives around the cemetery yielded no recollection of where the grave might be, as time renders memory misty. No familiar landmarks protruded from a dramatically altered landscape. The mystery enshrouding the location of his burial plot was as thick as that of his life. Stopping at the cemetery office, we secured a plot map designating the place where he lay, a map to the man of mystery and abuse. Navigating the thin, winding roads, a landmark finally leapt out from the oblivion of a grave lost. "I recognize that oak tree," Dad muttered. "He's there, by that oak. I remember that."

The car rolled up a slight gravel berm. The sound of crunching gravel slowed and stopped. Suddenly, time vanished for Dad. It was May 1941 all over again. My father paused, fumbled to put the keys away, and reached for the car door. We stepped out into another May day just like that one fifty-eight years ago.

Walking around the car, up a slight grass berm, and into a sea of granite headstones, the memories rolled in a torrential deluge, bringing up with them other assorted memories long forgotten to the thickening mist of time. Recalling tombstones of distant family members that were adjacent to his father's, he seemed to be reconstructing a lineage that would culminate in his father, somehow trying to connect with his own father through a larger ancestry. Dad worked his way to his father across the resting places of other distant relatives, all the while working his way across the resting places of his own pain that lay buried deep in the plot of his heart.

There was a tension in his heart, I think, the desire to quickly find the grave and deal with whatever emotions it was to bring. This was wed with the equally powerful desire to keep his father deep in his own past where his father could not reach into the present. There was a disturbing sense that the power of his father might somehow rise up out of the grave and seize him again, emotionally hurling him back to pool halls and front porches.

Emotional meandering grew as he navigated various headstones and stepped ever closer to the grave. A collision of past and present sent emotional reverberations through my father. "Here it is," my father said abruptly. Silence fell. Fifty-eight years suddenly surged and truncated in that single moment. He teetered in swelling emotion, knelt, and brushed back the grass that had grown around the headstone, wanting, it seemed, to reach out and love his dad in the only way that was left for him to do it.

Then, ever so gently, he ran his fingers across the name engraved in the cool granite and down past the date. He pressed a trembling palm against the name etched across the edifice. Trembling fingers dropped to his side, reflecting a moment that no one could join him in. For the briefest moment, Dad was alone with his father. Tears welled in the corner of eyes softened by the years. "I should have come before," he said. "I waited too long ... I waited too long."

### How Many Days?

The young man posited the question, "What must I do to inherit eternal life?" (Mark 10:17). His riches had not waved off the question, suggesting his awareness that riches are confined to the finite and are unable to purchase even a single square inch of the infinite. His acquired assets had not insulated him from larger things. Wealth was not a guarantor either for eternal life or against the inevitability of death. It left the most fundamental issue of life abjectly untouched and unaltered; money could not buy off death or purchase so much as an additional tick of the clock.

Earthly power was stifled, stymied, and wholly helpless when it came to matters of eternity. The various trappings of power, prestige, wealth, and wisdom were useless—a preponderance of illusions that wielded nothing but the illusion itself. And here was this rich, young ruler wrestling with the preponderance of those realities. Wealth found itself kneeling, and power fell prostrate before God disguised as an itinerant preacher out of Nazareth, asking about the one thing that exceeded his grasp and lay far outside his sphere of influence. "What must I do to inherit eternal life?"

The children had only begun to disperse when the rich young man had approached. They had been a splendid lesson in simplicity. Jesus' animated response to His play with them filled his words and spilled over His syntax. "Anyone who will not receive the kingdom of God like a little child will never enter it" (Mark 10:15).

Could it really be that simple? Could it be that all that God is and all that God wants can be distilled down to that? Is that not the mind-boggling wonder of the infinite? The staggering truth of all eternity rests in the ability of a God who has no end to pack all of His endless vastness into the simplicity manifest in the life of a child. Only God could do that, and in the apprehending of that fact, eternity is revealed for the simplest of us to see. No wealth. No power. No wisdom. No prestige. Access to God is the absence of earthly resources or means that are obtainable by men. It's nothing but pure faith, the sole and single ointment of heaven.

It's so phenomenally simple and rudimentary that it can only be fully grasped by eyes unspoiled and untainted by the allures of life. It can be seized by the unsullied windows of souls untarnished, souls not yet caught in the vice grip of works, achievements, successes, and meritorious efforts that futilely work to purchase what only God can give. It's all the abject futility of the finite attempting to purchase the infinite, which in and of itself is an irreconcilable exchange rate. The task is to reclaim the eyes of a child when adulthood has hazed them foggy and thick with the distorting mist of life.

This young ruler was resplendent, draped in chains of thick gold and sleek silver. Deep fabrics dyed in the riches of bedazzling colors bespoke their cost. Wraps of silk edged in decorative threads wound themselves lightly around his frame, obvious imports purchased from wealthy merchants. Perfumes laced the air with thin and buoyant aromas of distant lands. The nard of earth was generously lavished on him, rendering his skin soft, supple, and clear. Rings wrapped long fingers in variant jewels set deep in settings of precious metals that caught bits of sunlight and effortlessly threw them in a dazzling dance of golden light.

His entourage surrounded him, servants adept and poised to meet every need. The laughter of dispersing children was only now fading into the background. Simplicity in the form of playful children had brushed up against complexity for a brief moment, skipping off in the joy and abandon that riches and power had found irritatingly elusive. So elusive that they are sought from this impoverished Nazarene.

In the end, it would be simplicity and simplicity alone that will have been able to grasp this Savior. Faith meeting fortune, innocence meeting influence, in it all power meeting perfection where the fortunes of the world fell in dry rot at the feet of the young man. The fading sounds of children embodied that for which this rich young man sought, but even though it was so very close, it would elude him. That for which he knelt before Jesus to obtain was within earshot, little more than a decision of surrender away. But he would not seize it because he could not grasp it.

A bronze Galilean stood before the rich young man. There was nothing of earth's manufactured magnificence in Him. Isaiah had long ago said that "He had no beauty or majesty to attract us to him, nothing in his appearance that we should desire him" (Isaiah 53:2). Weathered with callused hands broad and strong, feet dusty and worn from walking the long and arduous back roads of man's pain. His eyes were set soft with a hint of the eternal lying deep in a slight sparkle. Discerning, His eyes cut through the self-placating decor the young man had wrapped his life in. Riches and power had coalesced in an unseasoned mind unable to balance their weight and passion.

Moreover, the rich young man had come seeking a two-fold existence, acquiring and holding the treasures of earth and the treasures of heaven in a joint venture that would secure him both. He was voraciously seeking to find an answer that would permit his privilege and gain God's graces. He wanted the best of both worlds and, in the wanting, assumed that such an arrangement was possible. In fact, holding both was likely more destructive than holding one or the other, as holding both was holding onto the atrocious lie that man could simultaneously possess both heaven and earth and be true to both. In the end, he would have neither. Such a posture relieves us of choice and allows us to avoid commitment, for commitment to everything is commitment to nothing.

The sound of children had now faded; innocence had wafted off on a slight breeze that ruffled the folds of Jesus' robe. Jesus paused and then scanned the attendants. His gaze shifted to the young man, and upon his eyes, he drew down and centered. Drawing a firm and confident breath, he said, "You know the commandments. Do not murder, do not commit adultery, do not steal, do not give false testimony, do not defraud, honor your father and mother" (Mark 10:19).

Legalism could answer in the affirmative, and it did. It seemed for the briefest of moments that the rich young ruler had achieved his goal and been granted permission to live out his life in both worlds with a commitment to both. Nothing would be lost. Such is the goal of man, to live life as a buffet from which he can make his assorted choices and have each affirmed as congruent with all the other choices. In this manner, we are never put in a position of having to deny ourselves or become subservient to anything other than our own passions. Oscar Wilde wrote, "Selfishness is not living as one wishes to live, it is asking others to live as one wishes to live." And that request was being made of Jesus that day.

"Teacher," he declared, "all these I have kept since I was a boy" (Mark 10:20). At that point, God was everything this young man wanted Him to be. Nothing had to die. There would be no graves to visit, for nothing needed to be buried.

The rich young ruler paused and then began to stand, assuming that everything had been said. Jesus stared long and hard at the young man, feeling a love for him commensurate with the young man's misdirected love for his own wealth. And then the words of Jesus fell terribly hard. "One thing you lack," he said. "Go, sell everything you have and give to the poor, and you will have treasure in heaven. Then come, follow me" (Mark 10:21).

It did not happen. The power of this world's hold and its short-sighted rationale was too much. The rich young man was far too deep in the world to become deep in God, for you cannot be "deep" in both.

Scripture never again mentions this young man. We do not know where his life went from that moment. Apparently, it did not intersect with Jesus or the disciples from that point forward. We can assume that this encounter rolled through the young man's mind many times in the years that followed. The effects of that rolling are left for the unwieldy wide spaces of speculation.

How many times had he forced the memory out of his head so that it would not impede his efforts to secure additional wealth or extend the scope of his influence in political affairs? How many times did he go to the temple but find it empty because legalistic religion had not been enough that day so long ago? And because of that, how many times did he attempt to force a contrived religion that would somehow surpass or invalidate what Jesus had told him that day? How many times did he see a poor person on some dusty street corner and find himself back at the feet of Jesus? And how many times did he throw a few coins in their direction, hoping that somehow compromise would suffice to both please God and soothe his own distraught conscience? For how many years did he fight the existence of that moment and, by virtue of that, forfeit the very living he sought?

Most importantly, how many times did it dawn on him that he died the day he refused to follow Jesus' commands and that no amount of money or power could ever resurrect him? Did he realize that without facing the death that occurred on that day, he was merely existing under the guise of living? Did he realize that in order to live, he had to go back and reclaim something from that time? I wonder if he ever visited that grave in his heart before his own death. Did he go back and revisit a moment lost in order to reclaim it? Did he ever go back in order to go forward? If he had, he would have lived. History is completely silent on the subject.

### Grandpa's Grave and Reclamation

Within ten minutes, we had strolled leisurely back to the car. Ten minutes had apparently been enough. Ten minutes altered fifty-eight years. Dad went back in time, and because he went back, he now went forward. Something died in 1941 that he reclaimed in 1999 because he went back to it. Dad's step was lighter, his affect clearer, his eyes were somehow sharper. Dropping into the driver's seat and adjusting his seatbelt, he put the key in the ignition and then dropped both hands into his lap. Turning toward me, he paused to again collect his words, tilted his head a bit, and said, "Thanks for thinking of this." What had been buried in him for fifty-eight years was no longer buried. And he was different because of it. He was alive.

### Pondering Point

There are things that we bury because we prefer them buried. Somehow, we feel that both they and we are better off in that state. But that's often not the case. Living means connecting with what we've buried because we haven't resolved whatever it was that we buried. Whether that's a person, a belief, a choice, a relationship, a fear, a past, or the future, it really doesn't matter all that much. These things may die, but they're not necessarily dead. They are truly dead when we bring ourselves back to what we refused to bring to closure and deal with it, as did my father.

**THOUGHTS**
- For how many years have I buried something and refused to return to it?
- How many things have I buried?
- In what ways has the burial affected me?
- And what are those things that I refuse to go back to?

CHAPTER 12

# PINE TREES AND SLIPS OF PAPER
## Seeing Birth in Death

*"The kingdom of heaven is like treasure hidden in a field. When a man found it, he hid it again, and then in his joy went and sold all he had and bought that field."*
Matthew 13:44

*"The death of what's dead is the birth of what's living."*
~ Arlo Guthrie

**THEY WERE SEVENTY YEARS OLD,** as near as we could figure. They had silently stood guard at the foot of the yawning front porch, planted long before I had been born by people now long dead. Standing as proud sentinels for seven long decades, they had flanked the weathered cement steps that ascended our massive front porch. Their lush evergreen boughs had gracefully wrapped the steps much like a scarf of great finery.

These proud evergreens had faithfully stood by through the seasons, recording the process of our growing. They stood by in summer's thick, sultry humidity as my brothers and I sat on the wide porch swing, gliding deep into the temperate nights. In the transition of fall, they would watch as the three of us raked mounds of brightly colored leaves from around them, only to scatter them in wild and frenzied leaf fights. They waited in winter's chill until we would trudge down the long cement sidewalk and laboriously move drifts of wind-swept snow from the cements steps that were their charge. In the spring, they gracefully lifted their bows as under my mother's careful supervision my brothers and I planted clusters of geraniums and brilliant marigolds beneath their canopies before scurrying off to play with our friends. Inevitably, they came full circle, heralding summer's first days by tolerating three mischievous boys errantly rummaging through their foliage looking for bugs to add to their glass jar collections.

Childhood vanished in a whirlwind of time that seemed to pass without notice, despite the sometimes-tumultuous nature of its passing. Time unabated rolls on to whatever sits waiting in the future. The year 1993 arrived all too quickly, finding me twelve years removed from the day that I had left home and had moved away from the two, faithful evergreens. Those twelve years had handed me three college degrees, a beautiful wife, and a bright-eyed daughter. By all standards, they had been fruitful, adding to my life many blessings that caused me to miss what had diminished and had begun to die along the way.

I returned home. Time had marked its advance, leaving deep footprints in its wake. They were a cruel reminder that we are on this side of eternity. The two evergreen sentries were marked deeply, having been trounced by the footprints of time. Watching those three boys for those many years had exhausted them. Our departure into adulthood, it seemed, had diminished them. It was as if their purpose had been fulfilled, and now they had nothing left to do but slip into oblivion. They stood diseased and dying, beyond redemption, holding our precious history in boughs now slumped and browned. There was no alternative but to remove them, finalizing death that was well on its way.

With chainsaws in hand, we approached the two faithful evergreens. Standing before them, I wished they could speak. I so wished that they could speak of events to which they had borne witness. I craved a few final moments where, together, we could free our memories to run and leap and laugh in recounting many of the marvelous moments held deep in their branches. It seemed that to conclude their lives respectfully meant sharing in memories shared. There needed to be a celebration of everything that had been in order to properly celebrate everything that they were. It was not to be.

The chainsaws roared to life, the nature of their personalities not cherishing life as they were designed to end life and quickly dispose of it by cutting it neatly into cordwood piles. They seemed entirely hardened and cold, being all about business and nothing about nostalgia or the coddling warmth of memory. With famished teeth, they gorged themselves on the heartwood of one and then the other evergreen sentinel. Clouds of sawdust enveloped with the bluish exhaust of famished chainsaws seemed to create a veil of death that surrounded the morbid scene. In a matter of moments, both evergreens were helplessly prone on the ground, dead. Part of me was dead too.

The chainsaws fell silent. The carnage lay around us in savagely broken limbs, mounds of dead needles, and an air of deathly quiet. A gaping hole in the canopy left the sky quizzically peering in as if something was missing. Then, a thin slip of paper, caught in the swirling breeze produced from the falling boughs, was blown in a spiraling arc. It seemed to pirouette and curtsy in some airborne dance before bowing to gravity and concluding its dance amid the fallen branches strewn on the ground. Landing softly, it was a message from the past.

Deepak Chopra wisely said, "We are not victims of aging, sickness, and death. These are part of the scenery, not the seer, who is immune to any form of change. This seer is the spirit, the expression of eternal being." There is something eternal in everything. That eternal piece or part is not subject to decay, as that is not its design. Rather, it is entirely caught up into increasing levels of wonder, perfection, and glory. I do not know how the piece of paper had stayed in the evergreen for so long. It was not possible, or so it seemed, but it collided with my life as part of those eternal things.

It was dated April 18, 1971. Miraculously, for some twenty-two years it had remained lodged deep in the evergreen's branches. Faded and mottled by two decades of rain and snow and sun, it was a check, but it was so much more. Faded pen strokes in circular cursive graced the front. It was barely legible, but it was clear enough to provide a precious hint as to its origins. Squinting, I could still read the amount and the name. It was made out for the grand sum of $1.25, the cost of a week's worth of newspapers. The name inscribed on it was mine. Incredibly, it was a check written to me from one of my customers on my old paper route. Somehow, I had lost it over two decades ago. And somehow, some way, the evergreen had held it for me.

Holding this brittle and weathered check in my hands with the raw smell of the chainsaw exhaust still thick in the air around me, I was transported back to a warm, wonderful time in my life. My old paper route and the faces of many of my old customers rolled warmly and easily through my head. Suddenly, cherished memories flooded every recess of my mind, throwing me back to a time both precious and cherished.

I recalled old Mr. Hock with his cigar and bathrobe greeting me at his door every Saturday morning. More often than not, the cigar was unlit, which always made me wonder why he kept it clinched in his mouth. Then there was Mrs. Ryan, who always gave me hefty bags of fruit and mints at Christmas with a twenty-dollar bill tucked in among the treasures for good measure. Mrs. Tilly, who always seemed older than old, counting out her pennies on her worn Formica kitchen table in order to make certain that she'd count out fifty of them for a tip for me.

I recalled Mrs. Bland, who bleached her hair to unrealistic shades of blonde and who wore skin-tight clothes in a failed attempt to halt the aging that had obviously already overtaken her. She always tipped too. The Sawyers: I always hoped that one of the daughters would come to the door on Saturdays to pay the bill, as I was rather fond of them. I was a boy, after all. And the Clarks with six Siamese cats that seemed to be something of a feline gang intent on inflicting harm on me. You never knew if they wanted to love you or mutilate you.

Across the street, there lived Mrs. Warren with six romping Pomeranians. Watching her walk them was like watching six dogs trying to figure out how to go six different directions all at once. I thought it would be great fun to put those six cats and six dogs in an enclosed space and see what happened. I'd have wagered on the cats. There was my sturdy, fire-engine red, ever-faithful Western Flyer bicycle with its three massive baskets that served as my constant companion on the paper route. The two of us were indeed an awesome team, covering literally thousands of miles and delivering thousands of newspapers together during those five wonderful years.

### LIFE FROM DEATH

Jesus blurted out the completely improbable words, "Lazarus, come out!" (John 11:43). The action was both implausible and incomprehensible, a seeming setup for embarrassment. Mary and Martha had likely found the whole event uncomfortable as well, fearing that it would terminate in the gross disgrace and abject humiliation of their friend Jesus. "I know that he will rise again in the resurrection at the last day" (John 11:24), Mary told Jesus. Even a correct application of truth can often limit our understanding of a God who can regale truth with even greater truths and astound us in what He can do. And so, any thought of "resurrection" for them was likely connected to something far different from what was about to transpire. Their conceptualization of God was about to be shattered by His reality.

## A Step to Lazarus

Loosely knit flocks of sparrows flitted in bobbing arches across a sky mottled with frothy clouds. Their spirited chirping set the cadence to their anxious flight. The sun threw thick shadows that were embossed by the torrential golden sunlight raining round about them. Tall grasses waved in gentle waltzes with a soft breeze, fully satisfied with the simplicity of a simple existence. Bees droned in lumbering arches, weighed with the nectared bounty of the sea of wildflowers that lay strewn across the grassy landscape. Hills of content meandered out to the edges of the horizon, washed in ever thin hues of blue until they rolled off the horizon's precipice. Life was lavishly spread in abundance across warm meadows.

It was not life, but death that pressed weary feet shod in leather sandals cracked by long roads trod in hurried steps both panicked and pensive. A motley group of weathered messengers arrived exhausted and out of breath. Parched, hungry, and layered in the dust of a hasty journey, they shook the accumulated filth out of weary robes. Eyes bloodshot and framed red by the collective wear of sun and gritty windblown sands drew themselves up from the dusty folds of faded robes and scanned the group for the object of their journey.

Jesus' predominance was obvious. Something about Him lent an indescribable air of a bit of something all of us were intended to be, that something calls out an invitation to all of us from somewhere but is at the same time far greater than any of us. And so they hurriedly made their way to Him with a plea of the most urgent sort. Lips chapped and dry drew a touch of moisture into a parched mouth and said, "Lord, the one you love is sick" (John 11:3). The message having been said in breathless urgency, their eyes searched those of Jesus, hoping to draw from them the compassion and urgency that would stave off death.

Jesus paused and then placed a broad hand on the exhausted messenger. Squinting with an intensity that would accentuate His words and drive them deep into a frightening soul, He said, "This sickness will not end in death. No, it is for God's glory so that God's Son may be glorified through it" (John 11:4). Tears of relief edged burning eyes, then collected in tiny pools at their corners and traced rivulets of glistening release down cheeks burnt deep red by the wind and sun of a panicked journey.

Wiping damp faces with the sleeves of worn robes, the fatigue of the journey somehow dissipated, the answer having re-energized the messengers with a mix of relief and hope that drove any physical fatigue into full submission. Glancing at each other, they drew themselves into a state of excited composure, looked at Jesus with the anticipation of children expecting some wonderful event for which they cannot contain themselves, and urged Jesus' immediate departure. But Jesus waited ... for two agonizing days.

Jesus' agenda and the cadence of His work were not based in or on the need to outdistance death, somehow fearing that should death beat Him to His destination, all would be lost. Such a posture would assume the superiority of death. Therefore, death must be outflanked, for if death claims the prize first, death will have won. And in the winning, the victory would be irrevocable. But death did not set the agenda that day or any day. Jesus set the agenda. The men who had come to get him, however, had no idea of agenda setting and who set it.

The setting of such an agenda was incomprehensible to the messengers, leaving them stupefied, forcing them to live two excruciating days of razor-sharp anxiety. Their comprehension was one of a race, that whoever reached Lazarus first would be the victor. It's likely that they did not doubt Jesus' ability to turn back the frigid hands of death. But they likely doubted His ability to take back a life from death's hands once death had laid its claim. Death was an irrevocable finality from which nothing returned. For two days, they sat on the sidelines of a race they felt they must win, watching adversity take to the track uncontested, rapidly closing in on the finish line without so much as a challenge from Jesus. Those forty-eight hours were deluged with confusion, anxiety, and frustration.

## **ABSURDITY**

We can believe to a point, but absurdity is that point beyond which faith wanes and then fails. Absurdity is often nothing more than God minus faith. Absurdity is our inability to release the infinite to be the infinite. Conversely, it is the refusal of the infinite to abide by our finite structures so that we might be able to force some pattern upon God that we find predictable. We imagine the impossible and what the impossible might be in a given situation. And then we assume that our conceptualization of the impossible is indeed accurate. Having fabricated our idea of the impossible, we then naturally assume that whatever we've imagined is what God will do. But the very conceptualization of the impossible is in and of itself impossible, creating a finite space within which the infinite is supposed to function. Such a supposition is ridiculous.

But eventually, Jesus set out—two long days later. The journey terminated in what the messengers had both suspected and dreaded. Lazarus had died. The news hit them with a force of both grief and anger that toppled them emotionally. Their feelings proved right, their concerns about the delay were validated. The error of this prophet was verified, and His poor judgment was confirmed. Shaking heads were weighed by sorrow and anger over this prophet who did not heed the call of reason and by being so grossly negligent let a friend die.

We feel that sometimes God needs to sit up and listen, recognizing that at times even He may miss the slightest piece of information that had somehow escaped His notice. There are times when a little bit of advice might even be good for God. Maybe there are times when we know better, even though those times might be rare. Such were the feelings of the messengers and those who had awaited His arrival. Jesus was too late, and circumstances now lay beyond even Him.

But Jesus did not have to contemplate His own limits, because there were none. "Take away the stone" (John 11:39) was His response. In our estimation, even God can take on too much with His need for restraint outdistancing His own common sense. We want to Him to stop, think, and heed our advice in order to save Him from the folly of the infinite having gone too far and therefore doing something stupid and looking stupid in the doing.

"But Lord ... by this time there is a bad odor, for he has been there four days" (John 11:39).

Even the crowd was held captive by the limitation of their own limitations, saying, "Could not he who opened the eyes of the blind man have kept this man from dying?" (John 11:37). The presumption was that death had placed Lazarus beyond the reach of Jesus. There was assumed a threshold beyond which all is irretrievable. Everyone felt that there was a final line of some sort that no one could reach across. It was believed that Jesus could thwart someone from reaching that threshold, but once it was crossed, it was even beyond His grasp. Death was that threshold. It was the irretrievable finality.

G. M. Trevelyan said, "Never tell a young person that anything cannot be done. God may have been waiting centuries for someone ignorant enough of the impossible to do that very thing." The human drama could be made far more vigorous and profoundly more miraculous if we simply added a pinch of ignorance from time to time.

I wonder if somewhere in the back of their minds that day, these thoughts voiced a plea for restraint, that the tomb would remain sealed and embarrassment be avoided. But the words were spoken. The intent of Jesus' action was made public. There was no room to turn back now. In the end, the man walks out of the tomb alive—impossibly alive. Jesus calmly reached across the chasm of death and effortlessly pulled Lazarus back to this side. What was believed to be irretrievable was well within the reach of Jesus. "Is the Lord's arm too short?" (Numbers 11:23) says the Lord.

## SLIPS OF PAPER

My father's hand set on my shoulder. I snapped back across those two long decades and dropped into the present moment filled with chainsaw exhaust, sawdust, and death. Crinkled, faded, and weathered stiff, I held a precious bit of history. The trees would of necessity be cut up and used for firewood. Despite my desire to once again pick bugs from their branches, to plant flowers under their boughs, and to climb their heights to view the ends of the earth, that was not to be. In the march of time, we are born, we live, and we die. So it was with the evergreen sentries.

The trees, however, gave me something that did not need to die. They gave me something not bound by their lives or restricted by the finiteness of their existence. They gave me memories. They handed me a living piece of myself, forgotten except for a tiny slip of paper. Weakened by their death, I found untold strength in their memories.

## PONDERING POINT

Had the trees not come down, the legacy tucked away on the slip of paper deep in their branches would not have been mine. It was there all along, hidden within them the entire time. But it was only released to me at their death. And so it is with loss and death in our lives. Something greater, a morsel of the eternal, is released to us to illustrate a God who is on a scandalous mission to unceasingly create. And what greater display and more magnificent exercise of creative power than to create in the midst of the very thing that seems to so completely destroy, that which is death? God is the infinite genius, not only building life from life, as that is too easy, but also crafting life out of the raw material of loss and death.

**A Thought**
- Do I see the footprint of the eternal behind aging and death?
- What has been released to me in a recent death?
- Do I look for life out of death?
- Can I view death as actually birthing life?

CHAPTER 13

# TWO THIN ONES
## Purposefully Gain to Purposefully Give

> *"In everything I did, I showed you that by this kind of hard work we must help the weak, remembering the words the Lord Jesus himself said: 'It is more blessed to give than to receive.'"*
>
> Acts 20:35

> *"To give anything less than your best is to sacrifice the gift."*
>
> ~ Steve Prefontaine

**A SINGLE QUARTER AND A** lonely nickel lay in his palm, the sum total adding up to a mere thirty cents. Such a scant sum is humorously marginal and of little monetary value. Practically speaking, thirty cents buys a handful of nothing.

Eddie's hands were gnarled, his tendons stiffly drawing fingers up in a claw-like grasp that somehow seemed both pathetic and wicked at the same time. Emaciated, his hands seemed little more than skin tightly drawn over skeletal protrusions that might have been the creation of some artist set on a fiendish agenda. Two coins were precariously cradled in a violently spastic palm framed by a larger body of morbid deformity. It was the stuff of cerebral palsy.

His body was indeed a larger manifestation of his contorted hands. Gnarled, twisted, and spastic, his limbs were atrophied thin, giving them the illusion of brittleness and fragility. Skin skirted slight sinews of sparse muscle and wrapped itself tight around numerous bony protrusions. His spinal cord was drawn irresistibly forward, having wrestled with gravity and having lost. It all rendered him a collapsed lump of spastic humanity. Pencil-thin legs were helplessly draped over metal footrests that velcroed two tremulous feet into submission. A thin rivulet of mucus traced an errant line down a stubbled chin, eventually coursing a path down a soaked shirt.

His voice was likewise muted by the gross contortions that rendered his vocal cords inoperable. He had been born into this condition, knowing nothing other than this skeletal and spastic depravity. Eddie was forever shackled to a wheelchair by a terribly dysfunctional body that held him as some kind of innocent prisoner who had committed no crime worthy of this kind of imprisonment—or any imprisonment, for that matter. I stood before him somehow ashamed that I should be privileged to have a healthy body when he did not. And in the midst of this spastic mound of deformed humanity, he held out a quarter and a nickel.

Over the years, I came to deeply cherish Eddie. Actually, I came to love him. His was always a smile and the extension of a spastic hand in friendship no matter what might have beset him. He had a broken laugh, deeply marred by cerebral palsy but overlaid with the joy and wild laughter of heaven itself. Sometimes, the best place to see perfection is deep in imperfection, because perfection is freest in that kind of place.

Eddie's hope was relentless. Grieved by the pain in my life that I sometimes shared with him, he would lay an erratic hand on my arm, look up to heaven, and then back at me and then at heaven again. And then he would bow a bobbing head. Without words, he would pray for me in a manner that words could never hope to imitate. I never heard what he said. I didn't need to. Few have prayed so powerfully, so genuinely, and with such absolute conviction that he was heard and that the answer was already well on its way. The weakness of his body was more than made up for by the phenomenal strength of his spirit.

A tattered Bible stood watch at his bedside. I would affix his glasses on his face with a tight band around his head so that the gross motor movements of his head and neck would not throw them to the floor. As I turned the pages for him, he would read for hours, saturating himself in God. Finding a favorite passage, he would laugh with the very joy of the angels themselves, so much so that I often coveted the freedom that was neither touched nor diminished by his physical imprisonment. He was remarkable. And in his terribly spastic hand, he held out this quarter and this nickel.

"Thirty cents. For what?" I asked. Several bumbling guesses later, as I tried to interpret his gesture, I finally understood. He wanted me to give it to the church. It was thirty cents—a lonely quarter and a tarnished nickel—that, once given, left his pockets entirely empty except for lint and love. It was an offering of inestimable proportions. Everything within me said "no" because sometimes sacrifice like that is far too hard to watch and too difficult to permit.

I don't have the strength to let someone else sacrifice like that because I don't have the strength to do it myself. So I told Eddie to keep it for something else. His choice ignored reason, and I put that choice right in front of him. Yet, I had yet to learn that when it comes to the purest kind of sacrifice, reason itself must at times be sacrificed. As Aime Cesaire put it, "Reason, I sacrifice you to the evening breeze." Such was Eddie's life, and such were his actions. I am inestimably changed because they were.

His commitment to sacrifice for his God overcame the limitations of his spastic frame, causing him to nearly rise out of his wheelchair while waving the coinage in my face. I melted. Right there I watched sacrifice and commitment come together in a spastic life, and I was grieved because of my response to him.

I took the coins from his spastic palm. He settled back into his chair. A contorted smile instantly drew itself from ear to ear as his irrepressible laugh filled the room and skipped down the hallway of the facility, reminiscent of the unfettered spirit from which it sprang. I told him that I would see that it got to the church.

What followed was one of those inexplicable moments. Heading out the door of the facility, I was taken with an irritating curiosity. Pausing in one of those life moments when we pause because something indefinable is crossing our path and seizing our spirits, I turned and went back to the office. Walking to the patient files, I pulled the patient accounts. Scrolling down, I came to Eddie's name and drew out a yellowed ledger. The balance on his account registered the balance of his heart ... thirty cents. That was all he had. The thirty cents that I held in a sweaty palm was it. That lonely quarter and tarnished nickel didn't just empty his pockets, they emptied him of everything. The ledger of his life now stood at zero. Suddenly, the two coins became priceless. Instantly, they weighed heavily in my hand and shook me to the core of my heart. I found myself in the middle of a dizzying collision where a handicapped man gave away all that he had in order to gain everything that he needed. I scooped up the ledger, seized the file, and returned to Eddie's room.

He knew before I got there. He knew before I walked in the door. He nodded, and I knew. It was all he had. They were the sum total of his assets. And that was the very source of his elation, the fact that he had given himself in his entirety and had left nothing unto himself that would diminish what God does in a life when we abandon ourselves entirely to Him. He laughed and motioned me out of his room. I knelt, placed my hand on a boney shoulder, looked into the deep eyes of faith set in a terribly deformed body, and said, "Eddie, you are a remarkable man." And he was.

## A Temple and an Offering

Two coins that were nearly paper thin. They were the smallest currency in circulation. A "lepton," which rightly translates "thin one." They dropped into the collection box, their weight so slight that they barely made a sound. Their value was so insignificant that they would make no real difference to the cause for which they were given. Immediately, they were engulfed in a mound of gold and silver coinage. They would sink into obscurity as they quickly drowned in the profoundly greater gifts that drew these two coins down into the murky depths of fiscal irrelevancy.

Once she had dropped them in the collection box, the thin and fragile woman drew a threadbare wrap around herself, turned, and shuffled into obscurity. Setting out on a course of hopelessness, the compass of her life was set for a bearing of destitution. But history had been made, and a core truth had been observed and heralded. She would never know that this act of private obedience would become public for generations. She would have no idea. She left the temple and walked into history.

Flocks of pigeons were stirred, bursting into flight; they were launched into the gaping possibilities of a vacant sky. Circling, returning, and approaching again, their wings beat the air before they lit on lofty marble precipices. Hundreds of feet above the sprawling courtyard, the view of the Judean countryside rolled off to distant horizons and spilled over their edges, leaving one with a sense of engulfing magnitude. A ram's horn muscled itself into the scene. Its bellow was uneven, ancient, and haunting. At the sound of it, pigeons exploded, scattering from their lofty precipices yet again. Cascading down the temple wall, the call flooded the courtyard, bounced back, returned yet again, and breeched the marbled walls. It rolled deep and unabated, its surge gradually dissipating far out in the expanse of the Judean countryside.

Smoke rose and curled listlessly against the lucid blue sky. The scent of the morning sacrifices drifted through the cool calm, being distilled before dissipating into the clean morning air. The drawn lowing of cattle bellowed soft and soothing. Erratic bleating of innumerable sheep set a more intrusive tempo. The velvet cooing of doves gave the scene a soft edge. An occasional wild fluttering of caged wings was reminiscent of the soul and sin, where one desires to soar and the other desires to shackle. Musty odors wafted through the soft air of a new day. Offal permeated the morning, the scent of thick coats of animals that were destined for sacrifice.

There were so many animals that the odor was pungent at times. Hoofs, hollow and tentative, treaded down cobbled surfaces, their sounds echoing off smooth marble stones, thereby doubling the auditory experience. Long shadows wrapped cloaked arms around colonnades, giving them the first hug of a new day. Having spread across the courtyard, they now found themselves in a gradual retreat in morning's advance. On the yawning expanse of this grand pavilion of marble and colonnades, hundreds milled about, enraptured in a mix of curiosity and worship.

An event was set to unfold in the Court of the Women. Thirteen collection boxes shaped as trumpets were set about. Adjacent to this place was the Gate Beautiful. Against its cool marbled walls, Jesus sat; the protracted arguments and residual tensions from His recent encounter still reverberating through the colonnades of the Court of the Gentiles that sat on the other side of the gate. His authority had been squarely questioned. There was a story of a vineyard, a rebuffed owner, and the vinegar-like taste of condemnation that had set His spirit on edge and had shaped His response. A host of carefully crafted trick questions were thrown at Him. There were stealthy conversations about Caesar's image, the resurrection, and marriage. All of them were shrewd nets woven and then cast to capture Him in the mire of their duplicity. The nets had not been crafted nearly big enough. More than that, they had been cast awkwardly.

Yet, the hardness of men in light of such a great gift continues to illustrate the fact that God is far too immense to be perceived by men unless God gives them the means to do so. Can it be true that men can see God and still not see God? These men did exactly that. Having been missed, Jesus relocated to the Gate Beautiful. Disciples in tow now milled about close by. They equated following Jesus with some sort of euphoria and celebrity. They had not yet comprehended that great sacrifice was unconditionally woven into that very following.

It was likely here, with all of these assorted dynamics playing on and off each other that Jesus first saw the woman. Here He caught a glimpse of her. He saw in her that which was so woefully absent in His detractors and is so very fundamental to an authentic walk with God. He settled and watched the scene play out with a frail actress at center stage, an actress who had no idea that she was on any stage at all. And then a principle unfolded, nearly undetected, as is the manner in which most things of value in life unfold.

Who she was, where she came from, and the intricacies of her life are unrecorded and left for speculation. The woman walked into and out of the pages of Scripture in the space of a few simple verses. "All these others made offerings that they'll never miss ..." (Luke 21:4, The Message), Jesus said.

Is that not the difference? Calculated giving is weighed and measured against life's balance sheets of both risk and loss. Decisions are most often designed to insulate the giver from the potential peril of chance. An act of sacrifice that has been gutted of the very essence of sacrifice is no sacrifice at all. It may be giving, but it has nothing of the greater gift of sacrifice inherent within it. Giving that in the end leaves something of myself to myself is giving tainted by greed. It is giving that is calculated so that I am able to perpetuate a false sense of security. In doing so, I limit what God can do through what I give.

If I somehow fit in this story of this unknown woman, I am everyone else that pushed past the widow that day. In the flurry of my life, I throw a few coins at God in the name of sacrifice. And then I am on to other demands that litter my life, that forcefully elbow themselves into my heart, and that arrogantly cram themselves into my schedule. Hers was a faith, a focus, and a core theme that has eluded me. Hers was an abandonment that was unrelentingly total, that left nothing for her to hold onto other than the faith that precipitated and prompted the act: a golden and purified faith for which I thirst. I grasp, fumble, and strain for that kind of faith. In the end, I am only able to grasp it in thin threads that snap too easily.

Jesus pointedly commented on her action, saying that "she gave extravagantly what she couldn't afford – she gave her all!" (Luke 21:4, The Message). And so she set out that day both thin and gaunt. Her face was irreparably drawn, deeply etched, and roughly furrowed. A tattered collection of mismatched wraps was tightly drawn around a thin body that was frail from loss. She was a widow, and in the death of her husband, she lived out and walked within an endless, impoverished angst. Jagged lacerations had cut deep flesh wounds across her soul. Hers was a heart that had been seared by the white hot heat of loss.

She lived the crippling kind of woundedness that's left when life strikes in ways that defy all of the desperate pleadings for some explanation that might somehow soothe a battered soul. Some souls are sharply bent by the weight of the unbearable. At times like these, we often wish our souls would simply snap and give us relief even if the relief meant the end of ourselves. It's likely that tears came frequently to her soul and cascaded down her weathered face. A feeble hand, trembling, brushed them aside yet again. She drew a breath, stiffened her resolve, and set out into the morning.

She was intent on giving what she couldn't afford. Shuffling through winding streets, she pushed past cloisters of gathered people, drew aside for heavy pack animals, and circumvented vendors loudly hailing the proclaimed benefit of their wares. Two thin coins held tightly in bony hands. Hers was a rush to sacrifice, knowing that any hope for her life lay there and there alone.

The market was not full of things that she would have liked, but things that she, in her desperation, needed. The purchase of a few morsels of food to quell the sharp pangs of hunger, a sparse piece of weary fabric to better hold the cold at bay, or maybe a vial of pasty opaque ointment to sooth chapped skin. Two thin coins could have purchased a bit of one of these. But no, it would not be. She passed the vendors and refused to trade sacrifice for "stuff." Her steps were firm. The temple was in view, and God was in mind.

She was misplaced in that place. Nothing of grandeur defined her. She stood in stark contrast to the majesty of the temple that surrounded her and raised itself boastfully into the Judean sky. It diminished her, and it truncated her. The compilation of everything that encircled her made her smaller and of less import than she already was. For certain, she was brave. Some resolute thread ran through her soul and had tied a knot in her heart, casting a plumb line into the depths of God's heart. All of that had drawn her here to give out of the vast resources of impoverishment. The ram's horn bellowed again. The pigeons burst into flight. She found a place in line.

She was a widow, poor and likely alone. The lack of resources suggested no extended family. She was isolated, impoverished, destitute. Her earthly resources were tapped out and non-existent. And so she stood, meaningless and vividly invisible to those around her. It was not recognized, even by her, that earthly impoverishment empties the vault of the soul to make room for the wealth of heaven. It was those around her who stood impoverished, while she stood deep and dripping with eternal riches. It was all starkly visible to Jesus. While it was irrelevant in the larger scheme of things, it was terribly relevant to God. The majesty of the temple and the power of the rich appeared to render her as nothing.

Flowing robes that were lavish and richly ornamental fluttered in a gentle breeze. Rings littered various hands. Each one sparkled in luminescent gold settings set deep with precious stones. Silks and imported fabrics woven into ornate wraps abounded in the courtyard.

The thick scent of costly spices and variant nards floated about, rending the air sweet and flowery. Servants in attendance were constantly being dispatched on errands of presumed importance. Positions of power awaited many of those in line, with lavish homes to which they would retire at day's end standing ready for their return. Henri Frederic Amiel wrote, "Sacrifice, which is the passion of great souls, has never been the law of societies." Therefore, it is missed in the very societies in which it is exhibited. Such was the case on this day.

In sharp contrast to the surrounding splendor, the widow stood there with two thin coins. No one knew it, and no one saw it, but poverty and prosperity had been reversed. The line moved. She shuffled in cadence with it, being the richest of them all but having no idea whatsoever that she was.

It is inherent in us to judge and to evaluate. When we observe something, we apply some standard and then draw conclusions based on the standard that's spun from our anemic and shallow sense of life and living. We rate, compartmentalize, ascribe value, and label. And so it was with this woman. Bedraggled and threadbare, she moved in pensive and muted steps in this line of humanity, holding two thin coins in brittle fingers. Her life was held in defining contrast to those around her in that line and those in society. She was disheveled and seemingly undeserving. Yet, she was a marvelous and cherished daughter of God.

The same kind of evaluation was apparently performed in the minds of the disciples. She had been labeled, and the nature of the label has caused them to move on, blatantly disregarding and discounting her. They could not see in her anything other than what world saw, and so they missed the magnificence of the riches in the poverty.

She reached the collection box, fingered the worn metal, and dropped in the coins. She paused, clasped weathered hands, uttered a brief prayer of faith and desperation, turned, and was gone for the rest of time. The moment was only seconds in duration, but its lessons are nothing less than eternal.

Jesus drew the disciples back to her. He reevaluated her and then sent their worlds careening. He handed them different eyes, which opened up a radical vision. She was more than everything around her. The things encompassing her that seemed to diminish her were in reality dwarfed by her. She towered over that which towered over her. She was the embodiment of God's heart, as was Eddie. It was a grand reversal that the world couldn't see because the world couldn't apply any other standard to her other than its own. With only one standard to apply, reversal was not possible because there's nothing to reverse to.

It was so easy to see that it was passed over and therefore became invisible because it was simply too visible. The temple and its decor paled in comparison. But none of this found a place to settle or to root in the hearts of rural Galileans unfamiliar with such architectural splendor. They were caught up in the magnificent constructs of men, and they missed the greater wonders of a heart bent on sacrifice. Their eyes turned from the widow to the temple. In response to it all, Jesus said that the temple will "be thrown down" (Luke 21:6). The story of the widow remained when the temple did not because one is of God, and the other is only a monument to a perception of Him.

### THE SUFFOCATION OF CALCULATION

Sadly so, I am calculating. Calculation renders abandonment impossible. Calculation is control, pure and simple. It is balancing risk and assessing outcomes as a means of attempting to achieve safe sacrifice. This search for safe sacrifice, which is an oxymoron indeed, is one that is so calculated that I must hold the principle entirely separate from the reality simply because they are irreconcilable. I sacrifice within the bounds that I have calculated as safe, prudent, and wise. And when I do that, I am not sacrificing anything other than the joy of genuine sacrifice.

With the essence of the principle having been made clear to me, I must abandon myself to God and incur whatever intentional risk there might be in that abandonment. The principle's application to my life is lost in the consideration of how I can manage it safely. What was done that day, the profound nature of this single abandoned soul, was clear. I can speculate on how to mirror the abandonment of the widow in my life and my actions. Theological and philosophical contemplations are easy. But bringing it home into the heart of my actions and how I live that out in my life ... that is difficult. Playing the role in my head is flawless. Living the role out in my heart is something I fumble with. Not being able to match my heart and actions with this woman or the sacrifices of Eddie is devastating. And I am disgusted with myself.

Whatever I hold is thin anyway, thin in that I hold it only for a moment. Anything that I hold that is not of God is not eternal; therefore, it's always thin. It will not follow me; therefore, holding it is useless. It's thin because it is never really mine. It's simply on loan to me. But more so, whatever I hold leaves just that much less room for heaven in my soul. Every nook and cranny of my life that is taken up with the stuff of this world leaves just that much less room for the stuff of eternity.

God looks for vacancies as much as He is interested in orchestrating evictions. He searches and fills the space that I have intentionally made through the aggressive disposal of all the worldly items that once occupied that space. I would be a fool not to clear out the vault of my soul despite all the horrendous fears that scream the insanity of such an action. Once that is done, I may then fling open the door of my soul, point to the emptiness I have created, and plead that God take up residence in every bit of the space that's there. And take residence, He does; gladly, every time.

And so, I intentionally move past life's vendors that offer me nothing eternal, only that which would fill space that I must leave for God. My eyes are focused on something greater. My heart is set in the grip of sacrifice. I enter the presence of God and walk into the courtyard. The horn blows, and pigeons explode in frenzied flight. I approach the collection box, and whatever thin part of myself I possess, I drop it in. I hand it over. I give it to Him—all of it. And then a weathered life pauses in prayer, thanking Him that I have this precious opportunity. Then I walk away. It is here in the success of my determination that God moves, reaches, and then descends. He sees me from the gate and acknowledges my actions as "extravagant." Now I am His, totally, as Eddie is His, as this woman was His. Being His is the only way to be with God.

Eddie knew that. Eddie was that. As I walked out of his room I realized the gift I had been given. Holding his file, I looked at the account balance again: thirty cents. I looked at the two thin coins, a gift of totality where nothing was held back in order to sacrifice with safety. No calculating, just abandonment; sweeping the vault of his handicapped life entirely clean so that none of the imperishable riches of heaven would find themselves crowded out by the impoverished treasures of this life. And I realized that my account ledger needs to be lived just like this. Just like Eddie, at the end of the day the ledger that renders that tally of this life's accumulations needs to read "zero." And when it does, no ledger is large enough to record the riches that God pours into that emptied vault.

### Pondering Point

"Do not store up for yourselves treasures on earth, where moth and rust destroy, and where thieves break in and steal. But store up treasures in heaven" (Matthew 6:19-20). Where are your assets? Our investments speak to our priorities and to the nature of our hearts. Our assets speak to the real gods that we serve, despite who we say we might serve. And so, where are your assets? What does your ledger read? There is immeasurable power in a sacrificed life. The joy and security we seek is not found in assimilating, but in abandoning. Not in gathering but disbursing, holding the treasures of this world loosely so that they can be poured out constantly and consistently so that heaven can be poured in. And it is here that we find real riches, real living.

## A Thought
- Where are my assets?
- What are my assets?
- Do I collect and acquire, or do I give flagrantly?
- Am I willing to abandon my attempts to accumulate life in order that I might gain life?

CHAPTER 14

# A RED RYDER BB GUN
## The Plain Power of Legacy

*"I will perpetuate your memory through all generations; therefore the nations will praise you for ever and ever."*

Psalm 45:17

*"The greatest use of life is to spend it for something that will outlast it."*

~ William James

**THE DEPTHS OF UNCLE BILL'S** basement were a winding catacomb of endless adventure for a five-year-old boy. It consisted of dark causeways encased in aging brick and crumbling mortar. The expanse of it was laced heavily with silky cobwebs that drew together en masse in corners and hung from rough-hewn ceiling timbers. Descending into Uncle Bill's basement was a wild adventure every time I went down the creaking steps.

Scant windows, foggy with an ancient film of dirt and inattention, sat high, embedded in the cold brick walls, giving a hint that the world outside wasn't quite as foreboding. Pieces of leftover life were strewn about in various rooms, the discarded and the decaying, things that had fallen into the abyss of time and were waiting to be washed out into the endlessness of eternity past. That basement was filled with everything that the imagination of a young boy could squeeze into its dampness and darkness.

Uncle Bill had an impulsive way about him—those moments when his child side leapt out of him to do something adventurous, devious, and scandalous. He was always cooking up something that was likely to be enormously fun. One day, standing in the kitchen, Uncle Bill smiled that mischievous smile and motioned me to the basement steps. "I want to show you something," he whispered. It seemed that we were preparing to do something so fun that we were likely to get in trouble for it. How could a five-year-old kid resist?

We slipped down the creaking steps into the bowels of the brick and mortar beast. Flipping a switch, a bare bulb hanging in a ceramic socket warmed to life, casting an anemic glow that threw pale shadows into the deep dark. Just outside the first room at the bottom of the steps, Uncle Bill stopped. With that elfish smile, he reached behind a door and said, "I want you to see this."

It was dusty and somewhat rusted, but it was absolutely beautiful, the envy of any young boy. If a five-year-old male is ever lustful, it's for one of these. Somehow, it was a culmination of all my cowboy fantasies. With it, young boys became heroes, charged fearlessly into uncharted wilderness, singlehandedly repelled the enemy, rescued the girl, and saved the day. Indeed, it was the holy grail of just about any boy my age.

He tenderly held it in his callused hands. Pondering it, he turned it this way and that as if he were savoring a rare treasure. It was clear that it had unlocked a floodgate of memories that swept him in warm currents of memory and drew him back into time. There was a reflective pause and then that elfish grin of his unfurled across his face as he carefully set up the moment. "Yup, I've had this a long time," he said. "A long time." In that dramatic kind of way, he said, "I shot a few cats with it. I remember shooting a squirrel or two that got into the attic. There were a couple times I lined up some tin cans and shot them too ... yea, I've had this a long time." By this time, drama had been nudged aside as the sweetness of a host of warm recollections handily supplanted it.

As for me, my five-year-old palms were sweating. My forehead was damp with perspiration. My heart was racing. I was standing completely still but panting as if I'd run a mile at some break-neck speed. For all I know, I may have been drooling.

And then something transpired that I only recognized decades later. It was an ascent to manhood. A rite of passage transpired deep in the darkness and musty air of that cold brick and mortar basement. Completely hidden away from the rest of the world, it was just me and Uncle Bill. A moment of silence fell, and his eyes met mine. A firm determination had now set in them. The child had departed from his eyes, and the man had returned. The elfish grin had moved aside from Uncle Bill's face, being replaced by a hint of squared determination as if something reverenced was about to happen. A passage was indeed developing.

And then without any forewarning, Uncle Bill handed me the BB gun, the Red Ryder BB gun. He set it squarely into my small, untried, five-year-old hands. Patting it several times, he said, "Treat it with respect." Then he turned and headed for the steps.

An unknown author wrote, "If you have any doubts that you have what it takes at the beginning, you'll know by the end that you do." I didn't know that I had what it took, but Uncle Bill did. The most impactful part of receiving a legacy lies in not realizing that you're ready to receive it. The most impactful part of passing along a legacy is realizing that the person receiving it doesn't realize they're ready, which makes the recipient sufficiently grateful to receive the power that comes with it.

There was an encounter with a man whose life was ending while mine was beginning, and on each of our respective journeys, we collided in a way that makes collisions marvelous. I just stood there, aghast and in paralysis. Uncle Bill stopped on the steps, turned, and smiled that knowing smile. "Come on," he motioned with a sweep of a large hand. And we climbed the steps together. Not a boy and a man, but a young man and an older man. That day, at that moment, he had begun the process of ushering me into manhood. But he had done more ... much more. He had handed me a precious piece of himself. He had left something of himself with me, and I did not know it. I did not understand it ... until ...

## DEATH CAME

At five, I did not know what cancer was, much less death. Those things were not any part of my world at five years of age. Six months or so passed. Mom and Dad sat us in the living room with a solace and seriousness I had never seen in them. With the deftness and tenderness that had so marked them, they told my brother and me that Uncle Bill had this thing called cancer. The word *death* was not used, but it was clear anyway.

At five, I had no introduction to death. Its face was strange and imperceptible. Its role and purpose in the landscape of a five-year-old life was far too premature to determine. Arriving long before its time, it was alien in a young life where death was yet on a distant horizon far on the other end of life, yet indiscernible and unintelligible from my vantage point. But whatever it was, it was coming. It was unstoppable. And it was coming for Uncle Bill.

At five, I watched death as it advanced and laid claim to him. Over the months, it pulled him down to an emaciated shadow of himself. The palette of his life was painted in rich colors: Pacific War veteran, stalwart in character, an avid outdoorsman, a man of integrity and raw strength. He told jokes with an arid dryness about them that made them hilarious every single time. He had a touch that was everything of love and nothing less than love.

Now he was weak, washed in pale whites and bedridden. He became skeletal and emaciated, barely able to wrap his fingers around my hand. His commanding voice diminished to a mere whisper that was hardly audible. But he faced death as a man. Not with some fake, superficial, macho game-face. But with courage, firm confidence, and resolute focus.

Finally one night, the word came. A late phone call taken by my father was filled with subdued tones and choked words. I listened as he stammered to find the right words. That was something my father never struggled with, but he did that night. With shallow steps, he walked into the living room and fell into my mother's embrace. Crouched at the top of the steps as a silent observer, I knew death had arrived, that it had taken Uncle Bill, and that it had fled on shadowy feet. It had left our living room clouded in black. It was finally over. I touched my heart and found a hole, my first one. I crawled up the steps, buried myself deep in the thick blankets, and cried myself into a restless sleep.

Deep into the nights, I would cry, holding tenaciously to a large stuffed dog until I wore him threadbare. His fur was stained with the tears of a five-year-old in a deep dark that he knew nothing about. The Red Ryder BB gun stood as a silent sentry at my bedside. Uncle Bill passed into the next life, and I passed out of innocence.

It took several decades before I understood the legacy of Uncle Bill. Standing in that damp brick and mortar basement, he helped me take a step toward manhood. It was a private and privileged rite of passage. It was carried out alone, just the two of us. But there was more to it all. He knew he was going to die. Whether he knew specifically or simply as one of those things of the deep soul, I believe he knew. And when he handed me the Red Ryder BB gun, he was handing me a part of himself. He was indeed leaving something that would outlast him, something that would fill a bit of that hole he left behind. It was a precious piece of himself that would roll through the decades ahead in his stead. But even more than that, he was investing something of himself in that young life. Something that would grow with me, move with me, and serve to shape me. His blessing and a bit of his legacy would do all that and more.

## The Passing of a Legacy

The night was thick and heavy. A stifling pensiveness filled the upper room. It was all mysterious indeed. The foreboding of something that could not be identified hung in the air. There was a strange juxtaposition where the celebratory anticipation of kingship melded with a deeply unsettling sense of pending disaster. The two contrary feelings wafted around the room as irreconcilable and were therefore assumed to be the product of frightened minds and nothing more. However, one would prevail.

The city had swelled with streams of countless pilgrims. Endless lumbering caravans stretched in thin, wavering lines over distant horizons. Perspiring pack animals laden with bulky provisions struggled against heavy loads. Unwieldy and cumbersome, they wound down tight streets. The push and shove of sweaty congestion seemed to press toward a million different destinations all at the same time. The braying of donkeys and lowing of cattle mixed and were laced with innumerable conversations in Hebrew, Greek, and Aramaic. Squealing children punctuated the air. Vendors were huddled on corners, hawking their wares with sweeping gestures and intrusive voices extolling the fabricated qualities of their product. Streets and alleys coursed with the faithful, the sounds of their lives mixed into an unintelligible din that rose above the controlled mayhem.

Then it came, suffocating and suppressing every lesser sound, reasserting its supremacy in its muscular tones. The blast of the ram's horn bellowed from the lofty temple tower, falling from the precipice. It reminded the coursing minions of the purpose for their journey.

Rising thick and weighty, it rolled out of the temple, breeched the temple walls, coursed across the sea of rooftops, and inundated the city streets in a swell of sound. The final bellow surged over the city walls and crashed into the countryside, gradually dissipating among the far-flung hills, valleys, and groves that surrounded Jerusalem. Suddenly, it fell silent, and the din of compacted humanity resumed.

Evening had fallen without notice. The day began to drift aimlessly into yesterday. Thousands of tents dotted the green hills and valleys surrounding the city. Their rippling cloth structures seemed as scattered wildflowers tossed in a soft and supple meadow. Their bleached canvas absorbed the last faint oranges and pastel mauves of a sun having drawn down the backside of a sleepy horizon. Fires sparked to life, sending entangling threads of smoke into a drowsy sky. The murmuring of a vast contingent of humanity settled and floated intermittently on a tepid breeze that massaged the surrounding hills.

Tens of thousands of pilgrims brushed off the excitement and surrendered to the fatigue of celebration. An occasional rooster called into the fading pastels of a day gone sleepy. The barking of dogs wafted lazily across the expanses. The cry of an infant pierced the dusk and elicited the soothing words of a loving mother. Conversations, blurred and faint, were carried on the winds of twilight. Birds settled in various groves and fluffed feathers to sleep. A flock of pigeons sought a night's roost against the fading mauves of a sleepy dusk.

Three blasts of the trumpet rose in soft succession, declaring the coming of the new day for Israel. Three stars had now been seen in the East as tradition declared it. Slowly the trumpet dissipated into the fading light of day, and everything fell silent except for the soft murmuring of a world celebrating the Passover feast. A lamb, bitter herbs, and unleavened bread were everywhere. The collection of sacred traditions harkened back to a hurried night in Egypt filled with the wailing of firstborn dead and blood on doorposts. A world soon drifted off to sleep, now resting in anticipation of the weeklong celebration that lay before it.

In the sacred fury and flurry of it all, the disciples had gathered. An upper room was painted in the temporal yellows and golds of flickering lamps bearing olive oil. The table had been set in a manner ornate but simple. The cluster of variant conversations meandered across topics both meaningful and those of simple chatty verbiage.

However, everything appeared in order except a servant at the door, which would have been an obvious omission. There was no one to wash the men's feet upon their entrance. This oddity created a moment of discomfort and disorientation. Such was the custom of washing one's feet upon entrance into a home that its absence was disturbing and unsettling. Confused glances marked bearded faces. Hushed comments yielded no answers to the oversight. There was no ready explanation, so it was assumed to be an error of omission. But, by this time the issue had passed, its absence being absorbed into the evening with little trace. The meal proceeded.

In citing this event, Scripture reads, "so he got up from the meal, took off his outer clothing, and wrapped a towel around his waist" (John 13:4). A sharp departure from tradition transpired at this point, jostling those gathered and sending a wave of unmanageable discomfort through the room. Throughout the landscape that spilled out from the room, across the city, and out beyond into the innumerable tents and temporary abodes scattered as a sea of wildflowers, Passover lambs were being eaten, celebrating the release from bondage. This very celebration was about to fall into irrelevance as the final Passover lamb prepared for His own sacrifice.

Jesus knew that death was pending, that it was less than twenty-four hours removed. He knew that it would occur at the blast of the last ram's horns designating the third daily sacrifice on the morrow. Tomorrow, it would signal the last sacrifice of the day. But this year, it would signal the last sacrifice for all of eternity. Jesus knew He would be that sacrifice. Knowing that, He was about to leave a legacy.

We are told that He "poured water into a basin and began to wash his disciples' feet, drying them with the towel that was wrapped around him" (John 13:5). There was no immediate response from any of them. It was too far removed from the norm, too illogical to wrap their minds around. A master never washed the feet of his servants. It was so grossly out of character with their world that they were emotionally hamstrung.

Yet He knelt before each of them, taking their feet in His hands, caressing them, washing them, and then drying them—the Creator washing the feet of the created. The Infinite loving the finite so infinitely that He displaced Himself in order to take that love to a wholly incomprehensible and radically new level. When faced with an infinite love, the finite beings seated around that table were simply too limited to understand it. It was God shattering the very traditions that men had created to explain Him and contain Him. For in a handful of hours, God would restore every tragic implication of the fall. And He would shatter every box doing it.

And so He moved from disciple to disciple in the silence of the upper room. Flaming torches and the crackling fire were the sole competitors for the silence that saturated the room. The gentle swish of the towel in the basin and the soft sound of dripping water gave the moment a reality. His eyes were soft, but tense. There was within them the culmination of some grand event. It seemed the jubilant look of the victor, weighed and drawn with the anticipated price of the pending victory. His face seemed an odd mix of irrepressible joy and infinite pain that spoke from eyes set deep in love.

Jesus was entirely alone in all of this. He had to be, because human comprehension fell desperately short of plans so infinitely grand. For God to save man, He would have to leave man behind. And so He passed on a legacy, a piece of what He would endure and why He would endure it. Elias Canetti said, "When you write down your life, every page should contain something no one has ever heard about." No one had ever heard about God washing the feet of men. Yet, it was a legacy made bearable and understandable enough that mankind could grasp a thin thread of an infinite act that was only hours away. So it was communicated in the simple washing of feet.

It was an act that provided a sturdy container within which they could place the memory of this moment, the life of the One who shared it with them, and carry it securely with them into each of their futures. Having moved around the entire room in abject servant-hood with a simple towel and simple bowel in hand, He finally stood erect. It would be the swish of the towel today and the thud of spikes tomorrow. It was the stuff of sacrifice.

### THE LEGACY OF A LEGACY

It is not unimaginable to think that from that moment forward, every time their feet were washed, they saw Jesus stooped over with towel and basin in hand. When the roads were tough, at the end of the day, they would see Him. When the path stretched long and dusty, He would be there at road's end in the washing of the feet. And when the world set to rid itself of these apostles and refused to wash their feet, they remembered that neither were His washed that night. It is reasonable to believe that when they were called to sacrifice, the washing of their feet somehow held within that simple gesture something of the cross and its sacrifice. I cannot but imagine that this legacy, this memory, gave them hope at the end of many hopeless roads right down to the end of each of their roads.

### THE POWER OF LEGACY

It was now forty years later. Thanksgiving had just passed into another year, and the world was decorating itself for Christmas. The roads of my life all seemed to wind in hopelessness and to hopelessness. There was nothing on the horizon of my life to draw from, and so I reached back to Uncle Bill. His tombstone had been invaded by encroaching grasses and insensitive weeds. It sat on a slight rise, little more than a stone's throw from a mirrored pond with gliding geese leaving gentle wakes on its glass-like surface. I knelt, brushed back the grass, and pulled away the tenacious weeds from the bronzed edging of his head stone.

Gently, I placed my hand on the stone and read the inscription ten or fifteen times, my mind wandering back to a brick and mortar basement. I attempted to seize a legacy that I needed to prop me up and help me believe in the present, while granting me some shred of hope for the future. I realized, in the middle of that cemetery, that a legacy is not bound to the time in which it was given; it is for all time. It is not diminished either by use or by the obstacles that face me. It is a gift that is fresh every time, in every circumstance, and with the coming of every challenge. I thanked Uncle Bill for the Red Ryder BB gun, for a bit of him in me, for the fact that he took that priceless bit of time to pass something precious along to me. I thanked him for a legacy.

As I walked away from his grave, something went with me, something unexplainable and unexpected. It was as if I was not alone in a way that makes being alone entirely impossible. More than that, it was as if not being alone brought courage, hope, and some element of fortitude that I hadn't had as I first sat down at Uncle Bill's grave to talk with him. I reclaimed the legacy. I picked it up again, and it went with me. There is no doubt that his legacy gave me more than I would need for whatever it was that I might encounter, despite how big it might be. Legacy is another joining us to face the giants and forge a path toward new horizons. Jesus and Uncle Bill—I am so terribly thankful for the legacy that each left with me.

### Pondering Point

Legacy: the gift of a life shared. Whether it's packaged in precious moments or bundled across the expanse of years, a life shared leaves a legacy that gives us points from which to draw strength as we emulate the example of others. It lends us an identity in which to stand when life would cause us to question who we are. It affords us wisdom to borrow from the wisdom displayed by those before us, to emulate the courageous examples of others from which we can draw in life's onslaughts. It is a benchmark that makes hope feasible when all seems hopeless because others before us survived and thrived. It's a history that tells us that life is more than simply the difficult realities of the moment, but that life is about a journey traveled by others who have faith that we can finish what they began. It's a cross whose message was "I believe in you, and I have an incredible future for you." It is all a remarkable and precious legacy from the past, with an incredible promise for the future.

## A Thought
- What legacies have been passed on to me?
- How can I build upon a life of legacy in my own life by leaving a legacy in the life of another?
- What legacy do I want to create?
- When can I know that the legacy that I plan to pass on is worthy enough to build something into the life of the individual that I pass it on to so that it will not work to diminish the recipient?

**CHAPTER 15**

# A BLIZZARD OF BLOSSOMS
## Seeing Endings as Beginnings

*"He has made everything beautiful in its time. He has also set eternity in the human heart; yet no one can fathom what God has done from beginning to end."*

Ecclesiastes 3:11

*"In my end is my beginning."*

~T.S. Eliot

**AS A CHILD, I REVELED** in them while they lived, their life spilling into me as I rested in the broad embrace of their muscular boughs. As a young adult, I cried over them at their deaths. And as a person, I am forever changed in that they miraculously live again.

Spring is the beginning beyond the end. Lewis Grizzard wrote, "Springtime is the land awakening. The March winds are the morning yawn." It's the unexpected addendum to death that is, in reality, the first chapter of a never-ending story that leaves the rest of the preceding tale as a brief footnote. Spring says that real life can only be lived on the heels of death and that whatever transpired before is only the vaguest precursor. It's an eternal reality manifest in a natural cycle, rendering the reality and nature of eternity exposed in advance of our own arrival there.

As a child, I spent countless spring mornings lying in the tender emerald grass, engulfed in a sea of dandelions that seemed as spots of brilliant yellow pigment liberally splattered from an artist's palette. As the morning's sun peeked over a yawning horizon, I would stare up through branches dense with fresh, white cherry blossoms. Spring has its own snowfall, but that snowfall is made up of countless blossoms that are just as white as any snowfall winter might grace the world with. The blossoms were spring's heralding of fall's coming bounty. Life was emerging, not just for the sake of life or as some show of resilience or to illustrate a tired cycle that all of life is irreparably stuck in. Rather, life as manifest in the innumerable blossoms was to perpetuate life and build upon itself in the eternal expansion of life that will someday eclipse death altogether.

The sun seemed more golden early in the morning, its lucid brilliance not yet having been diminished by the demands of the coming day. As the sun reached over the horizon, its opulent rays fell on the cherry trees as a pure golden rain, dripping from the snow white cherry blossoms in twenty-four karat translucent droplets. Its light backlit each petal, transforming the cherry trees' branches into a dazzling white blizzard of blossoms.

The clean, buoyant breezes of spring drifted not far behind the advancing sun. They drew their warm fingers gently through the perfumed clouds of petals, teasing out robust aromatic waves and sending them softly breaking across my face. I found my body embraced in an invisible sweetness that spilled out beyond where I lay and gently rolled across the broad green stretches of tender grass.

Caught in this rich, airy bouquet, dozens of mesmerized bees droned trance-like from blossom to blossom. Legs heavy with nectar's golden dust, they sampled spring's sweet bounty until their transparent wings could barely lift them, finally lumbering off to unload their treasure at some secret destination. Their activity created a soothing hum of satisfaction, as if nature were taking a moment to take pleasure in itself. I would lie there, close my eyes, and breathe in every drop of the flood of life that washed in sweet charismatic swells over my soul.

By the time my adult years rolled around, the magnificent cherry trees had aged and diseased beyond redemption. Their once muscular trunks had fallen prey to the rot of age and the scourge of ants. Limbs that once invited young boys to endless adventure in the heights of their leafy canopy and a blue sky beyond creaked with years that had compromised their strength and altogether silenced the adventuresome tenor of their voices. Springs were now met with a few anemic leaves scattered across vast canopies now rendered largely bald. They had become skeletal, having no energy and too little life to respond to the soft summons of spring. Only a muted handful of blossoms dotted the starkly barren branches. Sap seeped from deep fissures that etched jagged lines up thick trunks. The trees wept, it seemed, in sticky rivulets of sorrow out of the futility of naked canopies. Death loomed, and they seemed to know it.

The waiting for death is dictated by the assumptions about death. We see it as the silent vigil of finality, where death is irrevocably tied to loss and we're just waiting for the loss. In reality, it is not the loss of the object itself. It's more about what we will lose in light of the loss. It is about our loss. The end always seems to loom bigger than the beginning that death spawns. Therefore, we see only the end. Sorrow does not afford us vision beyond the horizon where loss finally sets. Neither does faith. Faith, however, causes us to rely on Someone who sees beyond the edges of a darkening horizon where our losses have set. And He says that what is a sunset on this side of it all is a sunrise on the other.

On one fateful fall afternoon, with chainsaws in hand and with a lump in our throats, we approached the old cherry trees. Their horizon was darkening. With a single pull of the cord, one of the chainsaws roared to life, immediately joined by a second in a two-cycle chorus of death. Both united to spew a caustic blue-white cloud of exhaust into branches that for so many seasons had emanated rich perfumed clouds quite different from these. With a deafening roar, the chainsaw's ravaging teeth set about the business of finalizing the loss. In tandem, they bit into the ancient trunks, ruthlessly spewing bits of the trees' heartwood in every direction. Flakes and shavings blanketed the sullen ground around us as spots of brown pigment liberally splattered from death's palette.

With their aged trunks fatally undercut, one by one their wooden columns teetered, slow and almost reverently, as if resisting death would also be resisting the life that would follow. There was, it seemed, a willing obedience to a larger plan. With a deft measure of grace, they fell helplessly on the very ground that had been a privileged recipient of their blossoms for so many springs. With a few brief swipes of the chain saws, the trees were rendered a lifeless stack of cordwood.

The trees' histories as penned in their many rings lay naked and exposed at the end of each piece, citing the closing of one drama to make way for the next. Shutting off the chainsaw, I paused for a moment and wondered if the rings that marked each year of growth remembered the little boy that for so many years sat enthralled under their branches, or were they now little more than dead wood? Did they know? I set down the chainsaw, turned toward a darkening horizon, and cried.

## A Bit of Eternity

The sun threw a few last scant rays over the western horizon. Dusk assumed its place, obediently keeping pace with a sleepy sun, rolling up in its darkening folds the remnants of an exhausted day. The flurry of the Passover was settling over the city, drifting and then dissipating in the deepening dusk engulfing Jerusalem. The murmur of celebratory humanity caught in its own exhaustion was now sleepy and heavy. The day had been filled with celebration and sacrifice, ritual and rite, the mingling of multiple cultures descending on this city to remember, reflect, and recall. It was a celebration of unleavened bread, bitter herbs, blood on doorposts, and a hasty expulsion by a nation that woke to firstborn death. But for now, in the extending and deepening shadows engulfing the landscape, the city settled.

Another stream ran through the current of this particular Passover. It had, at this moment, pooled in Gethsemane, east across the city from here. Great drops of blood dripped from a forehead that spoke of the great angst of the Son of God facing the dark of day. Jesus was aware of the plan of redemption long before it unfolded, which replaced the anxiety of speculation with the chilling horror of certainty. He knew that soldiers would seize Him, and He knew the channel that the current of events would take that night as they flowed through the city.

It would flow through the house of the high priest: elegant, ornate and yet empty of everything that is of God. Then it would shift north through the Sanhedrin, deluged in the garments of tradition and blinded by religious fervor that had devolved into nothing but legalistic rigor. From there it would flow through Herod's palace, to the west. The marbled walls now rubbed soft in the milky thin moonlight awaited him. Pilate would step into its waters in the Antonia towers, but he would be unable to divert its flow. It would then be momentarily diverted to Herod and his coarse brutality and sadistic curiosity, only to be redirected back to Pilate. Then, coursing down the Via Dolorosa, it would crest on Golgotha, the pending terror of that place northwest just outside the city wall. It would finally ebb and pool in a chiseled and borrowed tomb a bit beyond there. Three days later, a spring of life would surge from the rock walls and burst open a tomb in its torrential power.

But, at that moment, Jesus was in Gethsemane. The soldiers were now on the way, possessing an edict from the religious leaders to seize God and then kill Him, though they did not recognize Him as such. The collision and resulting turbulent headwaters of a plan launched many millennia ago at the fall of mankind was only moments from happening.

What was Golgotha like the night before His death? What was it like that Thursday night before He ascended that hill? What was Golgotha like as it silently waited to be the place upon which God would be crucified in history's single most significant event? I wonder about that. It's not recorded in Scripture. To stand there that night, knowing what was unfolding directly across the city; knowing the crass and cruel events that would travel across the city and end right there on that gravel and rock hill. What would it be like to pick up a handful of gravel and run it through your fingers, knowing the kind of morbid horror that would unfold on the crest of this hill within a scant twenty-four hours?

The moon rose, washing Golgotha in a breathless pallor of death. The call of a roosting bird briefly broke the silence. Settling in, silence absorbed the hill once more. Various implements of death left by careless soldiers lay strewn about. Bones bleached in the moonlight cried with no voice, silently screaming the horror of those last moments. No one heard because no one listened. Its summit was saturated with death. Footprints of the dead covered its alien landscape. Blood spatter was dried and caked, left as an accounting of lives lost. It lay thick and coagulated, deep in the gravelly soil. It was strewn and spattered across rocks in wild gyrations as panicked bodies were pushed into the chasm of death. Fingers desperately clawed the precipice of that chasm, terrified in finding the battle useless. Life was forced out of them despite their frenzied efforts to hold onto that life. Cries, moans, pleading, and gasping lent a horrifying motif to the deaths that transpired there. The babblings of minds were seized in surrender to the caustic black face of death as they peered full faced into the abyss with shrieks that described what their souls saw. And then, they fell.

Always, silence fell. Eventually, death reigned … eventually. The abyss was repeatedly satisfied. On this hill, life would terminate, sometimes calmly, but most times with horrific panic. Whatever stories had been written about someone before their arrival on this hill, the final page of those stories would be written here. Innumerable books were closed and sealed, forever lost to the greater story of the ages. Lives and their accompanying stories dissipated in the backwash of history and were swept away in the undertow of time: gone. Such was the horror of this hill. On that night, it was particularly poignant because the next day, the incomprehensible would happen. On this hill, the infinite would surrender to death. God would die there tomorrow.

The moonlight had thickened a bit, moving across the hill in a pasty wash. On the far side of the city, the soldiers had likely seized Jesus by now. The river had now set its course to Golgotha. The night to come would be filled with beatings, accusations, and lies that were fabricated in the pit of hell and vomited into this river. Lacerations and contusions would mark that night and mark it deeply, spilling blood into the rising currents. He would drag a cross across the city and onto that hill now so silent, and here He too would die … right here. Like all the others who were forced to the crest of this hill, eventually He would die. And the event was now only hours away.

From here, this river would meander in rivulets of sorrow into a tomb just west of this hilltop. The final page would be written and the book would be closed, just like all the others … or so it seemed. Permanently sealed in a tomb and in the pages of history, like all the rest, He would be left to be caught in the backwash of history and the undertow of time. But the process and outcome of a typical execution would be radically different this time. No one suspected it, because God never died before. Instead, He would rewrite history, and He would commandeer time.

## A Gateway

Is not the faint voice of the eternal to be heard in death? Death leads to life, even in this temporal existence of ours. Somewhere, somehow, something arises out of the ashes of our losses to remind us that nothing ever ceases. Nothing ever vanishes. Nothing ever comes to *nothing*. God is always creating, even in the middle of the kind of devastation where we can't even remotely see that anything could possibly be created out of the ashes of whatever it was that was destroyed. His hand is incessantly recreating, renewing, rewriting, and revising faster than the devastation from whose ashes He draws up the raw material from which to recreate. Always!

"I am making everything new!" Jesus declares (Revelation 21:5). It's a declarative statement that demands the passing of the old to make way for the creating of the new. It's about grasping the incorruptible reality that the discarded shards, scraps, and remnants of that which has died and passed represent the stuff from which the new is miraculously shaped. And there lies the most profound of promises, that the passing of the old is not a tragic end in itself. Rather, it is a step to something new. A glorious promise that when set starkly against our immutable losses gives us immutable hope. Death is only an end that marks a beginning, and it exists only for that beginning, a promise that sows life with deep meaning and death with profound purpose.

"I tell you the truth, unless a kernel of wheat falls to the ground and dies, it remains only a single seed. But if it dies, it produces many seeds" (John 12:24). In dying, a seed, whatever that seed might be, produces life that is in excess of and superior to the death that birthed it. William Blake wrote, "He who binds to himself a joy does the winged life destroy; but he who kisses the joy as it flies lives in eternity's sunrise." A sunset on one side is a sunrise on the other that will rise eternally. What was to transpire on that hill would forever root and firmly establish this principle. It would declare it and forever seal it. History would pivot on that hill on the morrow and thank God it did.

## WINTER AND SPRING . . . AGAIN

With winter's snows having begun to seize the land once again, the cherry tree's trunk was left until spring's soft ground would allow us to fully uproot it. That was the plan anyway, errantly conceived out of the assumption that loss is just that—loss and nothing more. Into winter's dreary months we marched, frequently looking into the backyard where the old trees had been and to where I had spent so many wonderful spring mornings as a child. A gaping hole marked the landscape, just like the landscape of my heart.

Winter came, and winter went. One day after winter's snows had long vanished, I wandered back to the old cherry trees. The tender emerald grass had once again blanketed the landscape, bidding me to come and lie in them once more. The artist had once again returned from his prolonged absence. Taking his palette in hand, he again engulfed me in a sea of dandelions that seemed as spots of brilliant yellow pigment liberally splattered from his prolific palette. In its unfailing consistency, the sun stretched its golden fingers over a sleepy, spring-laden horizon. I laid there and realized that it was once again what it had been for so many, many wonderful years.

However, it suddenly became immensely and wrenchingly empty as I realized that there were no branches through which to watch spring unfold. The sun still seemed more golden in the morning, but there were no snow white cherry blossoms from which its opulent rays would drip. Its light searched for the soft white petals in order to marvelously backlight each one. Instead, the falling torrent of golden light fell helplessly through the air and formed dismayed luminous puddles on the ground all around me.

As with years past, the clean, buoyant breezes of spring reached out with their warm fingers, but they found no perfumed clouds of petals. My senses desperately reached out as well, but there were no robust aromatic waves to softly break across my face and generously roll across the broad stretches of green. Anticipating spring's nectar, the bees lumbered in from their secret destinations only to circle in confusion and then depart, leaving me in silence. My heart turned within me. The magnificent blizzard of blossoms was truly gone.

I could no longer stand the vacancy death had left in spring. Abruptly, I stood and turned to leave. As I did, I glanced at the two stumps that seemed to be nothing more than lifeless grave markers. They were graying monuments to an irretrievable past, a piece of death reminding me of what had died. Death sometimes haunts us even after it has passed by us and passed unto itself.

But, stubbornly poking up from each stump was a single, slim stem. It was not possible. I squinted and moved closer. Sure enough, life had begun the process of springing from death. I drew closer. On those tiny stems there protruded several plump buds. In time, they would produce a few small leaves and a small cluster of beautiful white blossoms. Taking another step closer, I knelt beside the old stumps and gently fingered the single stems. The trees were alive, creating a torrent of hope in my mind of springs to come that would once again be filled with a new blizzard of blossoms. Nothing was over. Wiping back tears, I realized that what had been dead was alive again. The beauty of what was, was to be once more. Death was a gateway to life; a sunset on this side is nothing other than a sunrise on the other.

Today, some thirty years after that wonderful moment of discovery, the cherry trees have completely regenerated themselves. They stand taller than they had during those many years that I as a child had sat underneath their magnificent, snow white branches. Now each spring, some three or more decades removed from those dreamy childhood mornings, I wander out to the old trees, lie in the thick emerald grass engulfed in a sea of dandelions, and once again revel in that most spectacular white blizzard of blossoms!

### Another Blizzard of Life

The tomb surged empty that Sunday morning, just a stone's throw away from Golgotha. The waters would gather, foam, and rise as an eternal torrent, bursting out of that tomb three days later. It would crest in a tidal wave that would inundate the entire world for all of time, finally ebbing off into the shoals of eternity, rendering this hill forever unneeded. Death can come, and it will. But it is now beaten. It had been seized, changed, and reshaped as a gateway to the eternal where loss is irrepressibly offset by the immutable life that now springs from it!

### Pondering Point

We associate death with permanence. Losses are seen as loss. Our view is skewed by the finite world in which we live. Too often, we don't associate and apply the eternal to life and living. The eternal is an extension beyond what our eyes see. What ends here begins there. What was gained, shaped, molded, and crafted goes on as did Jesus, and as did the two cherry trees.

### A Thought

- Can I begin to think beyond the temporal to the eternal?
- Am I willing to see the finite world in which I live as a river that rolls into eternity and beyond?
- How will that change my view of loss?
- How will that change my view of life?

CHAPTER 16

# "WHY ARE YOU DOING THIS?"
## Worth Unimagined

*"Rather, it should be that of your inner self, the unfading beauty of a gentle and quiet spirit, which is of great worth in God's sight."*
I Peter 3:4

*"It ain't what they call you; it's what you answer to."*
~ W.C. Fields

**I DREW BACK IN MY** seat with hands pressed hard on the steering wheel. I had seen ten patients in ten straight hours. My mind was a mushy and convoluted mix of thoughts, theories, sordid stories, and dark histories all bundled in assorted packages of grief, pain, loss, destitution, and hopelessness. I had been wrung dry and completely exhausted in the attempt to bring some shred of hope, some thin glint of light, some reason for living to those who daily fill my office—especially those who had filled it that day.

Facing the torrent of human pain, agony, degradation, abuse, hopelessness, fear, and futility day in and day out is my job. That's what I do. There's nothing heroic about it as it's simply meeting people where they are and joining them in whatever their journey might be. It's about walking alongside wounded humanity in their quest for healing, or hope of healing. But on wrenching days like this one, I wonder if I do it effectively at all. Did I make even the most imperceptible difference? Is anything or anyone really any better off because I poured myself out into ten lives in ten hours? Numbed and blunted, I leaned my head back on the headrest and navigated the flood of cars heading home as I was. I was lost in traffic while being entirely lost in thought, on the verge of the kind of collision that shapes lives instead of bending cars.

On these kinds of days, I question my worth and my value. I wonder if indeed I bring anything worthwhile to the lives around me. The result is that I end up looking back at myself through the mirrors of others, and I ask penetrating and painful questions about the validity of my life. The excruciating scourge of the human condition is to question the value of the human condition. Do I possess anything worthwhile or valuable? Do I count for something that gives legitimacy to my existence? Am I worth the resources that I use to sustain myself? Do I matter ... really?

We all look around us at some time. We survey the landscape of our lives and take some sort of inventory as to whatever it is that makes up that landscape. Often, most of what we see are the recurrent difficulties that constantly plague us, pain that is resistant to any prescription that we throw at it, stolen promises that have never been retrieved, shattered hopes that have shattered hope, and endless vacancies of every sort. We see time slipping away, taking with it both the time to reclaim our losses and the energy with which to do it. We see poor choices that bent the roads of our lives, turning them off in some abysmal direction that we've not been able to correct despite our frequently herculean efforts to do so. It seems that life is arrayed against us so much so that the best of our abilities and the most aggressive prayers are helpless against the onslaught.

We wonder what good are we, if any. We forget, as Elizabeth Gilbert wrote, "that once upon a time, in an unguarded moment, we recognized ourselves as a friend." Yet, if the best that our efforts result in are the sorry outcomes that lay scattered and strewn around us, what kind of friend are we? If our worlds continue to teeter and fall despite our efforts to prop them up and undergird them with something that will keep them upright, do our efforts matter? And what if it's all destined for destruction anyway? What if this is the route that life's going to take regardless of what we do to stop it? What if it's all in a timeless free fall and we're just a collection of puny self-proclaimed heroes pressing a naive battle that is not really a battle at all? What if life is something we've fooled ourselves into believing is a battle so that we can play the hero, only to find out it's not a battle and we're not a hero? If all of that is true, and I am genuinely irrelevant in the span of it all, then what am I worth?

Such days prompt such thoughts in a manner that makes the thoughts sharp and cutting. They pour through the ruptures forged by my frequently low self-esteem, deluging my mind, flooding my heart, spilling across the seat of my car, and pooling in puddles at my feet. The thoughts pound me like incessant waves at the forefront of an approaching hurricane with all the force of an emotional tidal surge, and they scream, "Am I worth anything?"

The traffic thins and my mind wanders.

## MY WORTH IN HIS ACTION

A thud. It reverberated through the air deep, thick, and thunderous. Somehow, it rolled beyond the cavernous street and out into eternity. Sweat and blood spattered across the arid dirt and gravel that surrounded the panicked scene. Dust rose from the impact of flesh meeting gravel and dirt, drifting and edging into dissipation. A hand, palm down, struck the ground in an exhausted effort to brace the fall and steady the weight of a teetering cross. The effort, however, was futile. The cross beam tilted and leaned precariously. The draw of gravity on thick timbers was irreversibly heavy. Sometimes we can't counter the gravity of the circumstances that befall us, so our lives teeter.

Blood, caked and coagulated in gouging lacerations, was embedded with the sticky filth of sweat, dirt, and the seeping of fresh blood. The only thing left was exhaustion, with death following feverishly on its heels. Jesus' body was sapped from a night of horrendous beating that layered beating upon beating until life had been driven so close to death that He was more the living dead. Death, in part, was already there. Jesus fell again. His hair was grimy with sweat. There was a fiendish embellishment of thorns that rested tangled and vine-like amidst clumps of stringy hair sopped in crimson. His face was in the dirt. His breath was heavy and labored.

The crowd that day was filled with a sordid mix of empathy and deep angst at the sight of the immutably suffering God face down in the gravel. Others were jeering, taunting and engaged in raucous mocking; kicking dirt, throwing gravel, and hurling insults as lethal projectiles that repeatedly struck Jesus' body and heart. Some were drawn by the titillating itch of curiosity that beckoned to them, raising them up on tiptoe with necks outstretched to watch this curious sight. The callousness of mankind was brazenly manifest and seen as blatantly heartless when held up against the love of God bleeding in the gravel. The pure, undiluted evil of the adversary seized the scene and spun it to ever-increasing levels of morbid insanity. The whole charade turned increasingly venomous and toxic. The wound had been inflicted, and the spiritual poison was now running through the very veins of God Himself.

Centurions, the seasoned veterans of innumerable crucifixions, pushed the beams upright, grabbed an unsuspecting bystander, and thrust him into the street. Confounded, Simon protested about being dragged into the middle of the morbidity. Pressed by centurions eager to get about the business of death, he stumbled and stepped to the center of the hard-packed street and to the center of history itself. Pensively, he set his own hand against the beam and steadied it.

Glancing into the mangled face he tried to avoid, he caught a glimpse, a flash of perfection that was wholly unmatched by the scene that swirled around him. There was a glimmer of something greater than everything that defined that moment. In the tangle of blood and gashes, there was something infinitely richer than all the filth that churned through the mass of sordid humanity in that street. A covert invasion was in progress, yet no one in the crowd suspected it. The price of the invasion of a fallen world was indescribable. It was a great assault, far beyond the scope and comprehension of the crowd. Something about this prophet was different. Something about this prophet refused to succumb to the evil dancing in crazed jubilation all around him.

The moment was suddenly broken as the centurions grabbed the dying man and pulled Him away from the cross ... only momentarily. Simon shouldered the beams and leveled the weight. His sandals pressed moist in the slough mix of blood and dirt. He drew a breath, and then stepped forward.

### We Were There

Somehow, I was there. All of us were. It was a pivotal event that extended the fortune and grace of the impossible to each of us. This event handed us hope sturdy enough and sufficiently robust to hold us firm when the world around us would do its level best to tear us down. My soul is so desperate for what it offered or what it meant, even though I would not feel its effects for thousands of years. But, I was there, for the act is timeless. It is rooted in all of eternity, not in the constant journey of the sun from one horizon to the other or the passing of the seasons that left this event to sit forever only in the confines of that day or of days like today. In His heart, I was there because it was an eternal moment.

**"WHY?"**

What would I have done had I been there? It would be at this moment on His way to the cross, before it was too late, before the spikes truly sealed the death that was now, at this point, well on its way. It would be at that very moment before the clock began to tick off the seconds of those last three hours of His life on the very cross He now carried. It would have to be before the thief, the sponge, the sour wine, the mockery, and the words "my God, my God."

Before all of that, I would want to kneel with Him at that moment on that street, on my knees, wholly prostate beside Him. I would want my face level with His, my hands claw-like in the grit and dirt right beside Him. I would want to say, to shout, "Why are you doing this? I'm not worth it! Do you hear? I'm not worth what's happening here!" I would want to scream every lewd bit of this madness out of existence. I would want to beg it off the pages of history, asking Him to obliterate me from all existence if that would stop the insanity that had seized all of creation. The core of my humanity would be screaming its worthlessness, that you, God, were somehow insane for doing this for me since the trade-off is no trade but a gross overestimate of my value against yours.

Glenn Beck wrote, "Sometimes the hardest part of the journey is believing you're worthy of the trip." In the face of this crass crucifixion with all of its macabre gore, bewildering brutality, and wildly gyrating evil, there's no question that I doubt that I'm worthy of Jesus taking the trip on my behalf. My own humanity is far too shallow to afford me even the remotest reconciliation between who God is, who I am, and His dying solely on behalf of who I am. I can't make it work anywhere in my soul or psyche. Therefore, I scream at the top of my voice that it all must stop!

Simply let me cease to exist! Cast me into the abyss of nothingness until any memory of me is extracted from every mind, every heart ... even your heart. Unwrite the history that brought me to this moment so that you can be released from this moment. Erase me. Annihilate me. Send me beyond oblivion, outside of creation itself. But don't do this. Please, do not do this. Don't ... because I love you too much." Impassioned and desperate, the created finds himself pleading for the life of the Creator. It is an absurdly odd disparity.

Would He smile? I doubt it. This is a moment of eternal horror and infinite seriousness. He was truly alone. It had all passed out of human hands. Of His own volition, He had unsheathed a sword and raised a banner, thrusting it deep into the ground and unfurling it so that it could not be taken up without a battle. His feet were now firmly planted. The challenge was declared, and there was no taking it back. "I will take mankind back!" There was before Him a sweeping spiritual battlefield, epic in scope. The hills were lacquered black and thick with horrendous demonic hordes that girded themselves for battle. The advance had begun in a manger in Bethlehem thirty-three years earlier. It would not stop now. It's manifestation in the physical realm was lying at my feet in the mangled body of God having come to redeem me. It was now to the death.

Would He somehow acknowledge my words? Maybe. But the task was bigger than my words and infinitely larger than my shallow human demand. Would He press on with the insistence that I was too valuable to cast into nothingness, that it was already decided? It was all beyond discussion or debate. His eyes were blackened and deeply swollen. Blood was trickling, seeping from a cruel crown and tracing errant lines around hollow sockets. But those eyes remained firm and profoundly resolute. They were human, but much more. Through lips swelled, cracked, and bloodied, He might murmur the words, "I love you too much." If not, He was thinking them in His soul and shouting them on the battlefield now engaged. The shout had been raised for all of us.

The cross began to move. Centurions lifted a shredded body to its feet. He stumbled off, listing under the effects of scourging, blood loss, and the siren sins of mankind. His attention was there on that hill, preparing to do final battle with the minions of hell and the sin of man. The crowd moved along, culling a mix of confusion, hatred, and simple spectators. Those who loved Him and those who hated Him found equal place in the crowd. There were those who didn't know Him but had found themselves consumed in the frenzy of a mindless crucifixion. Each one was the sole reason for God having His face in the gravel, and none of them knew it. Each one was the sole reason for the battle that none of them could see.

Limping along, a javelin prodded Jesus to quicken His pace. He stumbled again, paused, regained His balance, and resumed. And so it was the journey to the hill, to death, and to redemption.

### MY WORTH ... MY ROLE

I am not worth what He did. Not in what I see in myself. It's absurd. I hate the thought that I might be worth something that demanded what Jesus did, yet I am at the same time captivated by it. I sense a worth in myself I cannot even remotely comprehend. The unspeakable sacrifice of His actions evidence something in me that I can't see, but something His actions refuse to let me deny. I am taken beyond myself and forced to see something in me that my own eyes cannot.

It's the image of God stamped on my soul that makes me something of infinite worth; I am the son of the King. It's completely inexcusable, but I have forgotten my son-ship so entirely that I am convinced of my impoverishment. My soul is held hostage to an enemy force that I cannot reckon with and that insists upon my impoverishment. Yet, my worth demands my liberation. It's an eternal non-negotiable. The sword is unsheathed. The banner is planted and unfurled in the winds of eternity. The cry is raised, and the assault is engaged. The purpose of it all? The purpose is you and me. We are the rationale for a war that would claim the life of God.

It is not about what I am, or what I bring, or what I do, or what kind of day I have. It's about who God is. I am valuable because "I am fearfully and wonderfully made" (Psalm 139:14). He alone conceived of me, and then He alone crafted me. I am His handiwork, the product of the Master Artist and a manifestation of His limitless genius. I am not only born of God. I am designed by Him.

The thoughts lift me and lighten my mind. The traffic has cleared and so have my thoughts. It doesn't feel so heavy and hopeless now. My value is beyond what I do; rather, it is based on whose I am. And Him to whom we belong assessed our value as equal to His life. There a pricelessness in that.

The thud on that raucous street deep in the city was to be followed by another thud on a hilltop of death, as the cross would be dropped after reaching its destination. Deep, thick, thunderous the sound, even. A series of others were to follow as spikes were driven. Another thud as the cross was raised and dropped into an awaiting hole that would hold the cross upright for the whole of the world to see. Another thud would follow later as the rock sealed the tomb. And three days later, a final thud would rumble across time as the stone was rolled away. The battle was fought with infinite angst, the blood of the infinite God, and it ended in infinite victory. It was fought for you and for me because we are worth the battle.

**PONDERING POINT**

We don't want to admit it, but most of us don't like ourselves a whole lot. Once we get past the many fronts and facades we put up to spruce up our image, we often don't like what we see. Self-images are destroyed by hands both intentional and unintentional. By those who are supposed to have loved us as well as those who have no such compulsion. Our lives become splintered on the rocks of betrayal, abandonment, abuse, neglect, and other assorted maladies inflicted from without and absorbed within. Our self-image is taken captive, mirroring and applying to ourselves the abuse that others have perpetrated upon us. We errantly assume that their response to us is a genuine reflection of our worth and value. Most often, it is not. The sole and singular benchmark that bespeaks your value is the action of Jesus on your behalf. No other actions matter. We must see our reflection in His work, not in the many other voices that would diminish us.

## A Thought
- From who or what have I derived my sense of value?
- Have I accepted the actions of others toward me as a commentary on my value, or can I see those actions as reflective of that person's issues?
- Am I willing to look fully into the cross and apply that action as fully and comprehensively indicative of my value?
- Or will I choose to believe in my worthlessness because it demands so little of me?

**CHAPTER 17**

# AND IT IS SATURDAY
## Living in the In-Between of Life

*"Who went ahead of you on your journey, in fire by night and in a cloud by day, to search out places for you to camp and to show you the way you should go."*
Deuteronomy 1:33

*"We must be willing to get rid of the life we've planned, so as to have the life that is waiting for us."*
~ Joseph Campbell

**SHE SMEARED DEEP RED LIPSTICK** in thick layers over wrinkled lips. Having been applied with trembling hands, the waxy crimson set an errant course, wandering off the edges of her mouth onto adjacent skin. A dusting of rosy blush gave an aura of life to cheeks washed white and fallen with the weight of time. A lengthy string of fake pearls, faded in disappointment, encircled the tired folds of her aged neck. Clusters of them were conspicuously absent, although she appeared to take no note of it.

Thinned by time and colored a light ashen gray by the wash of pain, her hair was fluffed and sprayed into weak curls. Sparse lockets of hair set about her head in thin and precarious waves. A powder blue dress fell over a body drawn down from assorted maladies both physical and emotional. Her physique was emaciated beyond fragility, as if the slightest touch might break her. Loose skin was thrown over a bony frame with little flesh to draw it firm. A few last touches in a foggy mirror, and she headed for the door as she had hundreds of times before. Yet, it would be the same.

I didn't especially like working the adult unit at the psychiatric hospital. It wasn't that I feared working with psychotic adults. Rather, the shifts were predictably unpredictable, rending eight hours an experience that sporadically hurled and halted itself through moments of jarring chaos sometimes controlled but more often uncontrolled. I took blood pressure and played a litany of worn videos that had been seen a hundred times but never remembered. Catatonic patients sat steeped in drooling stupors in corners, living out their lives in deep shadows from which they could not escape. Some would frantically pace the hallways, thinking that they were going somewhere when in actuality they were living out a circuitous route that led from insanity back to insanity and on to insanity.

Cries of women traumatized by non-existent horrors rolled down sterile linoleum hallways, their shrieks a response to petrifying but entirely imaginary images that were the stuff of wild minds unleashed and unfettered. Others would approach with wringing hands, asking where the bus stop was, or if the fairies had come yet, or when the dance was going to begin. They would return every five minutes to ask the same questions as if they had never been asked and as if the things about which they asked were real. So many lives were seized helplessly in the grip of minds awash in an irrepressible torrent of life at its worst that was multiplied to insanity. I read to patients in order to calm rampant thoughts and sometimes just let them talk.

There was always a series of restraints where a handful of staff would tie down a convulsing body that left to its own devices would inflict injury or death. A weathered nurse would apply medication and chart yet another tragedy. We observed the patient as the drug asserted the control that the patient could not, slowly loosening the belts and cuffs one by one as the medication did what it was intended to do. Within moments, we were doing it all over again with another patient seized by psychosis and lost in a labyrinth of lunacy. It may be that insanity is the realization that sanity is a hope forever deferred, a longing that would never walk down the hall of one's life. It could be a long shift.

Double doors marked the boundary between the real world and their world. Two Plexiglas windows scratched blurry by hopeless hands allowed patients to peer out and the outside world to peer in, permitting an exchange of glances barely inches apart but light years distant. Each world saw itself as reality and subsequently feared the world on the other side. Those on the outside found themselves bracing fearful minds against the stark realization that insanity and mental bankruptcy, even in the best of circumstances, lurks only inches away. Those on the inside stared back through cavernous eyes that lived out the full horror of that truth, waiting for the arrival of sanity that for most would never come.

I passed through this door once when I began my shift and again when I ended it. It was a step from one world into an entirely different one. And one day, Emily stood on the other side of that door with the thick Plexiglas windows, with lipstick smeared, hair in weak curls, and wearing a powder blue dress draped in loose folds over her emaciated body. Staring out from her world into the one outside, her eyes were set with irresistible anticipation and excitement. Deep blue pools reached out in profound longing, desperate in their desire to connect to something on the other side. Each day, she would prepare herself in just the same way, meticulously tending to her reflection in that faded mirror, and then stand at those doors for hours waiting, every day.

Curfew and bedtime would come precisely at ten o'clock. "But I know he's coming," she would say in a thin voice of surrender, "he said he would be coming!" Even in the throes of disappointment, she was resistant. "I know he's coming," she would say in whimpered tones. In a solemn manner, we would escort her away from the doors with the thick Plexiglas windows and guide her fragile frame off to a lonesome bed. Female staff members prepared her for yet another night of deep disappointment. Martin Luther King Jr. said, "There can be no deep disappointment where there is not deep love." Once upon a time, her love had been sublimely deep. So was her loss. So was her disappointment.

Fathomless cries of her soul rose in muffled whimpers, and glistening lines traced errant paths down cheeks made warm by the thin dusting of rosy blush. Her slight frame, wracked yet again by deep disappointment, would obediently roll into bed and draw itself into a tiny fetal position. Her grief had torn her down from the inside out, rendering her an aged infant who needed to be tucked into bed by staff members who, night after night, grieved along with her. In a few moments, she would drift off to sleep. Exhausted by pain, she would find some fleeting escape in slumber.

One unusually quiet night before my shift ended, I checked her room. Escorted by a female staff member, I paused over her bed. A thin wash of light lay tentative across the room, passively leaking from a night light yellowed and weakened with age just like Emily. Two thin blankets lay draped over a body worn thin by grief and the ceaseless lathe of disappointment. Shallow breaths punctuated by slight sighs told me that not even sleep was a sure escape. Lipstick, blush, and thin curls drowned in disappointment mirrored a hopefully hopeless soul that found fitful sleep.

Next to her bed, cheap brass frames sported washed out photos of a distant time. In them, there stood a young woman who was strikingly beautiful and vivacious. Her hands were clasped in the hands of a young man who himself was sturdy and robust. Caught by the faded images, I attempted to see Emily in those photos, to correlate the depleted woman in the bed with the bright and lively woman in the photo. The incongruence made the attempt entirely fruitless. "That's her husband," my co-worker whispered in a tone laced with her own pain. And then there came a pause laden with the dread anticipation of what was about to be said next. She continued, "He died in 1969."

I fell into an emotional rift, in the emotional descent slowly but persistently drawing together what I knew. Recognizing the devastation and hoping it not to be the truth, I stammered and then said, "Is that who she waits for?" A muffled "yes" from the nurse struck me and set me back. As she pulled up a loose blanket and primped the bed, she muttered, "She's done that every night ... for years." My mind raced to do the math that would provide me some measure of her pain so that I might identify with the suffering of this poor woman. She had been traveling to the door of disappointment for thirteen long and lonely years.

Under my breath, I murmured what my heart was screaming, "She's waiting for someone who's never coming." Such a thought was the stark and skeletal epitome of hopelessness. She was unable not to hope, but her hope would always be gouged and gorged to death by the futility of an eternally empty hallway. Hers was a truly hopeless life, for her hope was embedded in something that would never come. He would never walk down that hallway, and he would never peer through the thick Plexiglas windows. Simply, he was not coming ... ever.

## SATURDAY

The terrific void between "what was" and the hope that "what was" might be restored was overwhelming. Both were encased in the unknown of a future that might yield neither. That void was accentuated by the sense that nothing may come, that the results of the painful events of the past may very well be what lay ahead. The "in-between" is that place between "what was" and "what is to come." What's gone is gone, and what's to be hasn't arrived yet, leaving the "in-between" a place of limbo. It's a place of sheer anticipation rendered stalled in suspended animation.

The disciples had experienced profound pain, loss, and personal devastation with no sign or hopeful indication of restoration anywhere in sight. Jesus was dead and buried. It was a reality that was clear and yet unbelievable all at the same disorienting time. It was indeed a point in life where desperation seeped through the crevices of their hearts, saturated their souls, swept over their minds, and suffocated their spirits, like Emily.

It was Saturday, though they hardly noticed it, or maybe didn't notice it at all. The news had swept Jerusalem in a tidal wave of emotions that ranged from jubilation to devastation. The dam had burst on this supposed Messiah. The disciples had thought it unthinkable that such a thing could happen. A sense of protection had surrounded Jesus, so strong that He had seemed invincible. This unimaginable saga of a dreamlike adventure with the Messiah had a sense of eternity woven throughout it. No one ever doubted it, so when eternity fell short, the disciples fell apart.

A week earlier, the crowds had jubilantly heralded Him a conquering King, swirling around Him in a frenzy of disappointed and delayed messianic prophecy with Jesus riding into Jerusalem in a blur of palm branches and praise. There was indeed an air of impregnability about it all. "The world has gone after him" (John 12:19) was an apt, albeit temporary observation of the very ones who would soon find envy the foodstuff of murder and who would turn that same world against Him in the satisfying of that appetite. There would be a collision on a cross that would leave the Son of Man dead.

A certain headiness had prevailed among Jesus' followers. A dozen simple Galileans had been swept up in something monumental, the likes of which they'd never seen and never anticipated being a part of. It was the greatest rush possible—until it came crashing down right at the very moment that kingship appeared consummated beyond rebuff. Suddenly and inexplicably, it fell with the thunder of heaven and the shaking of a shifting cosmos.

A rush of impossible events would follow, somehow linking themselves together in a torrid race of wrenching and contrary emotions from Gethsemane to the cross and then to a borrowed tomb. The legalistic waters of religiosity and the territorial currents of politics had converged in a turbulent headwater on a barren hilltop. Flesh was shredded, blood was spattered, hate was seething, and spikes were driven. Jesus fell to it all, drawing a final breath—as impossible and implausible as it seemed—and then was sealed in a tomb. That had been yesterday. And now, it was Saturday.

The reality had yet to sink in. Until it did, emotional paralysis dictated confusion, disorientation, and fear that fed and fueled even more paralysis. It was one of those places in life where everything upon which one has staked his life collapses, or so it seemed. Yet, nothing had really fallen, for what appears to collapse in our lives is little more than God making a hole of hopelessly impossible proportions so that the infinite God has enough elbow room to work a miracle. That's the stuff of God.

Scripture does not recount any events on the day between Jesus' death and His resurrection; the handful of wrenching hours sandwiched between the two greatest events in history. Lost in the magnitude of them, John lived that day, as did the other disciples, the women, the secret followers, and God Himself.

Those grueling hours were that space between the known of events past and the unknown of future events yet to occur, the abyss of uncertainty where written history has yet to be balanced by that which is yet to be written. It was likely a time of not knowing if events were indeed an end in and of themselves or if they were a portent of something to come. The paralysis of that "yesterday" had left no room for any hopeful speculation about tomorrow, as trauma affords nothing other than the trauma. Either way, when a life is in pain and turmoil, the unknown can be devastating. Such was Saturday.

We don't know where John and the others fled. The issue in fleeing is not the destination as much as it is the creating of distance between oneself and that from which one flees. Panic and fear too often combine to result in flight away from what has elicited the panic and fear. But whatever the place they fled to, it was behind locked doors. Events on that first Easter morning would suggest that they were assembled together at known locations, having stumbled into something with some familiarity when everything about them turned terribly unfamiliar. They apparently had not scattered or left the city.

It's likely that the disciples found hiding places, assuming that one crucifixion might stir appetites for more. Waiting for the feeding frenzy to wane sufficiently in order to slip out of the city, they likely contemplated a return to previous occupations as the blur of events left no room to contemplate anything other than that which they knew. The combined force of the events effectively sent them backward instead of forward, picking up old lives where they had left off since the path with Jesus had apparently terminated and trailed off at an empty tomb. In the turmoil of it all, they did not recognize that God's beginnings are so massive that they can look convincingly like endings.

These three years of life and travel and astonishment with Jesus had been relegated to a diversion, a dream, and a wild hope murdered in a chilling compilation of beatings, jagged gashes, torn cartilage, mangled tissue, and blood. Blood had been everywhere: across His body, tracing thin rivets down rough-hewn timbers, splattering across the ground and across John's soul. A tornado of emotions had whipped a gory vortex across his life, both decimating and pulverizing three years with Jesus in a bloody instant. It raged in a funnel cloud that spun his mind in an unabated torrent, exchanging obedience to Jesus for obedience to fear.

And so, John sat hunkered down somewhere in Jerusalem with the celebration of Passover filling and flooding the streets, not knowing what to do or what to think other than somehow try to do or think. He was abjectly mired in the dark of a lost soul that occurs when a friend dies who should not have died. No ... a friend was murdered. And it's Saturday.

### THE EMPTINESS OF MY SATURDAY

Right now, it's Saturday for me. Another, far different Saturday than that experienced by John holed up somewhere in Jerusalem, or Emily in a psychiatric hospital, but the destructive and damaging events of the past are resonating within my mind. Mine is an emotional death, possibly the death of much more, but I am not entirely sure because for me, at this moment, this is Saturday. I'm in between what was and what is yet to be, living squarely between a death of sorts and the unknown of the "what next?" It is my Saturday. If the "yet to be" is nothing more than what is transpiring right now, my future will be shrouded in the thick cold of bitter hopelessness. If it shifts ever so slightly, my future may be colored by the dark hues of personal devastation. A shift in a slightly different direction, and there may be jubilation.

But I don't know, for this is my Saturday, that "in-between" in which I have no alternative than to trust. I can feign control and attempt to alter circumstances toward a favorable outcome. I can go backwards and park my life in the last place where I felt safe and forfeit growth as a trade-off for comfort. I can attempt to deny it all and wash my mind and my heart clear in the sudsy rationalization that it never happened in the first place. But in my Saturdays, control is an illusion only, and I, like John, can only sit and hope. But, hope for what?

Life is full of in-betweens. The problem is that we forget that the in-betweens are transitions and that transitions were not meant to be the places within which we live. Aldous Huxley wrote, "There are things known and there are things unknown, and in between are the doors of perception." The in-between is simply a door to the next place. Transitions are not places that we should fear. Transitions are doors to brighter places that we simply can't see while we're passing through the door.

## SUNDAY . . . THE DAY AFTER

The sun had thrown only the first slight rays of light over the crest of the eastern horizon. Twilight is that time that really isn't night any longer, but it's not yet morning; it's that "in-between."

Mary had risen in the last blackness of the night, living the in-between of her own soul and of the day at the same disorienting time. Awakening early, she wound her way through darkened streets, out the northwest gate, past the hill as fresh with memories as the blood that lay spattered on the ground. She was driven by the passion to provide her Lord the semblance of a proper burial to offset, in some small way, the horrific degradation of Friday and the deep dark of yesterday. If this were to be an end, she would make it an honorable one, bringing the best of her humanity together with whatever shred of faith had survived yesterday. She was walking through a still garden with that bit of humanity and faith symbolically wrapped in a bundle of cloth and spices. It was her offering for her Lord. She would not allow yesterday to be an end, at least not for her, not yet. And because this was the cry of her heart, she would be the first to see the inexplicable beginning rise from an impossible ending.

She felt her way down wandering paths through the dew-laden garden. The silence of the crisp morning seemed to mimic the forever silence of death. Her feet crunched as lone footsteps on the hard-packed gravel. She remembered the tomb's location, having followed Joseph and Nicodemus there two days ago. Rapid steps were marked with pensiveness as she stumbled, caught herself, and regained her balance. Seeing His body would be fraught with terrible contradictions for her. She desperately desired to see Him once more, but seeing the corpse would only confirm the horrendous reality of His death. Seeing His body would cruelly validate that the memories she had come to vest her hope in were but a figment of her own imagination. Encountering God is always safe, but it always comes with great risk.

But, something was different. Something was wrong and out of place. She turned a corner that was ever so slightly illuminated in the thinness of that first early light. Pausing, she turned her head slightly, squinted, and stepped closer. The solemn stone, had it been moved or was the retreating darkness simply attempting to deceive her one final time before the light banished it? The morning light was slight but sufficiently revealing. She drew closer, looked deep, and confirmed that the stone had been moved, leaving the exposed entrance bared dark against morning's ascending light. Her natural assumption screamed through an already destitute soul ... the body had been stolen!

She was suddenly panicked and doubly grieved. They killed Jesus, and now they'd stolen Him as well! In a rush of contradictory and confusing emotions, she ran madly to Peter and John, the chaos and pain of Saturday now seemingly minor compared to this cold thievery. Chaos seized her mind, highjacked her heart, and drove her through a torrent of tears that blurred streets and ran down flushed cheeks. A wild flight traced a stumbling course through the sleepy corridors and dozing alleys, each stride punctuated by gasps for breath. Peter and John responded in kind, and a foot race back to the tomb ensued. Those who had roused early along the streets were puzzled by the

John arrived first, entirely out of breath. Taking in the situation rather than rushing into it, he stepped up to the entrance, bent over slightly, and peered in. Trauma rebelled against more traumas; the mind instinctively protects itself from more pain, and so he was pensive to believe that his Lord was raised because there was great risk in finding it not to be so. The brash and bold demeanor of Peter found full expression as he arrived and ran into the tomb without pause or hesitation. Indeed, there was no body, but here, life turned on one of those rare moments when we put ourselves before what appears lost and we allow ourselves to believe against all belief that God is not finished with what appears to be finished. Our fallen humanity screams that there is tremendous risk in believing such things, as disappointment is likely certain. In reality, believing in God incurs no risk despite the panicked screaming that fills our heads and our hearts.

The grave clothes had lain folded as if the use for which they were intended was of no value any longer and their purpose concluded. With their purpose finished, something eternal had been completed. There was a torrential contradiction in it all, as death is irrevocably permanent ... so are the grave clothes. But here, all of that had been temporary, everything had been reversed, their purpose now concluded when there was supposed to be no conclusion to their purpose. They were folded and put away, now relegated forever to the stuff of history.

History presumes a future; otherwise, history is nothing more than an endless present. In this tomb, what was presumed as an end was not. Something entirely contrary to the natural order had transpired in the damp confines of the tomb, and it could not have happened without Saturday. Saturday was not an end despite the completely convincing nature of the tomb. Saturday was not an end at all. Rather, it was simply the "in-between" within which that which was to be next was preparing itself to be. That afternoon, Jesus would appear to them. Indeed, Saturday was over.

### GOD HOLDS SUNDAY

And that's how I try to live: not knowing what Sunday will hold, but knowing that God holds Sunday. The fact that He holds Sunday assures its existence, and I can look forward to it from the dark confines of my Saturdays. If Sunday exists, it will come. What was dead and lost to me can be restored. Whether that will occur soon, in the distant future, or possibly in the life yet to come, I don't know. But the "not knowing" of Saturday builds the faith necessary for guaranteed "not yet" of Sunday to happen. A remarkable turn of events will mark the end of my Saturday and the beginning of a brand new day. And it is that hope that makes my Saturday bearable. That hope can even make the darkness and pain of my Saturday exciting, knowing that with God, Saturday is only a causeway to Sunday. Sunday is always and only a sunrise away.

### GOOD NIGHT, EMILY

Turning, I switched off the light in Emily's room and glanced back one final time. He's never coming, and she's desperate for him to come. She has shaped her entire life around that single hope, and she made it her sole reason for living, drawing from this single hope a thin thread that gives her a reason to live in a reasonless life. But he's not coming—ever.

And so it is with so much of the world out there and the world that we each have inside of us. Hopelessness pervades and consumes so many lives like Emily's. But this sole hope we have: the assuredness that Jesus is coming back and that He will boldly stride down the long hallways of our lives. He will peer through the thick glass rendered foggy by hands that have constantly pressed against it, He will throw wide the door and embrace us with an eternal embrace that exceeds everything we hoped for—everything we dreamt that moment would be. He is coming, and Saturday will be over.

## PONDERING POINT

How hopeless is your life? Often, lives are often dark, cold, foreboding, and devastating. And we wait for something that will never come, that will never be, that will never show up. We know it, but it's simply too painful to admit it, so we wait because not waiting admits to our soul that our hope will never arrive. But Jesus will come. He promises that "surely I will be with you always, to the very end of the age" (Matthew 28:20). And for the future, we have the assurance that "this same Jesus, who has been taken from you into heaven, will come back in the same way you have seen him go into heaven" (Acts 1:11). He will come at every point, in every place, at every time.

## A THOUGHT

- For what am I waiting?
- What have I pinned my hopes on?
- How desperate is my attachment to it?
- Do I live knowing that only Jesus Christ is the one sure thing that I can count on?

CHAPTER 18

# SNOWSCAPES OF THE HEART
## Looking Ahead by Not Looking Behind

*Jesus replied, "No one who puts a hand to the plow and looks back is fit for service in the kingdom of God."*

Luke 9:62

*"You must live in the present, launch yourself on every wave, find your eternity in each moment."*

~ Henry David Thoreau

**THE PHONE ON MY DESK** rang as it does many times each day. I haphazardly reached for it, fumbled the receiver, and then picked it up. Habitually, I recited my customary greeting. Sometimes we live life out of rote memory, which causes us to live a life of rote routine. It would seem that such routine really makes life bereft of anything that even approximates living. So I answered the phone much as I answer many things in life: in a mechanical manner.

On the other end, over a thousand miles away, death leapt into the receiver. Suddenly, my rote and mechanical way of navigating life fell apart. Death's gray fingers, frigid and experienced from the innumerable lives they have seized, thrust themselves through the miles of phone line. Pain is not bound by distance. It's not rendered less or somehow diminished the farther that we are away from it. Leaping out of the receiver in my hand, death's gray fingers drew down into a clenched fist that rammed all of its accumulated force into my heart. The distance vanished to nothing, and the arm holding the phone went limp.

I have emulated my father. As I grew and faced the complex realities of life, I would model his response to those realities as I had watched him face them. He had always performed with a deft air of grace and ease, handling life as if it were feather light. He had a natural tact about him that would allow him to navigate any situation to a solution, despite how impossible a solution might seemed to have been. It was only when I grappled with those same realities and was more than once sent reeling by the intensity of their strength did I realize how admirable my father's performance had been. How naive I had been to the steeled strength of the inner man that gave Dad the ability to be velvety soft on the outside and yet to forfeit absolutely nothing in life because of the underlying strength he possessed. I had no idea.

Death, however, was laying claim to this remarkable man. Something like an advancing army, cancer had stormed the shores of his body. A formidable beachhead had been established, and an advancing front followed a predictable yet deadly strategy. Stark x-rays bluntly mapped out the invasion. Reams of test results analyzed the onslaught. Medical jargon sterilized death. The line of demarcation between life and eternity was abruptly erased, suddenly redrawing it nearly at his feet. Slipping into an emotional abyss, the phone dropped to my desk, and my heart dropped somewhere outside of my body. I slid down in my chair, stared out the window into the fiery reds and pungent oranges of a brisk fall day, and recognized that winter was coming, and coming quickly.

As with all the other battles that have unleashed themselves against him, Dad faced the news with grace and ease. With the trembling receiver lifted back to my ear and with the hands of death now choking my heart, the grace and ease that he so easily exhibited eluded me. Once again, his remarkable strength was evident even in death. Did he not understand the intent of the enemy or the ground already seized? Could he not see that the first snowfall of his life was likely but a breath away? Had he taken refuge in the dullness of denial? I hung up the phone and cried.

That evening, I ascended the front porch of my home. Each step was weighed by a heavy heart to the point that I wondered if I could ascend the steps at all. Reaching for the door, I glanced over to notice my old sled leaning in one far corner of the front porch, patiently awaiting winter's first snowfall. Its wood was worn. Its steel frame and sturdy runners were coated with a scattered layer of rust. Its aged rope hung eagerly anticipating the tug that would allow it to draw the sled back up some hill for another wild run. I turned, looked, stepped over to the old sled, and gently ran my fingers down its frame, and in the emotional collision that followed, I fell into memory.

Suddenly, I fell into a storehouse of memories embedded in its wood and metal frame. A horde of memories surged from over the hidden horizon of my mind and instantly overwhelmed me in a warm and wonderful blitzkrieg. An army of recollections stormed the beaches of my heart. They were a liberating army, every one of them a commited comrade. The memories seemed to sweep me off the porch and transport me back in time to a very different and very wonderful winter.

Suddenly, I was there. The decades had melted as if they had never been. My father and I were careening down snow-covered hills, soaring on numerous occasions and landing in places other than where the sled landed. We collided into trees that didn't move, and people that did, accumulating a lengthy list of assorted victims that included bushes, rabbits, other sleds and, on one occasion, my father's '65 Dodge. Wild rides abruptly terminated in ditches or snow banks at the base of innumerable hills. Lying prone, laughing as we dug impacted snow out of our coats and pants, we would look up and recount in precise detail the errant path down the snowy hillside that told of our kamikaze-style ride. Soon, we were heading back to the top to do it all over again, repeating the wonderful cycle all day long.

Hot chocolate was dispensed steaming from the old camping thermos that was covered with assorted dents, each one attesting to a part of that thermos' journey. Mom had prepared everything perfectly before we had set out from home on our snowy adventure. Cold hands clutched warm, frothy cups that steamed against the frigid winter chill. It felt like Mom's warm kiss on a cold day. After quickly downing the thick, chocolaty sweetness, we would hit the hill again and again … and again.

Finally exhausted, with the sun drawing down on a frozen western horizon dense with naked trees, the chill in the air would turn razor sharp. Dad would warm up the old Dodge, knock the accumulated snow off the sled, throw it in the trunk, and say, "Let's go eat!" And off we'd go, rambling into the twilight of a deep winter's day to a home-cooked meal whose delicious aroma would warmly greet us at the door.

Falling into mounds of thick blankets at bedtime, my young mind would again recount every wild and errant ride down those hills until exhaustion would claim me and lull me off to sleep. A tired body and a heart rich with warm memories makes for deep sleep. And so I would drift off to sleep, a young boy having run down the snowscapes of life.

## THE FINAL HILL

This particular hilltop called Golgotha was not a place for snow sport. What was to culminate on this hilltop was shockingly unexpected. It was not something that had been contemplated as a possible outcome of everything they'd experienced. Where they were on that hill didn't correlate with where they had been for three years before it. Jesus wasn't supposed to die. He was supposed to be the revolutionary God out about the revolutionary business of restoring mankind for eternity. A crucifixion on an abandoned hilltop didn't match that agenda in the least.

Sometimes life is so glorious and impossibly wonderful that the nature of it all excludes an end. It seems that some things were just not meant to end, as that would suggest a cruelty far too horrible to embrace. Something about whatever it is that's transpiring should, by the virtue of its sheer wonder and goodness, go on indefinitely in order that the world might have the chance to romp in it forever and that others have ample opportunity to join in the romping. The decadence and darkness of the world is such that beauty and wonder seem only able to offset the darkness effectively if they are given permission to exist constantly and without end. But, life doesn't work that way.

Joseph of Arimathea's own journey taught him all of that. His religious and political prominence had not skewed a greater sense of life. Neither had it narrowed him down to a rigid piousness that saw only self-serving agendas and messianic proclamations that could be manipulated to one's favor politically or personally. His heart remained supple, and his eyes stayed untainted. He saw in this Jesus something authentic that made any risk to retrieve His body as entirely worth the risk. He had opposed putting Jesus to death and had risked much in taking that stance. But his efforts had failed, and a cross had prevailed. After the chaotic rush of humanity bent on inhumanity, all that was left was a lifeless corpse that Joseph felt compelled to provide a proper burial.

He pulled himself out of the delirium of a lost Messiah and the hopes that had tragically imploded at His death. Drawing himself up, he headed to the intimidating specter of the Antonia towers, the central ruling place of Pilate. Here, Rome had its imperial heel firmly planted in the very heart of the Jewish nation. Rome held nothing but disgust for the Jews, so it ruled them with an iron fist forged from the steel of disgust. An encounter would not be a welcomed one.

Stepping through the ornate colonnades of marble, Joseph moved deeper into the lair of the very people who participated in the carnage he wished to take down from the cross and bury. In such fashion, he went to Pilate in full societal view and requested the brutalized remnants of a dead man.

Oddly enough, it was easier than he presumed. His request to take down the body and bury it was granted. Perhaps Pilate's affable nature was a result of the fact that he was dealing with some irksome element of grief or guilt, having found himself forced into an act of carnage that somehow touched him. Maybe he simply wanted it over, with the body permanently sealed in the ground and all the political and religious rumblings sealed there as well. Maybe he wanted it all effectively shushed so that word of it all would die right there and not find some filtered route to Caesar, whose response would likely be irksome and potentially damaging for Pilate.

Proper protocol was followed as Pilate set out to confirm the death of this self-proclaimed Messiah before handing over the body. There was no sense in creating further turmoil by burying someone who wasn't actually dead. The macabre charade had engulfed the city and had embroiled the religious and political community to the point that the sentence had to be carried out to its grisly conclusion. The death was confirmed, the grisly conclusion had been achieved, the variant parties across the city were now settling in morbid satisfaction, and the request was granted. The empire moved on with other matters and effectively categorized this event as concluded. With permission in hand, Joseph quickened his stride and set out for a hilltop.

The things that are bad in life should be temporal, it seems. That which is bad dogs the steps of the good and at times seems to exist for the sole purpose of thwarting that which is pure and wholesome. "Bad" and "evil" seem to rest on the existence of the good and find their existence and their identity as based in being the nemesis of "good." They would seem to cease to exist at any time that good ceases to exist. Oddly, the very thing "bad" and "evil" seeks to destroy is the very thing that gives them reason for living.

"Good," however, has something timeless about it, something rooted deep in the core of the created order that gives it an immovable centrality. It is so because it originates and rests in the heart of God Himself. It roiled around in Joseph's head as an attempt to reconcile that which could not be reconciled—that good would prevail because it could do nothing less.

The seeds of these ideas spun in the heads of the disciples as well. Their confluence began in a death that was barely hours old. This assorted band of followers was sequestered in undisclosed locations of a city in celebration; the bond of their relationships forged over three years was groaning, tearing, yet at other times bringing comfort. The object of their devotion, the person whose life they cast everything away for and gave everything to, lay cold on a vertical beam on a hilltop. It ended where there was supposed to be no end.

Theirs was a mix of wild confusion jaded with blistering fear. Out of the traumatic details and events of that last day, little could be processed or teased out to make sense of the experience that terminated on that hilltop. Disorientation reigned supreme with little ability to intellectually climb out of the bottomless pit into which they had fallen. It was all paralysis. There was nothing else. They remained hidden and sequestered away while Joseph chose to expose himself right in front of Rome itself.

In the sordid mix of emotions and events, what was it like to take the body down? I wonder. The endeavor is impaled with great risk and thick with the pillaging disappointment that spins confusion about how everything was supposed to work. It involved stepping up to claim the cold remains of a vanquished Messiah in full view of the adversaries who had created an embittered union to remove Him. Each of those parties now sat in the solace of their separated palatial surroundings, digesting the effects of it all quite differently. Theirs was an air of pompous success, having rid the world of a fraudulent Messiah and having caused the mighty Roman Empire to bow in their demands to carry out the deed. The remnants of their shared venture still hung vertical on rugged beams, pasty with death and cold with pallor on a barren hilltop. It was over.

Joseph could not let it end this way. His was a mixture of allegiance and integrity that drew him to Pilate and then the hill. The death somehow had to be formalized so that it became real. Sometimes things have to be done so that the reality of the loss is verified. The body had to come down. It was the only right and respectable thing to do, and it forced the reality of the death into minds shrouded in denial.

And so, it was up the hill with wraps, spices, and all the dread of loss and feared retaliation of going up the hill in the first place. Then it was down the hill carrying all of that in addition to a limp body drained of all the promise that it once held. The blur spun through a disoriented heart and a traumatized mind, rendering the situation as something abjectly surreal, a script of horror in which Joseph unwillingly found himself. It was a weighty task, physically and emotionally. But Jesus' body had to come down from the hill one final time.

There was no thought, not a hint at all in the minds of any of those who ascended that hill that day and descended with Jesus' body that this was not the end. Reality and life experience as lived by hundreds of prior generations would provide ample evidence that this was the end. People who died had a tendency to stay dead. Getting the body from the hill was exactly about that. It was done to provide a proper end, a worthy end, and an end in keeping with who Jesus was. No one carried the body down to prepare it for a resurrection. No one wanted to spruce it up in order to prepare it for being alive again.

T. E. Lawrence wrote, "All men dream, but not equally. Those who dream by night in the dusty recesses of their minds, wake in the day to find that it was vanity: but the dreamers of the day are dangerous men, for they may act on their dreams with open eyes, to make them possible." Joseph and the others had fallen to the cursed constrictions of their own humanity and had awakened to find their dreams vanity. Subsequently, Jesus was carried down to be prepared for being entombed. Everyone had affixed a "period" on this last sentence of Jesus' life.

### A Hill Beaten

While Scripture doesn't recount it, I wonder if Jesus took time to stop and look at Golgotha after His resurrection, to let His eyes run across its rocky incline, its sharp edges, its wind-whipped summit, and its thinly sparse vegetation. It would seem quite plausible, and it would appear more than completely appropriate to stand entirely alive and gaze upon the hill where He was at one point entirely dead. There's something majestically circular about that kind of experience, where the divine does what simple humanity milling about it cannot comprehend. Yet even though simple humanity cannot comprehend it, by virtue of the cross, we can now fully participate in it.

Whether He took time to ponder that hill is unknown. Such kind of wonderment is left for a potentially inspiring kind of speculation. Yet, while He was carried away from Golgotha at one point, two days later He walked away from it without anyone coming to get Him. It did not end at that hill. That hill was nothing more than the place from which a chain of events was set in motion that would culminate in a resurrected Lord who by virtue of that very resurrection would grant us access to every hill in the endlessness of eternity of hills. His resurrection was a collision that resulted in the death of death and access to hills uncountable.

We don't die on hills. A last trip down any hill in our lives is not the last trip. In fact, in the expanse of eternity, any trip down any hill will be always be followed by another hill. That privilege of which we are entirely undeserving happened on one hill, which opened up all the hills of all of eternity.

## My Hill

The front porch and the sled ... I snapped back. The memories dissipated like an ascending vapor in a sympathetic breeze. I drew into the moment, and my head cleared. Staring at that old sled, I thought back over the many paths that my father and I have made down the numerous hills of life. They were wonderful paths full of fun, laughter, a dash of craziness, and a godly father.

Standing motionless, my eyes again welled with tears as I realized that it was a path whose completion was close at hand. The trips to the top were nearly over. The wild rides, the legacy of memory, and the greater legacy of life would remain as tracks in the snow, but they were over. With the frightening reality pounding my heart I wiped the glistening lines from my cheeks and attempted to suppress the lump in my throat.

And then I realized that because Jesus died on a hill but walked out of tomb, Dad would do the same. By His act, the hills of eternity await; in fact, they beckon. Cancer may take Dad's body, but it cannot take him. Out there in the expanse of eternity, there are an infinite number of hills to be ridden, innumerable hills rising up in the untarnished landscape of eternity. There will be an infinite amount of time to sled down each one, to create memories that will far exceed those made in this life.

Death on one hill granted me the possibility and hope of innumerable memories on a sea of hills in another place.

It is out on the hills of eternity, if we can imagine them, that I will come to know my father in a manner so perfect and so comprehensive that it will be as if I had never known him at all. The sum of this life's memories are but the barest precursor that gives me only the faintest hint of what life with Dad will hold there. Khalil Gibran wrote, "Yesterday is but today's memory, and tomorrow is today's dream." Such a thought frames death, it gives meaning to life as that preparatory moment in the breadth of eternity, and it implants impeccable hope. Hope in the face of phone calls and hills.

I laid both hands on the timeworn frame of the old sled, drew a staggered breath, and said, "Thanks, Dad." Turning, I paused and uttered, "Thank you, God." Wiping away several final tears, I turned and opened the door, fully confident that Christ's work on one hill insures the preservation of all hills for all of eternity.

### **Pondering Point**

We often frame our concept of life solely on the temporal nature that we observe in this life, adopting a myopic sense of finality in lieu of a boundless sense of eternity. We errantly assume that all of existence is marked by a fixed end point at which loss is irreparable. We embrace such an end because we cannot see beyond it. Our inability to see the eternal evidences render us numb to the realities. We succumb to the finite because we cannot grasp the magnitude of the infinite.

And so, loss becomes permanent. The permanence is devastating. It's devastating because life was not meant to be lived with the richness of living and then be utterly lost, rendering the living implausible and meaningless because, despite all of its potentiality, it will vanish. Life was meant to be cultivated here and then transferred to a place where it is forever celebrated and savored in all its beauty. Death, then, is not loss but a step into the fullest manifestation of living. Death is simply a step to an existence shared forever on the innumerable hills of eternity.

## A Thought
- Do I live with dusty dreams that end in vanity and death?
- Do I live with an eye on eternity, conceptualizing this life as a precursor to an existence where this life is fully and perfectly manifest?
- And if I do not, do I then strip this life of the wonder and anticipation that makes living everything that living can be?
- Am I willing to live more broadly than I could ever have imagined by living out the reality that life extends beyond any horizon I could imagine?

CHAPTER 19

# THE NEW ERA
## Impossible New Beginnings

*"The days are coming," declares the LORD, "when the reaper will be overtaken by the plowman and the planter by the one treading grapes. New wine will drip from the mountains and flow from all the hills ..."*

Amos 9:13

*"Nobody can go back and start a new beginning, but anyone can start today and make a new ending."*

~ Maria Robinson

**NEW YEAR'S DAY: THE FIRST** sunrise of the New Year had barely begun to stir the darkness and nudge the night off the pages of this new day. It arrived pensively, graced with a wisp of pastel pink in a thin wash on the eastern horizon. Barely discernible to the eye, it reflectively traced distant hills hereto hidden by the thick cloak of the night. Tentatively set against the black of the receding night, the morning gently pressed a warming shoulder into the dark, prodding it westward. Slowly ascending the backside of the eastern skyline, it peered over the horizon's crest in a mixed anticipation of what this

New Year might have brought. The air was cold and breathlessly still. The stars were silent, watching from their orbits far aloft. Nature was holding its breath.

The sun, gentle but steady, slightly widened the thin wash of pastel pink and edged it with splashes of powdery peach, mauves, and pools of soft gold. Oaks and maples, silhouetted as silent sentries, submitted to the greater miracle of the earth turning its face into the sun. Darkness still prevailed but found itself being rubbed warm into ever lighter hues of sky blue as the earth rolled over into another day.

The lone sound of my footsteps on loose gravel was free from the inhibitions and competition of other sounds that might have diminished it. Somehow, there was a sacredness that embellished the entire morning, a near holy sacredness that I was permitted to immerse myself in and wander through. T. S. Elliot said that "what we call the beginning is often the end. And to make an end is to make a beginning. The end is where we start from." The end of the old year made for the beginning of the new and all that was tightly packaged and deliberately imported within it.

Sure, my mind was heady with what the New Year might bring, but there was something among the trees and woven through the pastels of that morning that called in entirely hushed tones that something hallowed was afoot. The leash tugged, and the dog and I ventured out into the first light of this New Year. They were fresh steps taken into a new era.

We tend to anticipate new eras as opportunities for something new. We lavish upon them a sense that new years, new experiences, and new opportunities of whatever sort hold something for us within them that wasn't there before. There's some hesitantly hopeful intuitive inclination that suggests that something is available to us or open to us that didn't exist before. Somehow, we're not bound to the suffocating limits or the tight perimeters that hedged opportunity out and locked us in. We feel that it's a new day because life has availed us of new resources, expanded options, and a fresh shot at living.

So we tend to anticipate new eras for what we perceive they bring. We hunger to have new opportunities imported in and old barriers pushed out. We passionately long to believe that the circles we run in and the well-worn paths that we trod day in and day out are not the sum total of life. We yearn with a deep groaning to believe that there's more to whatever's in the cramped and scantly sparse box we're living in. We want to believe that we've not yet "arrived." We're desperate to believe that there are a staggering host of unseen possibilities out there that allow us to arrive, knowing that arriving in one place does nothing but set us up to arrive in another place after that. New eras present us with the feeling that maybe there is more and maybe, whatever that more is, it's actually accessible to us.

### A New Era

Scripture does not recount Jesus walking out of the tomb, or those moments just before that event when He sat in the hollow of the tomb shaking off death and taking in life. Recounting that most momentous event appears to be an obvious omission in Scripture that in all likelihood was wholly intended as an omission. That moment has been left for speculation, possibly being too sacred even for Scripture itself. It was the final outcome of God colliding with mankind through Jesus in a manner that turned history on its head and handed mankind the expanse of eternity.

Maybe it was a moment exclusively for Jesus, that moment that He had anticipated from eternity past that only He could see through to an eternal conclusion that morning in that cave. Maybe it was not to be intruded upon. Possibly, it was left for simple wonderment with the clandestine mystery of the moment stirring speculation in those who would ponder it for countless centuries to come. Nonetheless, I can't help but wonder what that moment was like.

Curiously, God's plan played itself out in a cycle of gardens, which may indicate His passion for beauty and His commitment to ever-renewing growth. The plan of Jesus' death and resurrection had been intricately mapped out in eternity past. It was proclaimed in a perfect garden that fell when man's disobedience was seduced into action by a serpent's deception. It was a toxic alchemy that would rock and pummel the entire story of mankind. The final implementation of the plan was delivered with deep grief intermixed with an incarnate angst in yet another garden on the Mount of Olives that sat on the other side of the city. And now, it was completed forever in this garden where this tomb lay embraced.

The satanic rebellion had now been quelled on the cross with the din of battle having rolled into the annals of history and proclaimed eternally as God's victory. It had been terrifically horrific but entirely divine all at once. The cross represented the most sadistic means of execution ever devised by man, with the Son of God carrying out the most spectacular redemptive work of all of creation on it. The cross had been engulfed by the wildly spiraling insanity of jealously, the heady power-mongering of political intrigue, the gathered momentum of frenzied crowds, and the blood-lust of those who had abandoned civility for savagery. None of that impeded God's plan in the least. In fact, God bent it all and wove it into the completion of His plan. Despite the evil of those events, the work was perfectly completed.

The peace was now restored. Golgotha had fallen into silence and the horrible events into memory. Several days had passed, serving as a balm that had soothed the city back to some degree of sanity. Angels that had found themselves restrained at the sight of God on a cross were now released to seize the stone at the mount of the tomb. They effortlessly rolled it aside and stepped aside. The final obstacle in this eternal journey was now removed. The tomb was unsealed, and victory was sealed.

With the stone now removed, cool morning air drifted into the tomb, challenging the damp air of death and the proclamation of finality that death had, until this moment, held unchallenged. Death was subjected to an impossible experience that even it could not comprehend, having been diluted and then helplessly dissipated. A whiff of fresh air was caught by Jesus and drawn deeply into His lungs. He held it for a moment in silent triumph, and then exhaled, emptying Himself of air breathed by lungs once dead. It was the first breath since His last breath three days earlier on that cross, and his lungs were now drawing, expanding, and finding their rhythm once again. He was repeating the birth of a Bethlehem manger all over again. The cycle was now completed. He shifted on the cold stone ledge, rotated, and then slowly sat erect. God was arising, creation was sitting on the edge of its seat, and mankind was oblivious.

Slowly his hands reflexively emerged from the deep folds of His funeral wraps. The scent of the burial spices stirred and listed into the air as the wraps were teased, slowly removed, neatly folded, and gently placed on the stone ledge. The calluses of a carpenter were deep and thick, the broad hand of legacy written in callused skin and penetrating wounds. Strong hands that shaped wood, shaped lives, and shaped history by being nailed to wood itself. Hands that drove sickness out of weary bodies, brought light to blind eyes, ran across the gross disfigurement left by leprosy, made palsied legs strong, beckoned a disciple to tread on the waves, and clawed the soil in Gethsemane. They bore the marks of crucifixion, without which this second genesis moment would be impossible.

It was indeed the scars in incarnated flesh that probably drew the deepest reflection. Spikes had been driven with blows weighted by the sins of all mankind—combined, focused, and distilled into each fall of the mallet. The cross had been lifted with every sin of all mankind pressing as gravity of the kind exerted by the deepest black hole, with sin seizing the elevated body in tandem with gravity itself. The grief, horror, hatred, selfishness, abuse, abandonment, thievery, betrayal, loss, and fear of a thousand generations were all pressing down at one terrible moment. Every tear, every incident of abuse, every lie, every murder, every shred of depression, every moment of frustration, all of the shame and desperation and fear sustained by a thousand generations and more were there. Every ounce of it, every drop was running salty, burning fiery like own His sweat into wounds of ripped flesh.

A billion faces flashed before Him. A hundred billion tears came with them. Cries, moans ... the bruised and brutalized voices of the past, those seized in pain at that moment, and those yet to be seized by it. All of them were there. All of them were loved. All of them were being paid for and reckoned as gone. Their pain was now His, the immensity of it all obliterating the pain of torn flesh and spikes. "My God ..." But now, in the tomb, it was decisively declared over, forever.

He drew Himself into a standing position, thoughtfully scanned the rock walls, and then shifted His gaze outside. What transpired in that tomb was the inexplicable new dichotomy of living where death had taken life and interred it but was now forced to surrender it back again. Death, the great and unconquerable thief, now had to relinquish its captive to a life from which that life can never again be stolen. Death's hands were rendered slippery and arthritic, now unable to hold that which it seized, no matter how much it might tighten its grip. Life was now rendered but a step removed from whatever death might do, leaving death robbed of its own finality. A century and a half after Jesus' resurrection, Marcus Aurelius wrote, "It is not death that a man should fear, but he should fear never beginning to live." Mankind could now truly begin to live. And so, Jesus shifted His gaze outside.

A wisp of pastel pink in a thin wash on the eastern horizon greeted the planet rolling itself over into the new day. "It is indeed over," He whispered. "It is finished." He likely drew deep into the moment. "The people walking in darkness have seen a great light; on those living in the land of the shadow of death a light has dawned" (Isaiah 9:2). Indeed, the sunrise on that single morning hailed the dawning of an infinitely larger light, the promise of a dawn, of ever-increasing degrees of light that would dispel the darkness by allowing it no room.

It was perfect. I don't doubt that He uttered a word of profound thanks to His Father, drew into Himself the totality of what that moment meant, and smiled as only God can smile.

The full expanse of history would pivot on His next step. The millions now dead would, in those next steps, see their hopes finally fulfilled. The hope of billions unborn would rest squarely on this moment. Creation had paused before, it had gasped awestruck in the face of God's works many times in the past as He has lived large enough to fling entire galaxies into space, and yet be small enough to comfort crying children and touch grieving widows.

But no moment was like this one. For here and here alone, mankind was redeemed, and a creation living in the desperate agony of bondage was released. It was not about creating as much as it was recreating by releasing the creation. All that was before and all that would follow would draw its life, its sustenance, its hope from this single moment.

Angels waited outside. They were sentries at the first garden with flaming swords once drawn to keep sinful man out of that which man desired to return to after realizing too late the devastation of deception. The angelic sentries were now at a very different garden that would invite man back with God's redemption coming full circle. They had heralded Jesus' birth to shepherds in distant fields with splendor strewn across the night sky. They had knelt at His side after forty days of fasting, and they had restored Him. Only a few days before, with Jesus a lone figure and the disciples asleep, they stood beside Him in the garden, wiping great drops of blood from His brow.

The next day, they had stood on tiptoe, awaiting His command to surge forth and save Him from his own execution. He never summoned them. The spikes were driven, and the cross was raised. The words "my God, why have you forsaken me?" deafened the angels as those words pounded the cosmos and sent a violent tremor through the galleries of heaven. And the whole of the angelic host fell deathly silent as His last shallow breath was drawn and His body went limp. The intensity of their grief darkened the sky and shook the earth itself.

And now, in sentinel formation, they stood outside the tomb in reverent but wild anticipation of this next step. Jesus paused, His mind on the millions past and the billions to come. Creation was frozen and breathless. He drew His cloak around Himself, ran His fingers across the cold stone one final time ... and then He stepped out.

The sun, gentle but steady, slightly widened the thin wash of pastel pink and edged it with powdery peaches, mauves, and pools of soft gold. Oaks and maples were silhouetted as silent sentries. Darkness still prevailed but was being rubbed warm into ever lighter hues of sky blue. The lone sound of His footsteps on loose gravel was free from the inhibitions of other sounds that might have diminished it. The moment pulled Him, and He ventured into the first light of this new era. Heaven erupted in thunderous applause. The angels, lost in this final victory, bowed in deep and victorious reverence, witnesses of the steps across the millennia that culminated in that single step.

Shortly, He would meet the women. They would be the first to know. Already emotionally conflicted by the pronouncement of the angels, they were awaiting in angst. Then there would be the road to Emmaus, traveled incognito. After that, He would be off to Galilee and home. There would be the Sea of Galilee with another great catch of fish just like one three years prior. This time, Jesus would restore Peter over a home-cooked breakfast. What wild fun. Implausible reunions with doubting disciples wrapped in forty days and five hundred encounters. And then He would ascend to His real home at the right hand of His heavenly Father. It had begun.

The cosmos exhaled. Heaven was shaken again, but it was with the exhilaration of victory raised in thunderous applause, not the tremor of defeat. If God cannot defeat death, He cannot be God any place else. The tomb was indeed empty. Death was defeated. It was a new era.

## Embracing the New Era

A golden crescent bares a flaming edge and emerges from the womb of the earth. The sun peaks the expanse of the horizon. The wisp of pastel pink in a thin wash on the eastern horizon has now deluged the sky in a flood of deep peach, mauve, and glistening gold. I turned toward home. The birds begin to stir, energized by the first light, building to a raucous melody of simple joy high in lofty limbs. Squirrels dart about through the loamy leaf litter piled in the underbrush and scamper effortlessly up sturdy limbs. A slight breeze brushes my face. Nature awakens to a new year. It is already promising, ushered onto the stage of eternity as only God could do it, as only Jesus could do it on that day when He ushered in a new era.

## Pondering Point

In the flow of life, we often feel entombed. Constricted and constrained by forces and realities both within and without, we are subject to situations that render life little more than a living death. We sense no escape. We see no door, no point of exit, no way by which we are able to elude the confinement. And here, life closes down, devolving ever further into the abyss of futility. It shackles us with steeled chains of abject hopelessness.

Of our own devices, escape has been futile. Hope has been so disappointed that we refuse to hope. The risk of "hope deferred" (Proverbs 13:12) is too poignant and too painful. Such a realization forces us likewise to embrace our imprisonment. And if it is embraced, life turns intolerable. In all of this, it's realizing that Jesus walked out of a far greater tomb. Every one of our tombs are far inferior to that one. Since He walked out of His tomb, He can likewise walk us out of ours, whatever our tombs might be. And He extends just such an offer to you and to me.

## A Thought

- Have I surrendered to my tomb?
- Have I identified my tomb adequately enough to know what I'm surrendering?
- If I have, am I willing to risk believing one more time that freedom is possible?
- If so, am I willing to ask Jesus to roll away the stone and walk me out into the dawn of a new, exhilarating day?

**CHAPTER 20**

# THE MINER'S HUT
## Hints of Eternity Here and Now

*"He has made everything beautiful in its time. He has also set eternity in the human heart; yet no one can fathom what God has done from beginning to end."*

Ecclesiastes 3:11

*"What nature delivers to us is never stale. Because what nature creates has eternity in it."*

~ Isaac Bashevis Singer

**IT WAS NOT POSSIBLE—OR SO** it seemed. Sometimes things are too staggering to accept as true despite the fact that we can't argue the fact that they're true. At times, events in life draw us out to the barest fringes of our minds, and then they step beyond the fringes. When that happens, we find ourselves in places where reality and fact don't necessarily reconcile what we find there. This was one of those moments.

Granny had always been old, according to the standards of a pimple-faced teenager. The tattered edges of her life and the tattered edges of the photo that she held in her hand attested to the repeated handling of both by the hands of time. Sometimes, the handing was generous and kind. At other times, it was brutal and heartless. But both were tattered at their edges, which seemed to render them comrades of a most remarkable journey.

In black and white, the photo's images were flat both because of the lack of color but more so because the images seemed so rigid and archaic. Time was frozen on the photo's expanse. It was a window to another era, a portal to another time. I looked at it, desperately wishing I could step through it into the scene just as the camera had snapped the picture. I would have loved to walk into it at the very point where the participants relinquished their rigid poses and resumed their work, to have it happen right then with myself being a part of it. It would have been both magical and mysterious to erase the seventy years between the movement of that shutter, the capturing of the image on the film, and the moment within which I stood.

Granny was but twelve years of age when the shutter snapped the picture. Long pigtails draped down over half the length of her petite frame. Her diminutive physique was draped in a long dress wrapped corset-like around her waist and listlessly cascading to the ground. A slight smile betrayed the rigidity of posing for the camera. Her siblings and parents stood round about her in front of a clapboard farmhouse that was already aged by time; its sweeping front porch leaned slightly as if it had attempted to draw itself straight for the photo. Rough-hewn wooden shingles, dried and warped, seemed scattered across the roof. A window was ajar, slightly tilted in its frame. A split rail fence framed a sea of crops beyond. Chickens, having wandered into the photo, seemed not as distractions but as much a part of life as the people posing there. It somehow felt barren.

I glanced up from the picture into the soft, deeply wrinkled face of my grandmother. Furrowed lines etched her history across her brow, chronicling the vast sweep of time between the photo and that moment. Her hair was now washed white with time. The unmistakable musty scent of age proliferated, leaving her bearing the scents of time. Wrinkled hands, palms worn smooth from the decades of labor yet ahead of the girl with the pigtails, trembled slightly and uncontrollably. Abraham Lincoln said, "The best thing about the future is that it comes one day at a time." Indeed, it had. But the days that had brought the future into the present had flown by with unimaginable speed.

Tears drew up in the corners of weakened eyes, seeped through deep crevices, and traced thin lines down her mottled cheeks. "I remember when they took that picture," she mused. "It seems like yesterday." She appeared stunned by the vast gulf of time between that moment and the one that we shared together now. She had lived all of those years in between, yet she couldn't correlate how many had passed and how fast they had flown by.

I could not correlate the face before me with the one in the photo. They were so vastly different that they could not be one and the same. The difference seemed to be incomprehensively too vast to be attributed to the simple passing of time. That kind of change had to be attributed to something more than time. Time's work could not be so powerful as to change someone so completely. Could time indeed be that transforming? Or was it due to something that worked itself out in the conduit of time?

### The Irrepressible Flow of Time

Time. Its march toward the next minute is insatiable. It's always moving toward the next minute, the next hour, the next day, the next decade, and the next century. There is no change in time's cadence. Its pace is always exactly the same. It has no room for detours, no time for momentary respites, no places to pull up and catch its breath, and no tolerance for anything that would attempt to alter or impede it. It is obstinately insistent on a plodding pace that heeds no command, responds to no plea, and is deaf to both the good and bad that transpire within the span of its expanse.

However, its incessant flow is likewise transforming. Time is unable and unwilling to leave this moment the same in the next moment. This thin slice of time that marks the present moment irreversibly cascades into the past in an unstoppable torrent of time. On the front end of time, the future spills into the present through floodgates that are frozen open before cascading by us and flowing into the past.

And so we live in this wild, raging river of time. We cannot dam it. We are incapable of diverting it. The best of our efforts utterly fail at forcing it to pool in some reservoir long enough to savor life a little more fully, to hold the beauty of a moment longer than simply a moment. We are entirely unable to cherish what we have and who we have without watching all of it slip helplessly and haplessly through our fingers.

Yet, time itself creates a generous space within which change can transpire. Without time, there would be no vehicle upon which to hitch a ride and move from one place to the next. There would be no space within which to work out dreams, to fashion futures, and to build things that can ride the river of time far beyond our own lives. Time is the space and place within which our creativity can be exercised in a manner that births great things and creates great opportunities for a future not yet written. Yet, in affording us these privileges, time exacts a price from us. And that price is time itself.

Lost in her own history, my grandmother's trembling fingers softly ran across the black and white image on the faded photograph. She sat cherishing what she had accomplished, but what time had taken in the accomplishing was substantial. Part of her wished she could go back and apply the lessons of time that she had not had when the camera snapped the picture that day—hearken back past Vietnam, cross over the phenomena of the 1950s, and reach back beyond Korea. She wished she could roll back before Pearl Harbor, the Great Depression, and doughboys marching off to face a kaiser in a moonscape of trench warfare. It was before the model T, radio, and the miracle of flight achieved by the Wright brothers on a blustery Carolina beach. She went all the way back to her roots, back to the twelve-year-old girl in the picture.

She sighed, dabbed tear-stained cheeks, and collected herself. Clearing her throat, she laid down the photo, pressed a weathered hand against it one more time, and turned. "I want to show you something," she said. Reaching deep into a chest full of time worn mementos, she pulled out a thin volume. Its binding was frayed. The cover was slightly tattered with a handful of mottled stains. Yet legible on its dappled surface were the words, *The Miner's Hut.*

Carefully, she opened it and gently turned the first few pages. Again, she went back across time. But further, farther back to something immeasurably more powerful than even the photo. Closing the book, she pressed it between her hands and then held it to her chest as one would something indefinably precious. She hugged it as a life-long friend. Suddenly, two trembling hands held it out to me.

"This was my textbook from first grade."

How do you hold something so preciously sacred? How do you handle the past of another when they hand it to you? How do you receive a part of someone that is so much a part of them that you fear they're going to die in the handing over of it? She laid it in my hands. And with it fell the weight of her history.

Leaning back in her chair, she peered at me with soft eyes and said, "I want you to have it." With those words, my emotions collided with a wonderful and yet mysterious past that lay cradled in the palm of my hands. Tears welled up in my eyes. I paused. In disbelief, I gently opened it. On the first page, there were three, simple words. Written in pencil by young hands that were yet unfamiliar with words and a heart groping to learn were the words *cat, rat, mat*. It was the scribbling of a child sitting in a drafty one-room schoolhouse at the end of the nineteenth century, long before the events of the twentieth century had even begun to unfold.

I turned another page and saw the copyright date: 1870. The book marked the era of her father who lived as a Civil War veteran, a pioneer, and farmer scratching a living out of the loamy soils of Virginia and Ohio. My mind then leapt across two generations to that of my great-grandfather. Suddenly, I was something more. I became a part of those who had gone before me, able to borrow the richness of their lives to accentuate my own. The whole moment seemed to create a vehicle where I was carrying them within me, bringing to this generation the foundation they had laid in theirs, as hidden as that foundation had been. It was a gift to carry, a baton to pass along.

As I write this, the book is sitting before me. Calling out to me in silence, I can hear the voices of those gone before echoing across the rifts of time as they rise from its weary pages. Granny died in 1985. She wanted to be buried in the shade of a spreading oak, and so she was. Her gift to me immeasurable, her legacy is immutable and her memory precious. It lives today … right now.

### PERMANENCY

The breeze subtly drew gentle fingers through the folds of Jesus' cloak. A soft cascade of gentle golden rain poured from a generous blue sky. It traced His features and rolled off to inundate a hillside sown in generous greens. Thick grasses waved in unison in a waltz with the tepid breeze. Birds darted in a dance of frenzied flight. The soft drone of lumbering bees lent a gentle hum of satisfaction to it all. Wisps of cottony white clouds charted unknown paths of exploration and exploits across the endless ocean blue sky. Sweet scents of tender grasses and buoyant wildflowers blended in a warm aroma. It was all a tantalizing wisp of heaven slipping over into this world as Jesus did, brushing across their faces while brushing across His.

The eleven disciples stared and exchanged blank glances with each other. Their minds were unable to grasp it, to draw the miracle into their minds and accept it as real. They blinked and stared at Jesus, the eyes of their souls squinting to comprehend what logic would not allow them to understand. They saw Him die. It's one thing to know someone's dead, but it's another to witness that individual's death. There's something utterly convincing in watching death. The journey from life to death was an entirely familiar and wholly expected journey that every generation in existence had experienced right up to the termination of each generation. But doing it in reverse, leaping back across an endless chasm from death to life, that was incomprehensible.

Jesus' eyes and his voice, the mannerisms, the gestures, the lines of each feature that defined His face that were forever gone were now forever back. That bearded smile—so full, so indefinable, and so complete—was back. That glint, the manner of His gait, and the flavor of His voice. The dance of life in His eyes and the smoothness in the way He moved. The authority rendered sweet by His subtle humor and inundating compassion was there. It was all there. But there were additions now. The multiple scars that littered his body as demonstrations of brutality were new. They spoke as a testament to the instruments of death, the journey to death, and the return from death.

Three years of relationship, of a journey that was poignant and painful, precious and profound, had irrevocably terminated on a cross. It was over and settled, having spilt over the precipice of time and having been locked deep into the forever chasm of history. It was a chapter closed with the book sealed—as it was with any death. The disciples had begun to settle into the unwanted and uninvited reality that Jesus was dead and gone. They had begun the arduous process of shifting through reams of emotions and trauma and lost hopes and shattered imaginings and musings of what might had been if none of it had been.

Then, they had pulled together the shattered shards of shattered lives and had begun the process of reconstructing them. The pieces were too many and too broken, leaving any hope of reconstruction likewise shattered. So they let the pieces lie, and they returned to their old lives, believing that in doing so, enough pieces remained back there to rebuild lost lives. When we can't go forward, we often pick up the pieces of the past, because the pieces of the present are now too pulverized to take us anywhere. But now Jesus was back, and the hopelessly shattered pieces were no longer hopelessly shattered.

And then, He spoke the immutable words that surged across that hillside that day; they resonate deeply as I read them and write them. They allow me to reclaim my relationship with Granny and everyone who has gone before. Wonderful words of promise that supersede the river of time by handing me the promise of an eternity that eludes time. Jesus said, "And surely I will be with you always, to the very end of the age" (Matthew 28:20).

Is that not the security that each of us yearns for? The oddity of the toll of time is that relationship feels as if it should be permanent. It should be something that isn't to be lost or to succumb to the defiant river of time. Pain in loss of relationship is, I think, related to the deeply fundamental sense that relationships should not simply be for a time or a moment or even an era. Something essential and deeply central to our core cries out for the rightness of permanence. Relationships should have something of the indefinite about them, something eternal even.

"He has made everything beautiful in its time. He has also set eternity in the hearts of men," says the writer of Ecclesiastes 3:11. Time creates beauty. It shapes, molds, matures, and refines everything based on the infinite reflection from which everything has fallen. Time's extravagant brush paints lavishly beautiful strokes across the canvas of our lives. It adds rich chapters to our volumes. It relentlessly weaves richly colored threads into an ever deepening and widening tapestry. Life is supposed to be a song into which notes and stanzas are constantly penned in an ever deepening composition. Such things are not meant to be achieved and then lost. Gained and then forfeited. Built and then destroyed. Admired and then mourned over as we lose them. There is nothing of the eternal in that.

The grief is found in the wrenching incongruence that what is supposed to go on does not. Benjamin Franklin wrote, "Lost time is never found again." And each of us has lost plenty of it. What should not be lost *is*. What should be lasting is *not*. That which has been painstakingly crafted with the currency of years and sacrificial deposits of pain should be lasting. The costly investments that bleed us of our very lifeblood should construct a rich and promising foundation that holds ever-increasing promise. Yet, these are robbed of that very promise, through their demise, that lifeblood seemingly squandered. We are privileged to build great things only to hand them over to the demise of time. There is something wrong and unjust in it all, something that suggests permanence.

This awful, gnawing reality grinds against something inherently deep within us, something that cries out in the devastation of loss that should not be. Why? From where does that cry come? Why do we build and in the building beg that the eternal give permanence to what we build?

That passion arises from the small kernel of eternity that has been set in the hearts of men. That passion has been dulled by sin and muted by unbelief. Without a doubt, it has been rent and torn by our self-centered wanderings. We would be remiss to think that it has not been suffocated to near death by personal extravagance and arrogant defiance of God. Eternity suggests something that we can't create of our own energies and ingenuity, and too often we're too proud to admit to those limitations. So we briskly deny its existence in order to deny our limitations.

But that passion for permanence is there nonetheless. All of our power and assorted actions cannot kill it. Diminished, it still calls with a pervasive voice that we cannot silence. It still infiltrates our deepest selves and will not allow us to relinquish the eternal even if we think we don't believe in it. And when a relationship ends in death, our inability to reconcile a loss in the face of some right sense of permanence elicits wrenching grief. What is not supposed to be ... is.

"And surely I will be with you always, to the very end of the age" (Matthew 28:20). What sin terminated, Jesus restored, reconciling that sense of permanence. He handed back to us the assurance that what appears to end here will continue on in eternity. So fabulous is life and everything that makes up life that it could not possibly end as the river of time supposedly terminates into the lake of death. In reality, the lake of death is the reservoir of eternity. Life is far too complex and far too expansive to be held in the tiny pool of years that we have. It is profoundly detailed and fundamentally intricate in ways beyond human comprehension and termination. Life screams of the eternal. It shouts it, celebrates it, and reflects it in the depth of the human spirit and the wildness of a cosmos unrestrained by an end. And Jesus promises it in the fundamental relationship we have with Him.

## A Reminder That We Have Just Begun

*The Miner's Hut* is only a reminder. Not simply or solely a reminder of something that allows me to hold onto something I lost in the protesting defiance of the loss. Rather, it is a harbinger of what is yet to come, a reminder that the grave is not a sullen termination as much as the finality of death suggests. It is a declaration of a life lived and a promise of the resumption of that life. It's not a reminder of the past as much as a declaration that life will be fully manifest in a continuing future. *The Miner's Hut* is a recollection of people gone before me and a conviction that they continue in a stream I will eventually join them in. Indeed, *The Miner's Hut* is a reminder that one day Granny will again hold my hand, speak in soft tones, show me the photos, and tell me the stories. And for that, I can't wait.

## Pondering Point

We hold to many evidences and reminders of our past. Treasures and trinkets alike, we possess an array of memories and mementos. In these, we can embrace and celebrate our assorted histories. But we can also view them as a reminder that those lives and those histories will be fully revealed and made perfect in eternity. There, what we hold in our hands will be celebrated with an incomprehensible fullness, being all that they could never have been in this life. And so, as we hold to our past, may we see it as a promise and portent of our future. May we see the future as a glorious continuation of all the wonder and beauty extolled by our histories. May the future stand before us as a flagrant display of all that we've come from and all that time has taken from us now restored and made evident in stunning perfection.

## A Thought

- Am I so tedious about preserving the past and so caught up in the present that I can't see anything beyond either of them?
- How would my understanding of life be different if I saw eternity as the full and perfected manifestation of my past?
- How would I view my life if all that was good in my history was brought to fullness and I was allowed to live in its perfection forever?
- What would it be like if I realized that my past is only a precursor to eternity within which the past will be alive?

CONCLUSION

# A COLORLESS CANVAS
## A Collision of Color

*"And God said, 'Let there be light,' and there was light."*
Genesis 1:3

*"The rays of happiness, like those of light, are colorless when unbroken."*
~ Henry Wadsworth Longfellow

**SHE WAS NINETEEN WHEN THE** doctor clipped the x-ray onto the fluorescent panel in front of her. Even to the untrained eye, it was unmistakable. Like a venomous snake coiling its slithering body around its victim, cancer had wrapped its cold hands around her esophagus and thrust its pointed fingers deep into her lungs. Cancer was laying claim to her life. Her name was Wendy. Sitting in the waiting room only a few feet away, I was about to share in a journey that would affect my own journey forever.

At that moment in that darkened room a few steps away, with the black and misty gray shadows of that x-ray playing back across her face, Wendy's world stopped. Staring into the shades of gray and black, her entire existence imploded, suddenly becoming the sum total of that one muddled gray x-ray that silently screamed the tragic reality. The doctor took down the x-ray, held it for a moment, and walked away.

Months of treatments passed. Nights of wrenching pain when chemotherapy brought convulsions as it coursed through her body with its poison seeking out the cancer. Cold, hard tables upon which she laid as beams of invisible radiation were shot into her body, leaving her without hair and terribly emaciated from its cruel side effects. There were violent tremors and nights of wrenching vomiting. She was engulfed in deep hopelessness and disabling helplessness. The effort to save her became worse than the dying that she sought to avoid. Finally, the efforts of man played themselves out, placing her beyond the technology of men and at the mercy of cancer's cold hands and pointed fingers.

However, God is splendidly unpredictable. In one remarkable moment, He used the ugliness of cancer to birth a vision in her life. In His loving and perfect wisdom, He laid His hand on her dying body—not to heal it, but to place a picture in her mind that would birth a far greater healing. It was not a beautiful picture at all, but for Wendy, it was the perfect picture. It was the image of the x-ray that had cast its gray shadows on her face and her life so many months earlier.

Slowly, she began to see the world in that x-ray. Not the cancer that it revealed so profoundly, but the color. Much like that x-ray, she saw the world as filled with misty grays and blotches of black. The x-ray had no depth, no vibrancy, no brilliant hues. She realized that a world without Christ was veiled with those very same colors. Her life was not something stolen by this disease. It was the disease that showed her how much sin had stolen from the world and how gray it had left the landscape and humankind.

Wendy was an extremely gifted artist. She realized that this artistic gift had been given precisely for this moment. Weak and emaciated, she gathered her brushes, assembled her paints, and pulled her weakening body up to an easel. With one arm rendered useless due to prolonged radiation treatments, she took her good arm and put her brush to the canvas. Each painful stroke was filled with the compulsion to leave her world something of beauty, something that would lift out the brilliant colors that God has placed in her soul and splash them across a canvas for everyone to see.

For those last two months, she painted prolifically. I often sat beside her as she created works of art that had a life to them, that defied the death that was quickly overtaking her. She painted in a prolific mix of rich colors and beautiful tones. I sat and watched her pour into her paintings the very life force that she was losing.

The last painting that she began was never finished. The artist was to succumb to the cold hands of cancer before the piece was completed. It was a serene sketch of two Canadian geese smoothly breaking the mirrored surface of a lake. It was a painting that was full of potential and rich with possibility. However, it will never be finished. The life of the artist from which it sprung was spent before it could be given over to the painting.

### Gray and Flat

We all see many people who are gray and flat. We watch people pathetically going through the motions as if the motions provide the meaning of life. There are so many empty eyes, eyes from which the sparkle of life has long dissipated. There are legions of people who project the gray and flat of their own lives onto everything around them, thereby being able to see only gray and flat. The world is full of people who tragically assume that the gray and the flat is all there

What happens to us? We focus on things of little meaning. Things that look like they have meaning only because our culture says they do. Or things that must possess some shred of meaning because we've built our lives on them, and without them, we have nothing and are nothing. Things that help us understand where we are in relation to others. Things that give us a sense of purpose and meaning that in and of themselves are purposeless and meaningless. In the vastness that is the stuff of eternity, tangible things give our deepest insecurities something they can see, touch, and hold onto—because we aren't holding onto God. And these things too often become our focus.

Things ... what are they? They are, I think, parts of our lives that won't matter at the end of our lives. They won't enrich our experience but exist only to make our experience appear legitimate and worthwhile. They are made up of possessions that are believed to be a fuller expression of who we are, material objects that give us a tangible feeling that we are more than we appear to be. These *things* can be a degree of social standing that gives us a temporary sense of identity and worth. They come as achievements that gain us the admiration of others in order to fill our need for meaning and value. Often, they are career aspirations that give us some sense of purpose and direction. It's an assorted array of stuff that won't matter on the deathbed.

All of these things are the manifestation of deep human needs. They speak to something much deeper that these things can't meet, something hallowed and timeless. They are that eternal part of us that lies fathoms beyond the reach of all other things, which is why things never meet that need. It's the incessant urging of the human spirit for meaning and purpose. It's the need to attach ourselves to something infinitely beyond ourselves, the need to believe that we are a part of something much bigger. It's the desire to believe that there is a great plan of which we are a part. At its core, it's the desperate and insatiable need to have a collision with the divine God.

Possessions, social standing, careers, and achievements are crumb-like morsels in the midst of our starvation. We will always have to come back to them. They can only satisfy temporarily. In time, they become depleted, as they are far too small to meet the real needs in our lives. And so, we constantly need more of them. We need to set higher goals, move further up the corporate ladder, obtain more possessions, redouble our efforts, and work harder. And for what? For something that will not infinitely satisfy.

Like Wendy's cancer, it seems that the unnecessary stuff of life smothers the real stuff. It suffocates that deep-seated passion for living. We lose sight of the infinite, and we see only the gross limitations of what our hands can create. We breathe life in shallow breaths rather than breathing deeply. In time, we come to assume that this is natural. We are unable visualize anything different. Our minds become constricted and shackled to that which we know. What we don't know, we can't see and therefore assume doesn't exist. And so we exist because existing becomes confused with living, although it's assumed to be living. Existing that becomes all there is, is a tragic end in itself. Yet existing and living are radically different.

## A Collision with This "Jesus"

Jesus can be looked at through a myriad of lenses. We each bring our own view based on our histories, our pain, our personalities, or any of a thousand things that uniquely define us. We import those things into our thinking. Each of them shifts and subtly changes how see we life, how we see each other, and how we see this "Jesus."

Whether we watch His birth or observe Him go head-to-head with evil, hold children in His lap, call forth massive catches of fish for discouraged fisherman, point out the majesty of a destitute widow, see incalculable value in a life scarred by prostitution, or walk straight into the horror of a crucifixion, however we might see Him, we see someone who calls us out of the grays and into a life dripping with color. He calls us to an intimate and intentional collision with Him.

Even for the doubter who might strip Him of his divinity and label Him a good man or a prophet of some sort, even then, the power of His message and His example are profound. You can't look at what He did and what He said and not capture a glimpse of something far beyond the grays within which we live our lives.

This man, this "Jesus," brought vibrantly real life into our contrived and suffocated lives. He pointed to something that's irresistibly compelling because it's authentic. He tapped into something that each of us desperately yearns for. He demonstrated something that is so grand that it seems unbelievable, the stuff of fairytales, myth, and legend. He spoke of something that we would give everything we are and everything we have to walk in, to bask ourselves in the wonder and glory of it until we were soaked to our cores. We would do so, were it not for the fact that it's simply too grand to believe. It seems that the color is unbelievably vivid and therefore not believable until we collide with it.

With His words, His actions, and His parables, He scattered bits and pieces of something wonderful, something lost, something of eternity throughout the grayness of our lives. These shards and bits of color have refused to be consumed by the gray, and therefore they've lain in the furrows of humanity for somewhere around two thousand years. They have been harvested by those who have searched for them and gathered them. In the gathering, they have then sown them into the lives of others, much like Wendy's paintings were sown into other lives.

Sometimes, these bits of color seem contrived, as a means of countering the dullness of our lives, rather than being the very things from which this life emerged. Sometimes, they are plowed under in pursuit of forgeries or cheap substitutes. Sometimes, they are kicked aside in favor of attempts to create our own colors, which in turn are nothing but faded hues of something they simply cannot mimic.

Yet, it was this Jesus in all the many encounters that He had that illustrated rich color, translucent color, something dripping from the palette and paintbrush of eternity. We see in Him real color. And we have the invitation to share in that color, to have our lives painted in the exact same hues, to have Him run directly into us in a collision that spews and spreads the color of His life all over our lives.

Gray and flat, our x-rays hang before us, declaring the awful reality. They are flat and colorless. We can succumb to what they portray, and we can bow to the storms and turmoil that they illustrate. We can choose to believe that gray is all that there is, so we are reduced to coming up with as many shades of it as we can in order to believe that we're doing something productive.

Or we can choose to live. We can stand with God in defiance of what the x-rays portray, and we can choose something different. We can choose to seek God, as did Wendy. We can choose to accept the x-ray but to reject it as dictating our lives just as she did. We can make the choice to splash our lives with the infinite spectrum of rainbow hues that Jesus lived out as recalled in the stories passed down to us.

Today, Wendy's unfinished painting hangs in my office, forever uncompleted, as it should be. This unfinished painting reminds me that each life is full of potential and rich with possibility, just like that painting and the artist from whose soul it sprung. It is a wonderfully belligerent protest against the flat and gray in her own life. Better yet, it is a victory. It's the ability to live fully and to dare to do something different. To paint her life aggressively and purposefully with the very colors that had been so long absent.

The painting illustrated two geese coming home, as she went home. At nineteen, Wendy passed out of this world, full of color and life. Let us live with color and life as well. Let us bare ourselves to Jesus as a grayed canvas. And as we do, may we allow Him to splash the same colors across the canvas of our lives that He lived out Himself. May this book and the stories recited here give you a hint of how wonderful those colors truly are. May you see those colors in His actions and spilled out through His words. May you be generously bathed in them today so that when you go home, you do so aflame with God's glorious color. May you collide with this God in a life-transforming collision that throws His colors across your life so brilliantly that everything about your life is changed for as long as you live. May it be all of that and nothing less. May you be privileged to have an intimate collision!